White Masculinity in the Recent South

MAKING THE MODERN SOUTH
David Goldfield, Series Editor

EDITED BY
Trent Watts

WHITE MASCULINITY IN THE RECENT SOUTH

LOUISIANA STATE UNIVERSITY PRESS)（ Baton Rouge

PUBLISHED BY LOUISIANA STATE UNIVERSITY PRESS
Copyright © 2008 by Louisiana State University Press
All rights reserved
Manufactured in the United States of America
FIRST PRINTING

Designer: AMANDA MCDONALD SCALLAN
Typeface: WHITMAN, SCALA SANS AND IMPACT
Printer and binder: THOMSON-SHORE, INC.

Library of Congress Cataloging-in-Publication Data
White masculinity in the recent South / edited by Trent Watts. — 1st
printing.
    p. cm. — (Making the modern South)
  ISBN 978-0-8071-3314-9 (cloth : alk. paper) 1. Men, White—Southern
States. 2. Masculinity—Southern States. 3. Men—Southern States—
Social conditions. I. Watts, Trent, 1965–
 HQ1090.5.S68W45 2008
  305.38'809075—dc22

                                        2008004174

Epigraph to introduction reprinted with permission of Patterson Hood.
Material from Steve Estes, I Am a Man! Race, Manhood, and the Civil Rights
Movement (Chapel Hill: University of North Carolina Press, 2005), used
with permission of University of North Carolina Press.

Contents

Acknowledgments

Editing this collection has been a pleasure as well as an education. Thanks to series editor David Goldfield and Rand Dotson at Louisiana State University Press for believing in the project and for offering much-appreciated encouragement. Craig Friend provided a thorough and expert reading of the manuscript. I also wish to thank all the contributors for their good work and patience as this collection took form and made its way toward publication.

Without the support of friends and colleagues I would not have begun or completed this book. Kris Swenson helped me decide to put together this collection; she provided valuable conceptual advice in the book's early stages. Her midwesterner's perspective on the South helped me to see things about white southern men that I otherwise would have missed. I owe a great debt to the late Larry Vonalt, my former department chair at the University of Missouri–Rolla. He encouraged me to pursue this project and suggested several of the essay topics and contributors. I regret that Larry did not live to see this book published. Also, Ted Ownby has done more for me than anyone else in the profession. My thanks cannot begin to acknowledge how much his support has meant to me. At UMR, my colleagues Gene Doty, Jack Morgan, Kris Swenson, and Kate Drowne have provided good advice and sympathetic ears. Thanks also to my good friends Vance Poole and Marc Kilmer.

It's customary to thank one's family at this point and to offer the book as a sort of apology or recompense for time stolen from them. I, too, hope that this book seems to them worth some of what it cost. My parents provide love and support and a generous welcome every time I come back home to Mississippi. The older I get, the more I appreciate them and what they've done for me. My children, Jack and Ellie, are a source of great joy. Finally, I owe my wife, Jennifer, more than I can say here. She insisted that I finish this book so that we could move on to new projects and adventures. I appreciate her faith in me.

White Masculinity in the Recent South

Introduction

Telling White Men's Stories

TRENT WATTS

You think I'm dumb, maybe not too bright
You wonder how I sleep at night
Proud of the glory, stare down the shame
Duality of the Southern thing.
—PATTERSON HOOD, Drive-By Truckers, "The Southern Thing," *Southern Rock Opera* (Soul Dump Music, 2001)

During a 1991 trip to my southwest Mississippi hometown, my wife and I visited one of the city's main downtown businesses, a men's clothing store. The store's proprietor, a pillar of the First Baptist Church, was also an early and enthusiastic investor in local boy Bernie Ebbers's feloniously run telecommunications giant WorldCom, but that is another story. One of the businessman's sons recently had been misbehaving; he secretly dropped out of college, taking himself and his tuition refund on an extended holiday to Florida, where he raised hell and had a fine time. The proprietor acknowledged his son's misdeeds with frustration and resignation. "Down here, southern boys are like that," the man explained to my Midwestern wife. She did not press him about what he meant by the phrase "like that." Was it something like deceptive? Or maybe impulsive? Or perhaps something more positive, like spirited? In any case, people in my hometown enjoyed explaining things to her, including racial taxonomy, firearms, and gendered behavior. The businessman went on to explain that because southern boys were "like that," she would need to keep a close eye on me, too.

I must admit that I do not remember this incident with the same clarity as my ex-wife (but that too is another story). Growing up as a white male southerner meant that hell-raising young men were familiar characters, plentiful on the radio and television, in movies, jokes, and adults' cautionary tales, and, of course, in real life. So familiar to me was this type that nothing about the young man's story seemed odd or even particularly remarkable, although I was jealous of the fortunate son's good fortune. Looking back on it, however, the story of the hell-raising son seems to say important things about some principal characteristics of white southern manhood in recent decades. Suiting a tale from a Christ-haunted landscape, as Flannery O'Connor put it, the story followed a familiar, hallowed arc—that of the Prodigal Son. For in the businessman's account of his son, there was the suggestion—or hope, at least—that the wayward son would in fact sober up and face the world of adult male responsibilities. But there was also something about this period of wandering, especially among women, beer, and cars, which enabled or at least usefully accompanied the transition from boyhood to manhood. White southern masculinities, like other southern identities, often seem to contain such contradictions, or dualities. And the Prodigal Son narrative is but one type of white southern manhood. But it is a type that embodies a tension that this collection of essays seeks to explore: white manhood in the recent South is widely viewed as both natural *and* learned. Most white men in the South believe that they are "that way," as my hometown businessman put it, in some natural, irreducible sense, but they also firmly believe that manhood must be learned through rites of initiation and passage, and must be lived and displayed to one's peers and others in order to be fully realized.

In the years since World War II, the American South has exhibited a variety of models of white manhood and masculinity, the misbehaving good old boy included. But this collection of essays aims not only to examine such familiar stereotypes but also to move beyond those stereotypes and to demonstrate some of the multiple ways and places in which white men have acted upon their own and their culture's conceptions of white manhood. Sometimes overlooked is that many white southern men have chafed at definitions of masculinity that would appear to require them to be good old boys or racialist patriarchs or any of the other broad stereotypes. Several of the essays here feature biographical or autobiographical accounts of white men who have been troubled by or have overtly rejected the "ignorant, smirking, chest-out, crotch-forward triumphalism," as a journalist recently put it, that has too commonly characterized white manhood in the recent South.[1] But old ways still exercise a tenacious hold, and these essays also display the great degree to which many white men in the recent South have continued to define themselves against models, places, and traits regarded as feminine or as black. Even men who see nothing of themselves in the stereotypes of white southern masculinity that popular culture and everyday life in the South itself offer will recognize the prevalence and cultural weight of those models.

As these essays seek to show, white masculinity in the recent South has been compounded of materials handed down from the past. White southerners since William Byrd and Thomas Jefferson, to take two familiar examples, have perceived different and competing models of manhood and masculinity (elite and common, white and black), both within and outside of the region. Yet while models of white masculinity have deep roots in the South, they never have been a wholly indigenous growth. Before the end of the eighteenth century, northern and southern writers had established many still-potent stereotypes of American masculinity: the leisured and gracious southern gentleman (such as Byrd); the womanizing, drinking, gambling rapscallion (Byrd again); the hunting and fishing–addicted redneck; the money-loving, Puritan-inflected Yankee; and, of course, the black man, a figure of immense and protean complexity.[2] Regional stereotypes quickly hardened and gained broad currency, leading many white southern men by the nineteenth century to conclude that that they were superior to their northern countrymen. One thinks, for instance, of Civil War–era assertions by white southern men that the war was a necessary "vindication of our manhood," as Robert Toombs told the Georgia legislature in 1860, or that they could "whip the Yankees, five or six to one," as one former slave remembered.[3]

As long as Americans have held notions of a distinct North and South, white southern men have shaped and been shaped by broader American perceptions and representations of regional difference. From the 1830s through the Civil War, national reading audiences avidly consumed stories featuring southern white men from writers such as William Gilmore Simms, A. B. Longstreet, and Harriet Beecher Stowe. Their portraits of benevolent patriarchs, hell-raising and authority-defying frontiersmen, and callous plantation masters modeled varieties of southern manhood that are instantly familiar if seemingly contradictory, as in Simms's and Stowe's competing portraits of slave owners. In the post–Civil War years, as Nina Silber has shown, a national reading audience thrilled to stories of southern ladies courted by northern gentlemen. Northern writers captured broad national audiences with these parables of national reconciliation.[4] At the same time, southern writers such as Thomas Nelson Page and Thomas Dixon worked in the postwar years to advance a model of white southern manhood and male authority as honorable, masterful, dignified, and admirable.

In the years since World War II, print and electronic media have continued to disseminate and help to shape models of white masculinity, not only for southerners but also for the rest of the nation and beyond. To take perhaps the most obvious example, for millions of fans around the globe, Elvis—in whatever incarnation—is still King. Television, music, film, and now the Internet have offered a variety of images of white southern manhood. Some of these are quite favorable, such as former Alabama football coach Paul "Bear" Bryant, for instance, or NASCAR icon Richard Petty, but some are much less so, say, Birmingham Public Safety Commissioner Bull Conner or the menacing hill people from James Dickey's *Deliverance*. Representations of white southern men in the post–World War II years have tended strongly to fall back upon one of two models: the sinister character intent upon racial control (the locals in the film *Mississippi Burning*, for instance) or a more benign good old boy, whether he drinks, cusses, and raises hell, or not. The good old boy type has several variants: a comic sort, such as the lovable rustic, Andy Griffith, and the more serious patriotic, blue-collar (or blue-collar wannabe) redneck. The tendency to stereotype southern white men as either particularly good or particularly bad follows an American tendency since the Civil War, as many scholars have noted, to see the (white) South variously as the repository of the nation's virtues, its aberrant backwater, or its pathological doppelganger.[5]

In recent years, however, the redneck has slipped his southern moorings and has gone national. To millions of Americans, the redneck is benign and even beloved, a model of manhood as familiar and emulated in the Midwest and Far West, among other places, as in the South. Popular culture is suffused with musicians and comedians who embrace and revel in their self-professed redneck identity. Country music icon George Jones sings of the "High-Tech Redneck" (where "Mayberry meets Star Trek"),[6] comedian Jeff Foxworthy delights a national audience with "You Might Be a Redneck If" jokes and spin-off products, the 1970s television series *The Dukes of Hazzard* has been remade as a big-budget movie (2005), and NASCAR is no longer a regional curiosity by way of moonshine running. Charles Reagan Wilson argues that "the Southern working-class version of redneck is becoming the national version, and it's good-natured, it has humor and, in some ways, it's a performance."⁷ What happened? Perhaps the redneck's southernness no longer seems as worrisome for many Americans as it did forty or fifty years ago. Confederate flags on pickup trucks notwithstanding, this late-model redneck no longer targets African Americans with his humor or his ire—not publicly, at least. He now seems more harmless, like his near-cousin the good old boy, historically a sort of redneck, with many of the redneck's bad habits but without his white sheet and burning cross.

These days, good old boys and rednecks on television, in the movies, in popular music, and in the fiction of those who, like the late Mississippi writer Larry Brown, are fond of them, generally steer well clear of statements of prejudice against black Americans, unless the setting is clearly meant to be sometime in the bad old days. But the redneck has not gained national favor simply by foreswearing bigotry and violence, traits that a generation ago prompted Neil Young's critical song "Southern Man" (1970). Witness, for instance, the enthusiastic *amen* a national audience gave Oklahoma-born country singer Toby Keith's post–September 11 promise that America would put "a boot in the ass" of those who menace us, a barroom taunt raised to a comprehensive foreign policy statement. "It's the American way," sings Keith in "Courtesy of the Red, White, and Blue (The Angry American)" (2002).⁸ Clearly, a redneck's anger seems less threatening—admirable, even—to other Americans when it is directed not at black people but rather at accepted common enemies.

Consider, too, the wild popularity of Dan Whitney, who performs as Larry the Cable Guy, a thickly accented, apparently southern comedian. The Nebraska-born and Florida-raised Whitney's trademark is the ubiquitous if enigmatic slogan "Git-R-Done." At times his humor is self-deprecating, placing him firmly in the line of earlier rustic southern clowns; he jokes about his weight, his flatulence and poor hygiene, and his being henpecked by his wife. But his brand of comedy also targets the bogeymen of his *lumpen* (and many not so *lumpen*) conservative white audience: gays, environmentalists, Democrats, and Muslims. "I just read the latest gay marriage poll," he jokes. "Sixty percent of the country is against it, 30 percent is for it, and 10 percent of the country wants to smoke the pole [perform fellatio]!!! (If your [sic] not laughing at that then you're an uptight prick!)" Whitney asks: "Have ya seen that Al Gore movie *An Inconvenient Truth*? It's about global warming. I thought it was about him losing the presidency. Remember that speech when he's yelling the phrase, 'the president played on our fears'? Global warming is still a THEORY and NOT a fact. Hey[,] wait a minute . . . Is Al Gore 'playing on our fears'? NAW!! This is confusing." On Muslim prayer at the 2004 Republican convention: "Ya wanna pray to allah [sic] then drag yer flea infested ass over to where they pray to allah at!"[9]

Whitney and three other comedians (including Jeff Foxworthy, creator of the "You Might Be a Redneck If" line of jokes and merchandise) perform on television, subscription radio, and in live shows as the Blue Collar Comedy Tour. Thus, national audiences eagerly consume the redneck and good old boy repackaged as a blue collar man who is familiarly southern but not southern in a way that makes their target audience uneasy; he is hard-working, pragmatic, patriotic, and good-humored, but not a hater of African Americans or a symbol of other regional pathologies such as poverty, violence, or poor nutrition. As the nation has become more conservative in the last generation, "blue collar" (in actuality, millionaire) performers such as Larry the Cable Guy and Toby Keith mark the apotheosis of the white southern good old boy. No longer marginalized as either rustic clown or savage hillbilly, the "blue collar" man has become in the eyes of millions the most solid and patriotic of Americans. At the same time, the term *blue collar* has been neutered of any sense of the class solidarity that many Americans in the 1930s, for instance, might have understood the term as symbolizing. During his first term as president, Richard Nixon is supposed to have reversed the course of his economic commitments and famously declared that "we are all Keynesians now." When it comes to masculinity, many white American males now embrace an inner white southerner and apparently believe that we are all, to one degree or another, rednecks now.

This volume seeks to do what no other single work has done: to explore white southern manhood and masculinity in a variety of contexts in the years since World War II.[10] The essays have been chosen for their individual strengths and for the coherent yet nuanced picture they present of white southern masculinities. They were written by historians, literary critics, and scholars of film and environmental studies. In form they include cultural and social history, close readings of literary texts and music, interview, and autobiography. We hope that this book will find a broad audience among those interested in the South and in whiteness, men's, and regional studies, yet will be accessible to readers across the disciplines. To that end, the essays seek to be theoretically informed but still accessible.

This collection does not attempt a social history of white southern men. Neither is it a history of visual or textual representations of southern manhood. And there are many topics in the recent history of white southern manhood that are not the subjects of essays here: military veterans, military bases, or military schools, for instance. We do not examine NASCAR, the Christian Right in politics, or aging and elderly white southern men. Nor do we offer focused, extended explorations of normative white male heterosexuality. Further, this collection does not seek to impose any sort of interpretational orthodoxy, or to suggest that there is only one way to study manhood and masculinity in the recent South. Instead, these essays mean to provide suggestive models for future research. Finally, the essays do not directly engage the complex history of black manhood in the South, except obliquely to note how critically a sense (even if badly mistaken) of what black men were like shaped many white southern men's sense of self.

In recent decades, media and popular cultural images of white southern men, like representations of the South generally, have displayed a tendency toward extremes, either favorable or unfavorable. Images aside, white men still, of course, wield considerable political, social, and economic power in the South, so much so that it seems almost too obvious a point to make. It may well be, though, that probing at those images, as the essays in this collection do, might help explain why white masculinity and white men remain so culturally powerful in the contemporary South. But are white men powerful in the South because of their race or because of their gender? Two unoriginal points are worth restating here. First, a white southern man does not cleave neatly along planes of race and gender. Like other people, southerners do not so consciously and discretely categorize their lives, so historians should be cautious about isolating these categories of identity. The southern stories in this collection are almost always about both race and gender. Second, with all this talk of power and mastery, it is important to remember that white southern men do not form a monolithic cabal dedicated to oppressing white women, black people, and other racial minorities in the South. Working-class, white, southern men understand that no one has handed them the keys to the region. All white southern men's lives are lived individually and as members of families and communities. It is often analytically useful to consider white southern men as a group, but they are no more homogeneous than any other group historians might consider.

Historically, white southern manhood in its idealized forms has been structured around two core values, mastery and independence; the ideals are some-times in tension, sometimes complementary. Patriarchal, racialized notions of mastery are probably more commonly associated with the colonial or antebellum South than with the twentieth-century South.[11] And it is worth saying again that the ambitions of mastery and independence were not reality for most white south-ern men, let alone African Americans, American Indians, and white southern women. But to many white southern men the idea that their identity is founded upon legitimate claims to power and control has proved and continues to prove persuasive. As the research of Glenda Gilmore, Stephen Kantrowitz, and Nancy MacLean has demonstrated, late-nineteenth and early twentieth-century southern politics and culture were shaped by the determination of many white men to com-bat perceived threats to prerogatives due them because of their race and gender.[12] Their responses to these perceived threats included public lynching of black men, prickly sensitivity to criticism of southern institutions, and a fierce loyalty to a whites-only Democratic party.

These days few white southern men aspire to the ownership or overt legal and social subordination of African Americans; if they do, they keep quiet about it. How much hearts and minds have changed is not easy to say; at the very least, white southerners' ways of speaking publicly about race have changed significantly since the 1960s, and that transformation should not be discounted. On the other hand, that is not to say that the past is the past and that race no longer matters or should no longer be discussed in the South simply because most white southerners no longer openly express beliefs about racial difference and racial privilege. Among other reasons, a sense of mastery and control was historically too central to white manhood to be so quickly displaced. These days, however, notions of mastery in the South are more likely to manifest themselves in terms of gender rather than of race. Indeed, one can detect among many black and white southern men and some southern women a sense, expressed or tacit, that male authority is natural and benevolent, and sanctioned by history or some higher authority. White male political, economic, and social power thus seems so natural and right—no matter how individually elusive—to most white southern men that those who question it are seen as troublemakers who insist on bringing race into everything.

But if racial privilege is no longer overtly defended by white southern men, or is acknowledged as an unfortunate but abandoned relic of the bad old days, the same cannot be said of public assertions of differences and prerogatives based upon gender. Two actions by the Southern Baptist Convention (SBC) in the 1990s neatly illustrate white southerners' complicated understandings of race and gender. The SBC is hardly the entire white South. But with churches containing more than 16 million adherents, one historian of religion has argued, "no other major denomination has shaped white southern religion and culture as powerfully and as long."[13] In 1995 the SBC adopted a "Resolution on Racial Reconciliation" that "unwaveringly denounce[d] racism, in all its forms, as deplorable sin." Commonly referred to as the SBC's "apology for slavery," the document is more broad-reaching than that label might indicate. Acknowledging the central role slavery played in the creation of the SBC, as well as Baptist participation and complicity in the institution, the resolution goes on to recognize Baptist opposition to the civil rights movement and the continuing corrosive effects of racism on the United States and on the mission of the SBC.[14] Such a resolution would have been unthinkable a generation earlier, and the SBC's acknowledgment that race matters in the present and not simply as a historical problem, marks an uncharacteristically frank way for white people to speak about race in the recent South.

White southerners, Southern Baptists included, have in the main repudiated assertions that racial difference sanctions separate roles or differential power for white and black people. When it comes to gender, the story is different. Like many other Americans, many white southerners assert the reality or the innateness of gender difference. Such differences legitimate, even mandate, social distinctions based upon gender. Three years after the SBC adopted its "Resolution of Racial Reconciliation," Southern Baptists met in Salt Lake City. The most noted event of their 1998 convention was the adoption of a family amendment to the Baptist Faith and Message; written in 1925 and revised in 1963 and 2000, the document is the statement of the denomination's fundamental beliefs and teachings. An essential difference between the "Resolution on Racial Reconciliation" and the Baptist Faith and Message is worth noting. A resolution is by SBC definition "an expression of opinion or concern, as compared to a motion, which calls for action. A resolution is not used to direct an entity of the Southern Baptist Convention to specific action other than to communicate the opinion or concern expressed."[15] The Faith and Message, on the other hand, is a definitive statement of Baptist belief about fundamental theological matters. In this nonliturgical church with a devolved ecclesiastical polity, the Faith and Message is akin to catechism and papal encyclical. The 1998 amendment of the Baptist Faith and Message demonstrated the veer to the right the SBC had taken in the 1980s and 1990s. Of the Faith and Message's eighteen sections, the eighteenth states the denomination's understanding of the role of husband and wife, and merits quoting at length:

> The husband and wife are of equal worth before God, since both are created in God's image. The marriage relationship models the way God related to His people. A husband is to love his wife as Christ loved the church. He has the God-given responsibility to provide for, to protect, and to lead his family. A wife is to submit herself graciously to the servant leadership of her husband even as the church willingly submits to the headship of Christ. She, being in the image of God as is her husband and thus equal to him, has the God-given responsibility to respect her husband and to serve as his helper in managing the household and nurturing the next generation.[16]

According to the Southern Baptist Convention, then, a woman should submit to her husband, respecting him and serving him. They are partners, the SBC says, as Christ and the church are partners; such a partnership, however, no good Baptist would characterize as an alliance of equals. A defense of gender subordination based upon scripture was thus made central to Southern Baptist teaching. Three years earlier, however, the SBC apologized for its history of defending racial subordination through citation of scripture, calling that practice sin.

If mastery has lain and continues to lie at the heart of definitions of white southern manhood, another of its key values has been the ideal of independence, usually defined in economic terms. Far from unique to the South, aspiration to land ownership or independent producer status animated generations of eighteenth- and nineteenth-century white American men. Jefferson famously wrote that those "who labor in the earth are the chosen people of God, if ever he had a chosen people." "Dependence," which Jefferson equated with the nonownership of land, "begets subservience and venality, suffocat[ing] the germ of virtue."[17] The ideal of freedom from the control of other men has always carried a cultural as well as an economic valence, of course. Often expressed in egalitarian terms, this component of white southern manhood insists that one (white) man is as good as another, at least if he is willing to comport himself in socially sanctioned ways.

This ideal of independent performative white manhood has also been embodied in the figure of the hell-raising good old boy: hard-drinking, hard-fighting, and most of all, contemptuous of restraint or outside interference, whether by the government or his "betters." This figure appears early on in William Byrd's stereotypes of his Carolina neighbors and continues in real and fictional varieties such as the rough frontiersmen of Old Southwestern humor, moonshiners, many NASCAR drivers and fans, and pickup truck enthusiasts displaying gun racks and the Confederate flag. In *The Mind of the South*, W. J. Cash argued that the southern frontiersman displayed a tendency toward "a kind of mounting exultancy, which issued in a tendency to frisk and cavort, to posture, to play the slashing hell of a fellow."[18] Cash is best read as a suggestive rather than an authoritative source, of course, but a good many white southerners still adopt a "boys will be boys" attitude toward mild transgressions (adolescent or later) involving alcohol, women, and motorized vehicles.

Consider, for instance, the hard life and fast times of legendary country singer George Jones. Jones, "the Possum," is no stranger to such transgressions. If anything, Jones's brushes with the law, outstanding arrest warrants, marital discord, and journeys into and out of drug and alcohol abuse have increased his popularity as a sort of "honky-tonk Orpheus, returned from the dead." Jones, widely considered the finest voice in country music, seems to many fans and observers an embodiment of the hard living his songs chronicle. Even his hair, wrote one journalist, is "like a sculptured pinnacle of incongruous permanence atop a distinctly mortal shell." In repose, the wrinkles around his eyes "seemed less the natural carvings of age than the ravages of mortification . . . they were like the scars of a clawing."[19] Jones stories are legion: one wife, country star Tammy Wynette, having grown frustrated with Jones' drinking, took the car keys so he could not drive to get more liquor. Jones drove the riding lawnmower instead. That one incident, as Barbara Ching has pointed out, has inspired more than one country song. Jones himself posed on a John Deere mower for the back cover of a 1996 album, *I Lived to Tell It All*.[20]

In 1982, to pick another from a cornucopia of incidents, Jones was stopped for speeding (ninety-one miles per hour) south of Jackson, Mississippi. Technically, Jones and his girlfriend were both driving; she was steering and he was operating the accelerator. Officers found that the car containing Jones, his girlfriend, and her sixteen-year-old daughter also contained traces of a white powder, which turned out to be cocaine. Arrested for cocaine possession and public drunkenness, the singer bristled at the officer's assumption that Jones was a drug dealer: "I've never once sold narcotics or illegal drugs," he said later. "I've given away plenty but never sold any." As punishment, Jones received the relatively light sentence of probation, provided he play a benefit concert.[21] Someone with less fame and less talent—someone less of a forgivable good old boy, in other words—might not have received the same sentence. Southern law does occasionally practice fond indulgence or at least understanding toward the erring or straying good old boy, and good old boys are always defined as white. Mainstream white southern culture gives other names to black men who misbehave with money, cars, drugs, guns, and booze: *thugs* or *felons,* for instance.

While recent mainstream models of white southern manhood have continued to valorize traditional virtues of mastery and independence, they have also carried specific and related messages about sexuality. The white South has long been attentive to sexual as well as racial boundaries. At the beginning of the twentieth century, white southern men defended a number of prerogatives when they lynched black men for alleged interracial sexual contact, whether violent or consensual. And during the civil rights battles of the 1950s and 1960s, white southern men often claimed that black male access to white women was the real issue at stake. Civil rights workers were attacked for purportedly flouting sexual as well as racial taboos. Of course, the distinction between sexual and racial matters has not always been entirely clear, either to white southerners or to historians, but those issues have always seemed gravely important. That is to say, sex of all kinds—between married people, between men or between women, or across the color line—has occurred in a culture in which categories of race and gender and sexual practices are sometimes amorphous but always fraught with broader meanings.

For white southern men, sexuality has long been a briar patch, and historians have only begun to explore the subject.[22] With whom have white southerners thought they could properly engage in sexual relations? Is it possible to have sex with another man and remain a white southern man in good standing? What exactly constitutes sexual relations, as a recent president mused? Does sex without love make the sex more or less culturally palatable? Here again, white men's sexuality is complexly interrelated with questions of independence and mastery. One thinks, for instance, of the rednecks in *Deliverance,* who use sodomy to demasculinize and humiliate the suburban professional Atlanta men. Here, sodomy signifies power, control, and revenge rather than mutual sexual pleasure, of course. But the often-cited *Deliverance* example forcefully underscores an argument about sexuality that most southern white men have traditionally understood: that some instances of same-sex contact—depending upon one's role in the encounter—do not compromise one's manhood. Showering together in gym, and patting butts and holding hands on the football field, for instance, are viewed as wholesome rites of passage, and anyone noting the homosocial elements of these encounters invites condemnation as a troublemaker. At the same time, some heterosexual white southern men (and black men, too) have found it quite acceptable to have sex with other men as long as their role is active rather than passive. White male sexuality can even accommodate bestiality, as a host of barnyard jokes attests. The one great taboo has been that of public declaration of love for another man.

Perhaps, then, the most fundamental message that southern culture seems to deliver about manhood is that the southern man is presumed to be heterosexual. More precisely, normative heterosexuality has traditionally seemed to most white southern men (and women) a sine qua non of their identity. Former Louisiana governor and currently incarcerated felon Edwin Edwards famously said that nothing would bring him down except being caught in bed with a dead woman or a live man. While the federal government was more clever and persistent that Edwards imagined, he did have a point. If a white southern man aspires to elective office, the primary or secondary classroom, the pulpit, or the coaching field, he is still best advised not to be caught in bed with another man. And today, white schoolboys in the South (as in the rest of the country) freely toss around *gay, queer,* and *fag* as epithets, having learned that *nigger* cannot be said aloud anymore in most public contexts. So, then, at first glance it appears that white southerners have imagined and guarded sexual boundaries as vigilantly as and longer than they did racial boundaries. But the matter of sexual practices as a component of white southern male identity is more complicated than it might appear.

While a white southern man may be rich or poor, respectable or no account, how broad a palate of sexual expression is a white southern man allowed? Joel Williamson has said that in the South "a 'good woman' (white) cannot be a little bit bad, or a little bit masculine, anymore than she can be a little bit black."[23] Borrowing from Williamson, does it follow that a white southern man cannot be a little bit bad (if we take bad here to mean sexually transgressive) any more than he can be a little bit black? Has white southern culture defined sexual expression as rigorously as it has defined race? Does nonnormative sexual expression compromise a white southern man's claim to be a white man in the same way that uncertainty about race would traditionally have compromised that claim? Not always. Here is another case where southern stereotypes prove misleading.

Gay and bisexual white southern men have held positions of power and re-spect that were and continue to be denied to black men, provided that those white men's sexual transgressions were not accompanied by challenges to other cultural norms and provided, too, that those sexual practices were spoken about or not spoken about in certain ways. Bertram Wyatt-Brown suggests that "the South of the mid-twentieth century countenanced eccentrics of all kinds because they were rare enough to be harmless so long as public scandal did not erupt about them."[24] Broadly accepted or at least tolerated models of white manhood in the recent South accommodate sexual practices ranging from celibacy to faithful monogamy (straight and queer) to "epic fornication," as Blanche Du Bois put it. What ac-counts for this seeming hypocrisy or duplicity? It is vital not to overstate the white South's acceptance of a range of sexual expression. White southern men who love other men and wish to express that fact openly have traditionally found them-selves in a most difficult position. Public displays of affection between southern men (except on the athletic field) in most places draw stares, if not worse. And black and white southern adolescents struggling with their sexual identity find schools, churches, and other institution to be less supportive than they are in some other parts of the country.

The recent South, then, has neither warmly welcomed a continuum of af-fectional and sexual practices nor overtly accepted the malleability of gender. But white southern culture does at least tacitly accept a broader definition of sexuality than it does of race. It is and has been possible for a white southern man to love another man and still to embrace and claim his identity as a southern man; several essays in this collection make that point conclusively. Racial difference does not work the same way in the region.

Mainstream white male sexuality has been built in part upon notions of emo-tional and physical mastery of women. White southern men have also traditionally argued the need for the mastery of their own sexual impulses, or they have at least tacitly praised the ideal of sexual good behavior. Often they have lauded their own sexual restraint or mastery by damning the figure of the oversexualized black man. In *Black Monday* (1955), for instance, an attack on the Supreme Court's *Brown* decision, Judge Tom P. Brady argues that whites ought to dominate the South because of the inability of black men to govern the social order, much less them-selves. Brady's argument is a familiar one; no one, he argues, except the white southerner really understands the black southerner. "There is no substitute for daily association in learning the character, desires and habits of another human being." Again, not surprisingly, Brady's argument about knowledge and intimacy is rooted in a paternalistic perspective that positions white men as the patient, indulgent patrons of childlike black men:

> If you . . . have worked with them and among them, laughed at their ribald humor; if you have been stunned by their abysmal vulgarity and profanity; if you can find it in your heart to overlook their obscenity and depravity . . . and . . . have fed and clothed all of them and protected them from anyone *who would harm them* [emphasis in original] . . . if you have given him, in addition to his salary, extra money at Christmas and at other times in order that he might buy some presents for the three or four illegitimate children which he acknowledges as his own, THEN you are beginning to know the negro and his problems.[25]

William Alexander Percy, too, whose own sexuality was a complex, largely private matter, in *Lanterns on the Levee* shakes his paternalistic head over the energetic, profligate sexual habits of his chauffeur, Ford, who returned from Chicago with "a thrilling tale of how nearly he had been married against his vehement protest to a young lady for reasons insufficient surely in any enlightened community with an appreciation of romance." Brady's account is shot through with outrage at black political and social aspirations; Percy's is leavened by melancholy patriarchal observations about black southerners, whom he terms a "race in an alien world." Both men accept without question the inalienable right of white men to dominate the South because of their capacity for mastery and restraint.[26]

While economic and social conditions in the South changed dramatically in the twentieth century, broadly shared or at least broadly recognized notions of white southern manhood continue to be central to southern culture. The successes of the civil rights movement complicated definitions of white masculinity built upon overt racial dominance, even if racialism is still somehow present. And as the southern economy became in turn industrialized and consumerized, Jeffersonian and Jacksonian definitions of the white male as independent producer have seemed less applicable. Today's white southern male is far more likely to work in a Wal-Mart or an office building than he is to till his own forty acres. But white manhood in the South has proved remarkably resilient. As several of the essays in this collection point out, white manhood and masculinity is more likely these days to manifest itself along a broad cultural front: for instance, in arguments over flags and Confederate heritage, in allegiance to sports as a rite of adolescent passage, in gun ownership and hunting, or in a suspicion of sexual or political deviants.[27]

These essays seek to build upon the rich scholarship in the history of gender in the South that has developed over the last few decades. Scholars have produced particularly fine work on white southern manhood in the eighteenth and nineteenth centuries. Elliott Gorn and Bertram Wyatt-Brown have provided pioneering explanations of how gender worked for antebellum white southern males, and Ted Ownby's *Subduing Satan* (1990) has probably done more than any other single book to shape scholarly explorations of southern manhood.[28] Until recently, the amount of historical scholarship on the eighteenth and nineteenth centuries has been far greater than that examining the twentieth century.[29] But that situation is changing. Work on manhood and masculinity in the post–World War II South has flowered in recent years. For instance, the work of John Howard has illuminated the history of queer southern men. And recent work has shown the usefulness of considering manhood and masculinity along with race and class in assessing the impact of the civil rights movement on the region.[30] Thus, scholarship on gender in the South has reached a sufficient stage of maturity to allow for closer examination of more discrete periods, such as the South in the decades since World War II. White men in these years faced challenges to their authority from black southerners, white women, and from other white men who, in the face of broader social changes, no longer felt constrained to accept culturally dominant definitions of what a white man ought to do and to be. The post–World War II period represents a considerable challenge to white male authority, then, but most of the scholars represented in this collection would argue that the effects of this challenge should not be overstated. While normative models of white manhood have changed—in their public face, at least—white men's dominant position seems in some ways as secure as it did a generation or two ago.

What seems clear is that white manhood as it is lived in the contemporary South is still a complex, contingent historicized matter, as it always has been. Some white southern men, especially the kind who might contribute to a collection like this, consider their gender with a level of self-consciousness that earlier generations might not have done. But while some white southern men, conscious of living in a post–civil rights movement moment, appreciate the ways in which white manhood still has its privileges in the South, others do not.

The essays in this collection are gathered into four sections: institutions, racial matters, personal stories, and texts. The essays have been chosen and grouped in this way to provide coherence to the collection and to illustrate what the contributors see as principle themes and useful ways of considering the recent history of white southern manhood.

The first section, concerning institutions, illuminates how physical places and organizations—some obviously gendered male and others not—reinforce and transmit certain models of white manhood. A general conclusion to be drawn from these four essays is that white southern manhood has traditionally been learned and performed more deliberately than most white southerners might assume. Being a white southern man, whether straight or queer, has demanded space, rites of passage, and the approval of other like-minded men.

In "Church Camping and White Southern Manhood: Evangelical Males and Christian Primitivism, 1920s–1970s," Ted Ownby engages one of the white South's dominant institutions, the church, and traces the rise of church camps in the region. Camps organized especially for children became especially popular with post–World War II prosperity and growing fears about city life. Ownby analyzes the ideals presented to boys and girls in these camps, which were largely segregated by gender. Along with closeness to nature, wholesome play, and opportunities for character building, southern church camps showed a dramatic division between their goals for males and females. In Southern Baptist camps, girls aspired to the rank of queen, complete with a crown. In contrast, the ideal boy was an American Indian, with special knowledge of Indian language, dances, and skills. Boys competed to gain an Indian rank at what camps called the highlight of the camping season, the Council Ring. Ownby connects the popularity of the Council Ring during the 1950s and 1960s with the rise of the civil rights movement, which questioned many white men's ideals. Church men's groups, often called brotherhoods, helped organize the camps. These church brotherhoods, most of which were formed in the 1920s, served as a countermovement against the earlier organization and success of women's church groups in influencing church social life, finances, and especially missionary work. What ideals, asks Ownby, did church "brothers" uphold for themselves and for boys they wished to help become Christian men?

In some cases, physical places may subvert or challenge culturally dominant versions of white manhood. In "Where the Action Is: Interstate Rest Areas, the Creation of Gay Space, and the Recovery of a Lost Narrative," for instance, Brock Thompson examines two antigay controversies in the state of Arkansas in the 1990s. The first involved a sting operation at a rest stop between Conway and Little Rock which resulted in the arrests of eight men on various charges, including violation of the state's sodomy statute. The second initiative aimed to revise the state's 1977 antisodomy law in order to decriminalize homosexual activity. Efforts at revision met stiff resistance in the Arkansas legislature, with churches and other conservative religious organizations lobbying strenuously against revision, arguing that criminalizing homosexual activity served the interests of public health and morality. The effort to decriminalize gay sex eventually failed; homosexual activity and bestiality remained linked in Arkansas law. Both the rest stop sting operation and the sodomy statute battle, writes Thompson, were "not only over the use and misuse of a public place" but also demonstrate "the creation and facilitation of a gay identity and space in the thick of the American South."

Anthony James's essay, "Political Parties: College Social Fraternities, Manhood, and the Defense of Southern Traditionalism, 1945–1960," examines an institution that stands as an almost stereotypical bulwark of white male privilege. James sets his story within the broader national context of the immediate post–World War II period, when college social fraternities faced numerous calls to expunge their religious and racial discriminatory clauses. Most of the rhetoric and activity sparking racial and religious integration occurred in the Northeast. Southern fraternities responded by crafting an idealized version of Old South white masculinity, displayed in a variety of public forums. James examines how several college fraternities from the Universities of Alabama, Mississippi, and North Carolina created experiences and images that venerated the Old South through formal and informal parties, participation in annual college variety shows, and photographic self-presentations in college yearbooks. These social activities allowed fraternity members to construct an identity that both emphasized civilized white manhood and served as a paternalistic suave to the impending crisis of integration. Ironically, argues James, these festivities and entertainments also provided social space for southern white men to explore and perhaps embrace "otherness" to a much greater degree than would have been permissible otherwise.

The connection between group activity and white masculinity is further explored in Adam Watts's photo essay, "A Real Man's Place: Attitudes and Environment at a Southern Deer Camp." Watts provides a rich documentary argument for the connection between the natural environment, white male recreation, and ritual participation in rites of masculine passage. On maps or aerial photographs, and generally in the minds of the uninitiated, the deer camp can seem a speck lost in the woods. Visitors wonder at the isolation and, perhaps, at the rustic environment, and see no allure other than the camp's proximity to hunting land. What is the importance of the deer camp, asks Watts, that men will leave work, family, and home to spend a few days outside in the region's most miserable weather, eating potted meat—all in the name of hunting white-tailed deer? At the Clear Run Social Club in southwest Mississippi, there is more to the deer camp than an aggregation of shacks and camping trailers in varying states of disrepair. More, too, than the friendship of the members or their enthusiasm for the sport—indeed, some members rarely hunt. What makes this institution special (even sacred, some might say, given the number of hunters to be found sitting around a fire on any given Sunday morning) seems to be something like a collective sense of place where the roots of white southern masculinity remain firmly planted. At Clear Run there is what could be called a *man* ethic, much as there is in other institutions of southern white manhood—a specific model of the attitudes and experiences one must possess in order to become a man.

The second section of essays explores racial matters, showing white southern men responding directly to perceived challenges to their status and authority. Together, these essays prove that well-known stories such as massive resistance to segregation, black boycotts of white-owned businesses, or memorializations of the Confederate past are examined more fruitfully when gender is added to race as a category of analysis. These essays, perhaps more than others in the collection, demonstrate the great degree to which questions of race, gender and power have been interwoven in the recent South. White men—some more than others, of course—enjoy power and prerogatives based upon their gender as well as their race. A further contention of these essays—and of the collection as a whole—is that gender has been relatively neglected by people explaining power and authority in the recent South. Twentieth-century black and white southerners knew very well that race meant power or the lack of it. Racial prerogatives and discrimination, then, were a logical target of black and white southern reformers, and of the civil rights movement. Any comparison of the South today with the place a generation ago demonstrates several things, most obviously that southerners and observers of the South cannot agree how to characterize the main lines of the story we have witnessed: a story of progress over bigotry or a story of the tenacity of racial privilege.

No matter which story or which variant of the story one prefers, it is clear that race and stories of race figure centrally in the stories southerners tell about who they are and where they have been. Indeed, the focus on race in the South is sometimes so keen that gender is sometimes overlooked, discounted, or denied as a shaping factor in recent southern culture. It is perhaps revealing that when I presented earlier versions of my own essay in this volume at two conferences, members of both audiences argued that the story I told was "about race" and not "about gender." Other contributors to this volume report similar reactions to their attempts to analyze white manhood in the recent South. These essays and this collection as whole argue that white male power—especially when challenged—reveals itself as compounded of gender as well as of race. Historians' relative inattention to gender as a pillar of white male prerogative may help explain why the South today, while not the South of a generation ago, remains a region where young white men have at birth been dealt a better than average hand.

In "A Question of Honor: Masculinity and Massive Resistance to Integration," Steve Estes examines how in the 1950s southern white men faced a stiff challenge for control of a social order that they had dominated since the turn of the century. Many white men, argues Estes, worried that the "race mixers" in the NAACP and Supreme Court were determined to overturn a gender and racial hierarchy that rested on black disfranchisement and segregation. The white, predominantly male, members of the Citizens' Councils of America constituted the vanguard of "massive resistance" to racial integration in the South. Estes seeks to revise earlier accounts of massive resistance by analyzing the gendered nature of the debate between the Citizens' Councils and their opponents, revealing intersections between the segregationists' rhetoric of manhood and themes of southern honor, historical memory, social control, and racial violence. Massive resistance was not a "crisis of masculinity," concludes Estes, but it was a struggle for power often expressed in gendered terms. To retain their economic and social authority, white southern leaders in the Citizens' Councils demonized black men's sexuality and galvanized southern white men with ideals of whiteness, honor, and manhood. The violent extremism inspired by such masculinist rhetoric eventually gave civil rights officials and the federal government the moral authority to dismantle legal segregation and challenge white male supremacy in the South.

My own essay, "The Boycotting of Coach Rutter: Manhood, Race, and Authority in Post-1970 Mississippi," explores white masculine authority in the recent South through an event that disrupted the narratives of sport and benevolent white authority in a small southern town. The boycotting of Coach Hollis Rutter in 1988 in Brookhaven, Mississippi, demonstrates what happened when one coach's color blindness was placed in doubt. Rutter had a successful twenty-nine year coaching career at several Mississippi public high schools before and after racial integration. He came out of his first retirement to coach at two of the state's segregation academies, one in Greenwood and one in Brookhaven. When he was subsequently hired at Brookhaven High School as coach and athletic director, black Brookhavenites responded with an effective boycott of white-owned businesses. Rutter never coached the football team but served several years in an administrative position. His association with segregated institutions compromised the masculine authority that small-town football coaches in the Deep South generally exercise. Black citizens' use of the economic boycott proved particularly unsettling to whites, recalling the demands and tactics of the civil rights movement, predicated as it was upon the rejection of claims of benevolent white authority. The hiring and boycott tell us just how fragile the tacit agreement is that maintains the male homosocial bonds in integrated football as well as small-town narratives of placid, equitable race relations. Sports provide an arena in which teamwork and physical proximity of blacks and whites must operate in order to attain victories. In the Deep South, the success of integrated team sports requires that racial division be bridged or even ignored in the interests of an apparently seamless, "natural" masculinity. During the boycott, one of Coach Rutter's defenders voiced a common view of the southern coach's cultural significance: his job was "to turn boys into men."

Southern heritage groups and the neo-Confederate movement have drawn adherents and gained media and scholarly attention in recent years. Many commentators, however, see the story of these groups as a simple tale of white southerners refusing to come to terms with the twentieth century and a changed racial order. In "Neo-Confederates in the Basement: The League of the South and the Crusade Against Southern Emasculation," K. Michael Prince provides a subtle reading of the ideological content and political significance of one of the neo-Confederate movement's most articulate and ambitious organizations, the League of the South (LOS). Self-described southern traditionalists have resisted recent efforts in South Carolina, Mississippi, Georgia, and other southern states to remove Confederate symbols from state flags and other public spaces. Such traditionalism, argues Prince, amounts to more than a knee-jerk reaction against the civil rights movement. Prince distinguishes between traditionalist southerners who resent changes to state flags and Confederate monuments and true neo-Confederates such as the League of the South, whose message is a systematic critique of the contemporary American political, social, and economic order. Such a critique, says Prince, amounts to an alternative civil religion. One of the central tenets of the neo-Confederate civil religion is its sense of "true and proper manhood"—strong, courageous, responsible, and pious toward history, family, and tradition. To understand the LOS's appeal to certain white southern men and its desire for cultural and political separatism, argues Prince, it is essential to scrutinize its broad social critique and appeal to a traditional vision of masculinity.

In "'The Most Man in the World': Nathan Bedford Forrest and the Cult of Southern Masculinity," Court Carney explores the changing uses to which the figure of Forrest the Confederate cavalryman has been put since the Civil War. Forrest has always been consciously used as an icon of white southern manhood, as well as a symbol of the yeoman South's character and grievances. Carney demonstrates that Confederate contemporaries and the turn-of-the-century generation that memorialized the Lost Cause praised Forrest explicitly for what Carney calls his "virile heroism." In the 1930s, Agrarian Andrew Lytle took up the figure of Forrest to offer a class-based critique of the eastern South's neglect of the western South, during the Civil War and generally. Lytle, Carney writes, emphasized the class and racial implications of Forrest's masculinity, showing him to be "a paternal clan leader of the plain people of the South and a Klansman who served as the final protector of the Old South." Since World War II, Carney demonstrates, Forrest's connection to issues of masculinity became more pronounced as the general came to serve as a particular illustration of southern honor through virility and violence. The writer Shelby Foote did much to shape the post–World War II image of Forrest as a paradigm of southern manliness. By the late 1990s, due in large measure to Foote's work, the Forrest image had developed into a complicated symbol of southern honor and manhood as well as racial prejudice and intolerance. The general's military service obviously played a large role in this image as did his recalcitrant attitude of forgoing submission. Women played a role in honoring Forrest, but unlike Robert E. Lee or Stonewall Jackson, Forrest noticeably appealed more to men. By the late twentieth century, groups like the Sons of Confederate Veterans eclipsed the United Daughters of the Confederacy as gatekeepers of Confederate legitimacy, and Forrest (more than any other Civil War personality) personified virile and violent masculinity. Forrest became quite clearly, in the words of Foote, "the most man in the world." By downplaying the racially charged aspects of the general's life—he was an antebellum slave trader, a commanding officer during a racially motivated massacre, and an early leader of the Ku Klux Klan—Foote constructed a symbol of southern honor and masculinity that proved useful to many white southern men.

The third section of essays focuses on the lives of individual southern men through the lenses of documentary film, autobiography, and a careful reading of three recent memoirs. These essays demonstrate several essential points about white manhood in the recent South. First, white southern men's lives are lived individually as well as collectively; white men are as variable as any group a historian might study. The essays show how the forces of race, gender, class and family, and regional history shape white southern men. For some men these burdens of family and regional history have seemed almost overwhelming, leaving them with a sense that, for good or ill, being a white southern man is harder than it used to be. The essays further show the self-consciousness with which many southern men assess their gender and how they conform or fail to conform to the ideals their culture holds out for them. Even men who find little that is attractive in stereotypical ways of being a southern man find those models hard to avoid, or find that they are able to embrace certain components of white southern manhood, while rejecting unpalatable aspects.

In "White Southern Masculinity and *Southern Comfort:* An Interview with Kate Davis," independent filmmaker Kate Davis discusses with Larry Vonalt the making of *Southern Comfort,* winner of the Grand Prize for Documentary at the Sundance Film Festival in 2001. *Southern Comfort* is a ninety-minute documentary about a fifty-two-year-old female-to-male transsexual named Robert Eads, who lived in the back hills of Georgia, which he called "Bubba land." "A hillbilly and proud of it," Eads cut a striking figure—sharp-tongued, handsome, bearded, tobacco pipe in hand. Indeed, Eads passed so well as a male that members of the local Ku Klux Klan asked him to join. Though his home was nestled among tranquil hills dotted with hay bales, Eads confronted a world as hostile to him as if he were black in the antebellum South, argues Davis. Eads was diagnosed with uterine cancer and then turned away by over two dozen doctors who feared that taking on a transgendered patient might harm their practices. *Southern Comfort* follows the final year of Eads's life. In this interview, Davis discusses the making of *Southern Comfort,* as well as her broader interest in transgressive gender in the contemporary South.

Edwin Arnold's "Doctor's Son" is a rich autobiographical essay that explores the tensions and contradictions one southern boy experienced as he attempted to balance his culture's racial and cultural expectations against the domestic realities he experienced while growing up. The oldest son of a small-town Georgia general practitioner, Arnold grew up with certain expectations about the kind of life he ought to live. His father's profession brought Arnold social status, but his father's health and ability to practice medicine were compromised by a major heart attack and subsequent battles with severe depression. Arnold had to readjust to a life of financial and emotional stress, finding that his apparent social standing and domestic realities often contradicted one another. Determined that he would not display the sort of emotional weaknesses he perceived in his father, Arnold set about to prove himself as an independent southern male, based on images derived from film, literature, and his surroundings. Playing football, working in the local textile mill during the summers, protesting school and community restrictions, searching for ways to avoid the draft—all were efforts to distinguish himself as something more than the "doctor's boy." The essay also highlights the complexities of father/son relations among white southern males. As he grew older, writes Arnold, he came to recognize the courage his father demonstrated in his emotional and financial struggles.

Jim Watkins's "Drinking Poisoned Waters: Traumatized Masculinity and White Southern Identity in Contemporary Family Memoirs" examines white southern men's struggles to come to terms with fathers, family, and recent southern history in three memoirs: John Bentley Mays's *Power in the Blood* (1997), Clay Lewis's *Battlegrounds of Memory* (1998), and Lewis Nordan's *Boy with Loaded Gun* (1999). Each of these narratives, argues Watkins, represents white southern masculinity within the conventions of the emerging subgenre of the trauma recovery narrative, a category of life writing that is most often associated with female writers. For the majority of white autobiographers in the decades immediately following *Brown v. Board of Education*, southern racism is represented as a social or spiritual illness that contaminates the author's childhood experiences and renders her/him unable to perceive the world as it really is. Coming of age for these autobiographers and memoirists, then, typically takes place in the traumatic act of recognizing the immorality of social practices they have previously accepted as "normal" and "inevitable," a recognition that is often accompanied by a sense of displacement or alienation from their home communities. In more recent autobiographical narratives by white southern men, this basic pattern in which white (liberal) southern identity is implicitly conflated with the initial identification with, then rejection of, racism seems to have been replaced by a more subtle motif in which southernness is represented as an identification with an illusory image of a lost patriarchal order. Coming of age takes place in the traumatic recognition that the idea of the South which initially provided a matrix of values around which the protagonist's identity is centered is simply that: an idea. Yet, just as the earlier narratives feature a narrator/protagonist whose rejection of his community's social values paradoxically requires him to construct his identity in relation to that community, so too does the contemporary autobiographer's identity get constructed in relation to the community in which those values were initially promoted.

The final two essays examine representations of white southern manhood in fiction and music. The essays remind us that music and fiction in the South have been shaped by and have shaped ideas of what it means to be a white southern man. Both essays too suggest the broader national and international stage upon which white southern manhood was performed. In "Ratliff and the Demise of Male Mastery: Faulkner's Snopes Trilogy and Cold War Masculinity," Susan Donaldson provides a reading of the Snopes trilogy set within the context of midcentury U.S. cultural politics. Donaldson sees the trilogy as Faulkner's commentary on competing versions of white masculinity, as well as a meditation on male competition itself. Rightly or not, many midcentury Americans were convinced that the nation was experiencing a crisis in white masculinity. Faulkner was particularly troubled by postwar models of manhood that stressed getting and spending and domesticated conformity. Faulkner, like many other Americans, worried that such a model of postwar masculinity represented too radical a break with traditional models of manhood stressing production, entrepreneurship, and individualism.

But Faulkner was equally troubled, writes Donaldson, "by the personal costs of traditional masculine competitiveness—by what appeared to be the sheer vulnerability of a competitive form of manhood requiring an unending ordeal of display, performance, and achievement." Donaldson sees in the three Snopes novels—*The Hamlet* (1940), *The Town* (1957), and *The Mansion* (1959)—what she calls "a somewhat unsettling picture of Faulkner's own complicity in the discourse of cold war masculinity. For what wins out in Faulkner's saga of the Snopeses and their adversaries is not the competitive individualism of Flem Snopes but a reduced, domesticated, commodified form of masculinity represented by Gavin Stevens and his ally V. K. Ratliff—a masculinity signaling in some respects an acknowledged loss of mastery—for men in the Snopes novels and for Faulkner himself."

In "Where Has the Free Bird Flown? Lynyrd Skynyrd and White Southern Manhood," Barbara Ching explores representations of white southern manhood in the 1970s rock music of Lynyrd Skynyrd. Other scholars have defined and described the masculinity of southern rock by comparing it to country music. Ching, on the other hand, focuses on its contrast with other forms of country-inflected rock of the 1970s, particularly the California-identified rock of The Eagles. This contrast allows the defeat and anger of the marginalized southern male to be heard far more clearly than in scholarship that emphasizes southern rock's rebellion against the southern ideology of evangelical domesticity. By comparing the careers, reception, and lyrics of Lynyrd Skynyrd to those of The Eagles, Ching shows how the California-based "free birds" triumph in their relation to post-1960s hedonism, while southern rock now functions as a form of commemoration and angry longing, a tribute to a possibly valiant, but failed, attempt at liberation.

The range of topics and scholarly approaches in this collection suggest the exciting, evolving state of scholarship on manhood and masculinity in the recent South. Because the field is so dynamic, the historiography has not allowed for the sustained examination of a few problems, such as the debates over paternalism and patriarchy that have shaped gender scholarship on the antebellum South. Where, then, might new work profitably be directed? One clear trend in recent southern studies is the eagerness of scholars to broader their definitions of the South to embrace not only the Caribbean but also Central and South America.[31] Further, as the American South grows more culturally and racially diverse, it seems likely that definitions of white masculinity will become more complicated than older models based upon the subordination of black manhood. Scholars of white masculinity in the South will benefit as well from the increasing volume of work on black masculinity and on gender in other regions of the United States.[32] Such comparative work has a useful way of complicating comfortable stereotypes. The regional and transregional comparative scholarship is likely to yield many useful new insights on race and gender in the recent South, and there is no reason why students of southern masculinities ought not to adopt these comparative approaches. In the meantime, there is still much to occupy scholars of race and gender in the recent and more traditionally construed South. Beyond stereotypes of patriarchs and bubbas, there are still many untold stories about white manhood and masculinity.

NOTES

1. David Denby, "George & Me," *New Yorker*, June 28, 2004, 110. Denby's essay is a review of Michael Moore's documentary film *Fahrenheit 9/11*.

2. See Riché Richardson, *Black Masculinity and the U.S. South: From Uncle Tom to Gangsta* (Athens: University of Georgia Press, 2007).

3. Louis Hughes Autobiography; available at www.jmu.edu/madison/center/main_pages/madison_archives/era/african/life/hughes/chap3.htm (accessed May 12, 2006). Robert Toombs, "Speech to the Georgia Legislature," November 13, 1860; available at http://web.nu-z.net/~toombs/speech.html (accessed February 25, 2007).

4. See Nina Silber, *The Romance of Reunion: Northerners and the South, 1865–1900* (Chapel Hill: University of North Carolina Press, 1993).

5. A classic study of representations of the South in popular culture is Jack Temple Kirby, *Media-Made Dixie: The South in the American Imagination* (Baton Rouge: Louisiana State University Press, 1978). An excellent recent work is Allison Graham, *Framing the South: Hollywood, Television, and Race during the Civil Rights Struggle* (Baltimore: Johns Hopkins University Press, 2001); on representations of southern lawmen, see 154–65.

6. George Jones, "High-Tech Redneck," *High-Tech Redneck* (MCA, 1993).

7. See Patrik Jonsson, "'The Rise of the 'Redneck' Stirs Up Country Music," *Christian Science Monitor*, October 12, 2005.

8. Toby Keith, "Courtesy of the Red, White, and Blue (The Angry American)," *Unleashed* (Dreamworks Nashville, 2002). The complete stanza lyrics can be found at www.cowboylyrics.com/lyrics/keith-toby/courtesy-of-the-red-white-and-blue-10125.html (accessed June 27, 2007).

9. For the first two quotes, see "Larry the Cable Guy," available at www.larrythecableguy.com (accessed July 20, 2006); for the third quote, see "An Open Letter to Larry the Cable Guy," available at www.bobanddavid.com/david.asp?artID=183 (accessed July 20, 2006). For the Blue Collar Comedy group, see www.bluecollarcomedy.net (accessed July 20, 2006).

10. Standard histories of American manhood have little to say about the American South. See, for instance, E. Anthony Rotundo, *American Manhood: Transformations in Masculinity from the Revolution to the Modern Era* (New York: Basic Books, 1993); and Michael Kimmel, *Manhood in America: A Cultural History* (New York: Free Press, 1996). Collections with useful essays on gender and twentieth-century southern culture include Nancy Bercaw, ed., *Gender and the Southern Body Politic* (Jackson: University Press of Mississippi, 2000); Jane Dailey, Glenda Elizabeth Gilmore, and Bryant Simon, eds., *Jumpin' Jim Crow: Southern Politics from Civil War to Civil Rights* (Princeton: Princeton University Press, 2000); and Anne Goodwyn Jones and Susan V. Donaldson, eds., *Haunted Bodies: Gender and Southern Texts* (Charlottesville: University Press of Virginia, 1997).

11. The idea that white southern manhood in the antebellum South was built upon an ideal of honor and mastery is best represented in Bertram Wyatt-Brown, *Southern Honor: Ethics and Behavior in the Old South* (New York: Oxford University Press, 1982). See also Kenneth Greenberg, *Masters and Statesmen: The Political Culture of American Slavery* (Baltimore: Johns Hopkins University Press, 1985). On colonial paternalism, see Kathleen N. Brown, *Good Wives, Nasty Wenches, and Anxious Patriarchs* (Chapel Hill: University of North Carolina Press, 1996). On the paternal ideal in the antebellum South, see Stephanie McCurry, *Masters of Small Worlds: Yeoman Households, Gender Relations, and the Political Culture of the Antebellum South Carolina Low Country* (New York: Oxford University Press, 1995).

12. See Glenda E. Gilmore, *Gender and Jim Crow: Women and the Politics of White Supremacy in North Carolina, 1896–1920* (Chapel Hill: University of North Carolina Press, 1996); Stephen Kantrowitz, *Ben Tillman and the Reconstruction of White Supremacy* (Chapel Hill: University of North Carolina Press, 2000); and Nancy MacLean, *Behind the Mask of Chivalry: The Making of the Second Ku Klux Klan* (New York: Oxford University Press, 1994).

13. See Bill J. Leonard, "Southern Baptist Convention," in *Religion,* ed. Samuel S. Hill, vol. 1 of *The New Encyclopedia of Southern Culture,* Charles Reagan Wilson, general ed. (Chapel Hill: University of North Carolina Press, 2006), 214–16; quote at 214.

14. "Resolution on Racial Reconciliation on the 150th Anniversary of the Southern Baptism Convention," adopted June 1995; available at www.sbc.net/resolutions/amResolution.asp?ID=899 (accessed July 21, 2006).

15. See the Southern Baptist Convention's database of convention resolutions, available at www .sbc.net/resolutions/default.asp (accessed July 21, 2006).

16. For the text of the Southern Baptist Convention's Baptist Faith and Message and its revisions, see www.sbc.net/bfm/bfmcomparison.asp (accessed February 27, 2007).

17. Thomas Jefferson, *Notes on the State of Virginia,* in Jefferson, *Writings,* ed. Merrill D. Peterson (New York: Library of America, 1984), 290–91.

18. W. J. Cash, *The Mind of the South* (New York: Knopf, 1941), 48.

19. Nick Tosches, "The Devil in George Jones," *Texas Monthly* (July 1994), 64–74; quote at 64.

20. See Barbara Ching, *Wrong's What I Do Best: Hard Country Music and Contemporary Culture* (New York: Oxford University Press, 2001), 127, 157–58.

21. For Jones's account, see George Jones with Tom Carter, *I Lived to Tell It All* (New York: Villard, 1996), 306–9.

22. For a recent overview of southern sexual behavior, see Suzi Parker, *Sex in the South: Unbuckling*

the Bible Belt (Boston: Justin, Charles, 2003). Parker's work is entertaining, if not scholarly. "The first time a boy told me that he wanted to fuck me," she writes, "I was sitting in a church pew" (xi).

23. Joel Williamson, *The Crucible of Race: Black-White Relations in the American South Since Emancipation* (Oxford: Oxford University Press, 1984), 497.

24. Bertram Wyatt-Brown, *The House of Percy: Honor, Melancholy, and Imagination in a Southern Family* (New York: Oxford University Press, 1994), 299–300.

25. Tom P. Brady, *Black Monday: Segregation or Amalgamation . . . America Has Its Choice* (Winona, MS: Association of Citizens' Councils, 1955), 47–48.

26. William Alexander Percy, *Lanterns on the Levee: Recollections of a Planter's Son* [1941] (Baton Rouge: Louisiana State University Press, 1991), 288, 297. See also William Armstrong Percy III, "William Alexander Percy (1885–1942): His Homosexuality and Why It Matters," in *Carryin' On in the Lesbian and Gay South*, ed. John Howard (New York: New York University Press, 1997), 75–92.

27. See Ted Ownby, "Southern Manhood," in *American Masculinities: A Historical Encyclopedia*, ed. Bret E. Carroll (Thousand Oaks, CA: Sage, 2003), 429–33.

28. Elliott J. Gorn, "'Gouge and Bite, Pull Hair and Scratch': The Social Significance of Fighting in the Southern Backcountry," *American Historical Review* 90 (February 1985): 18–43; Ted Ownby, *Subduing Satan: Religion, Recreation and Manhood in the Rural South, 1865–1920* (Chapel Hill: University of North Carolina Press, 1990).

29. On the antebellum period, see Craig Thompson Friend and Lorri Glover, eds., *Southern Manhood: Perspectives on Masculinity in the Old South* (Athens: University of Georgia Press, 2004).

30. See John Howard, *Men like That: A Southern Queer History* (Chicago: University of Chicago Press, 1999); and Howard, *Carryin' On*.

31. See Jon Smith and Deborah Cohn, eds., *Look Away! The U.S. South in New World Studies* (Durham: Duke University Press, 2004); and Helen Taylor, *Circling Dixie: Contemporary Southern Culture through a Transatlantic Lens* (New Brunswick, NJ: Rutgers University Press, 2001).

32. See, for example, Matthew Basso, Laura McCall, and Dee Garceau, eds., *Across the Great Divide: Cultures of Manhood in the American West* (New York: Routledge, 2001); and Darlene Clark Hine and Earnestine Jenkins, *A Question of Manhood: A Reader in Black Men's History and Masculinity*, 2 vols. (Bloomington: Indiana University Press, 1999).

Church Camping and White Southern Manhood

Evangelical Males and Christian Primitivism, 1920s–1970s

TED OWNBY

Beginning in the 1920s, it became popular for evangelical white southerners to send their children to church-run camp. Enthusiasm for these camps peaked in the 1940s and 1950s. Most camps were segregated by gender, providing either separate places or separate times for male and female campers. The lessons camp organizers tried to teach young campers dramatized the religious ideals evangelicals hoped to instill in boys and girls. It is intriguing that southern people, for whom rural life had for so long been central to their identities, wanted to send their children out into the country. By sending children away from everyday institutions of home and church and school, evangelical adults highlighted what they hoped boys and girls could be beyond ordinary expectations. Camps are intriguing as liminal institutions because they ask campers to escape from parts of their lives to pursue some of the highest ideals of their culture. But what ideals, and how did they differ by gender? What did evangelical parents believe camping accomplished for their sons and daughters, and if they thought their children needed to get away from something, what were they hoping to see their children escape?

In the middle of the twentieth century, while southern culture was facing so many challenges and opportunities, leaders of church camps had dramatically different expectations for male and female behavior. Camps for girls, more than those for boys, emphasized the possibility for girls to become missionaries, one of the most dramatic ways in which evangelical females could claim independence outside male-run institutions. At the same time, intriguingly, some camps for girls offered a particularly vivid southern cultural ideal, asking young women to ascend a series of steps to become belles. While camps for girls offered this simultaneous challenge to and escapist celebration of traditional gender expectations, many camps for boys celebrated the outdoors as a place where young males could become like American Indians, with the particular goal of rising to become a kind of chief.

Gender ideals among white southerners have long emphasized dramatic contrasts, but within southern history, this dichotomy between the ideals of the female belle and the male Indian chief seems to have been a new one in the mid-twentieth century. The religion of white southern evangelicals had long been based on dramatic gender differences. For generations, women had made up a majority of church membership, and the language and many of the actions of church life suggested women had more affinity with religious morality than men did. In the churches that used disciplinary proceedings to raise questions of individual morality and to expel members who engaged in particular sins, congregations accused men of sinful behavior far more often than women.[1] And when white evangelical church groups turned more to politics, they supported prohibition and sometimes racial segregation laws in the name of the purity of women and home life.[2] Women were often the innovators in church life, leading the way with missionary associations, Sunday schools, fund-raising efforts, and calls for political action. But, while evangelicals believed women were more naturally religious than men, they did not put those women in charge. Men were the leaders and, especially, the speakers in all but a few denominations in the South.

Organized camps for children began in New England, New York, and Pennsylvania in the late 1800s, with encouragement first from the Chautauqua movement, then the YMCA, and then the Boy Scouts. The first church-sponsored camp for boys was a small affair in Rhode Island in 1880, and several church groups started camps in the 1890s. In 1912 the International Sunday School Association started its first permanent religious camp for children. One authority on church camps claims that "in 1923, 93% of all organized camping was in New England."[3] The growth of youth camping in the late nineteenth and early twentieth centuries was part of the muscular Christianity movement in the northeastern United States and England. That movement, sparked by fears of physical frailty and supposed feminization that accompanied urbanization, especially among professional classes, demanded a rugged, physical understanding of the godly life.

Camping for youth started slowly in the South, and muscular Christianity also grew slowly in the region. Southern church leaders early in the century worried occasionally that women dominated too many church activities, but those worries rarely stimulated new institutions for building manly muscles among Christians.[4] With the slow pace of urbanization and professionalization in their region, southern cultural leaders in the early twentieth century did not have the same worries about becoming effete and effeminate, and rural people were relatively slow to become interested in the possibilities of sending their children to rural camps.

When southern religious leaders started establishing camps for children, they drew on the northeastern model and on two older institutions, the camp meeting—a central icon in church life for some groups and in memory for others—and church-run assemblies, many of which began in the late 1800s and early 1900s as large gatherings of church members. The prototype for such church assemblies, the Methodist summer community in Ocean Grove, New Jersey, began in 1869.[5] The first such southern church camp started at Montreat, North Carolina, in 1897. It was the work of New England Congregationalists, who modeled it on the Ocean Grove community until Montreat became a Presbyterian camp in the early 1900s. Smaller but somewhat comparable southern institutions started in places like Epworth by the Sea in Georgia, Lake Junaluska in North Carolina, and Seaside in Mississippi for Methodists. Southern Baptists founded similar organizations in Ridgecrest in North Carolina, Mentone in Alabama, McCall in South Carolina, and the Gulf Coast Assembly in Mississippi.[6]

Those assemblies were set in either mountains or on beaches. Camps for children were, with few exceptions, in the mountains. Beginning in the 1920s, southern church organizations, Sunday School associations, missionary unions, and, occasionally, individual congregations began to establish camps exclusively for children. The earliest children's camps started in the early twentieth century for Presbyterians, the late 1920s for Southern Baptists, the 1930s for Methodists and Churches of Christ, the 1940s for Cumberland Presbyterians, and the 1950s for southern Pentecostal groups like the Church of God and the Assemblies of God.[7] Interest in church-related camping increased dramatically in the late 1940s and 1950s, with new camps beginning almost every year and with far more children than ever attending. For example, the Cumberland Presbyterians had nineteen camps in 1946 and fifty-six camps by 1958, with a total attendance of over 3,300.[8]

At first, southern evangelicals' camps had no distinctive emphases for males and females. The reason church leaders stated most often for starting and supporting camps was consistent with what Samuel Hill calls the central theme of evangelical theology.[9] Each individual is born a sinner and needs a conversion experience, whether at church, at revival meetings, at camp, or anywhere else. Therefore, statistics on camp conversions were required parts of the reports camps made to their state and national organizations, and those statistics were also fairly common in the advertisements camps ran in religious newspapers. For example, the 1966 advertisement for Short Mountain Youth Camp in central Tennessee read, "Many young people become Christians here when no one had been able to reach them before."[10]

The divisions and distinctive emphases within evangelical theology made their way into the goals and reports of the camps. With their roots in camp meetings, Methodists, Presbyterians, and Baptists reported numbers of people who attended the camps, the number converted, and the number of children rededicating their lives to Jesus. In 1955, Cumberland Presbyterians reported that 247 children and young people had conversion experiences, 186 rededicated their lives to Jesus, and 54 made commitments to church vocations.[11] Pentecostals added a category. As the *Pentecostal Gleaner* reported for youth camps in Arkansas in 1973, "Let us shout a big 'Praise the Lord' for the 91 saved and the 157 that were filled with the Holy Spirit."[12] On the other end of evangelical theology, the resolutely rationalist Churches of Christ upheld their distrust of emotional conversion experiences. An organizer of Church of Christ camps cautioned that at some camps that emphasized evangelistic preaching, "the young folk become so suggestible that many who are not really prepared for the step respond to the invitation and request baptism. This should be guarded against . . . Every decision should be based upon solid convictions as well as an emotional impulse."[13]

Along with the emphasis on conversion as the main point of living and the reason for evangelical institutions, religious camp leaders showed a perspective on childhood experience that was warmer and softer than the ideals that evangelicals had traditionally emphasized. This perspective, first appearing in the South in the Sunday School movement of the late nineteenth century,[14] stressed the need to preserve the basic innocence of children and worried about influences threatening that innocence. Camp leaders consistently said they wanted to make all of life Christian—children should enjoy Christian play, Christian food, Christian acquaintances, and, above all, a Christian natural world. Camps varied in their routines, but most had two or three gatherings a day for Bible study, Bible discussion, prayer, or preaching. All included substantial opportunities for play, and camp publications reminded counselors that, rather than emphasizing the need for conversion at every chance, they should nurture the basic goodness of children and turn every activity into a show of God's goodness.

Camp leaders showed considerable faith in the basic innocence of youth—not a surprising concept but one that was potentially at odds with evangelical emphases on original sin and universal participation in sinfulness. "Saving" children meant two things, not entirely separable and both important. Being saved meant having a conversion experience, and it also meant being separated from harmful influences. Anti-urban language of crisis was crucial to the expansion of church camping. As a camp counselor in Arkansas wrote in 1959, "It is impossible to pick up a newspaper or magazine today without reading or seeing a maze of crime reports." He hoped that with Christian camping, "perhaps a great step will have been taken toward the elimination of teenage crime in the world today."[15]

The best way to get away from harmful influences was to spend time on a mountain with other Christians. The Southern Baptists started their first denomination-wide camp for boys in Ridgecrest, North Carolina, in 1927, within three years of the South's two clearest statements of agrarian philosophy, the publication of *I'll Take My Stand* and the beginning of the Grand Ole Opry.[16] All three were intensely anti-urban, but of the three the camp probably used the most pastoral language. The 1938 brochure criticized "cities with their hurry and bustle, their activity and business" and waxed poetic about the natural world. Camp literature stressed that its chapel was "impressively situated beneath a natural arch of rhododendron trees. The only additions of man to this natural place of worship were the piecing together of rustic logs for bridge, seats, and pulpit. Here the campers can realize how the groves truly could have been God's first temples and instantly feel the spirit of reverence."[17] In 1946 a Cumberland Presbyterian writer promised that "the Spirit of the Summer Encampment" could lead to a "mountain-top experience" in "a place that is, as nearly as possible, representative of the Kingdom of God."[18] A Church of Christ writer urged that night-time devotionals "should be held in a quiet, dark place where the glories of the Heavens reflect a wonderful wisdom, magnitude and power of God. Here the campers can look up and see the same stars that probably caught the eyes of the apostles. They can hear the same amazing sounds of the animal world which have thrilled the ears of men of all ages. They can be lost in the vastness of the universe—yet made to realize that

God does love and care for them."[19] Camps consistently advertised their natural elements, often mixing descriptions of natural beauty with listings of opportunities for outdoor sports. Stressing an unchanging nature untouched by mankind suggested that mankind corrupts but that one could find innocence and purity in natural surroundings.

The topic of sending children to camp in the mountains is especially intriguing in light of the theology of evangelical Protestants. That theology rejects altars, shrines, and sacred places, believing that no time or place is especially sacred because human beings should seek and can communicate with God at all times and in all places. In evangelical theology, all people can commune with God anywhere, through prayer, Bible reading, and Christian commitment, so, in theory at least, they should not need a special place in the mountains in order to have a religious experience. On the other hand, mountains are important in biblical stories as being close to God and as places of potential piety separate from the busy, mundane world of commerce and compromise. By the early twentieth century, many Americans believed trips into the mountains allowed them to experience God in an emotionally compelling way. Significantly, the people who saw spirituality in the mountains most directly were many groups of Native Americans and naturalists, such as John Muir, who wanted to learn from both nature and Native American spirituality.[20]

Southern church camp leaders typically stressed that mountains offered separation from temptations and worries. Children were safer at camps, and organizers hoped they might be more receptive there to the possibility of a conversion experience. But camp organizers emphasized something more for boys and not for girls. For boys, church camps sometimes offered a connection to Native American tradition that is especially interesting because of the broader context of the South in the mid-twentieth century.

Historians of the recent South see two main developments during the twentieth century. One involves the growth of cities, the expansion of wealth, and the decline of the number of people making their living as farmers. The expansion of church camping for youth was clearly related to that change, with people taking advantage of camping opportunities as they worried about the moral effects of urbanization and mass culture. Unlike Vanderbilt agrarian writers' work and country music, camp literature never mentioned farming; untouched nature, rather than cultivated soil, was the ideal. It is easy to interpret the rise of church camping for children as a religious element of the rise of the Sun Belt South, with its increase in disposable wealth, decline in the number of families needing children at home to work on farms, and general increase in organized institutions for recreation. As with many Sun Belt institutions, camps were examples of northeastern imports into southern culture. But church camping for children was part of a phenomenon in which congregations and broader denominational organizations were expanding their influence into as many aspects of their members' lives as possible. In the early 1900s, many congregations still met once or twice a month, struggled to sustain Sunday Schools, and had at most two or three intrachurch organizations. But church activities expanded throughout the century and increased dramatically after World War II, and camping was an extension of the growth of youth groups like the Royal Ambassadors, the Girls Auxiliary, and the Royal Rangers.[21]

But what about the other major change in the twentieth-century South—African American migration to cities and African Americans' challenges to segregation and political disfranchisement? Might it be possible to see in white evangelicals' desire to separate children from threats to their innocence a desire to remove children from the fears whites had about blacks in the city and especially from the marches, controversy, and threats to white supremacy of the civil rights movement? Could sending white children into the wilderness be, among other things, a new form of making whiteness?[22] Was it only coincidence that at about the same time African Americans were taking to the streets, white children were heading for the hills?

At a time of clear crisis in southern life, the camps upheld dramatically different ideals for white boys and girls. One can track gender differences for Christian campers in the brochures for the two largest Southern Baptist camps—Camp Ridgecrest for Boys and Camp Crestridge for Girls. Located in the North Carolina mountains, both camps offered recreations ranging from riflery and basketball to swimming and weaving to the ubiquitous hiking through the woods. Horses were available for girls who wanted to ride, and some girls put on formal riding dress and top hat and took part in local competitions.

The distinguishing feature of Baptist girls' camping at Crestridge was the Council of Progress, in which campers moved up rank by rank by learning specific camping skills. The goal was to reach the rank of Belle. At the end of camping season, all girls who had achieved the rank of Belle could compete in a pageant for Queen Crester, "the camper who best typifies the spirit of Camp Crestridge for Girls."[23] Queen Crester had a court made up of favored girls of different age groups, and like other pageant winners she received a crown—in the 1950s, a paper crown and, beginning in 1967, a jeweled tiara.

The route to becoming a Belle had a complex series of historical associations. The first stage of the female camper was the Pilgrim, who wore a bonnet and a blue sash that symbolized truth. Next was the stage of Pioneer, significantly symbolized by a tomahawk and a green ribbon for growth. One moved on to become an Explorer, with a coonskin cap and a red ribbon for courage. Fourth was the stage of Trekker, symbolized by a staff, with a brown ribbon that somehow signified perseverance. The culmination of successful pilgrim work, pioneering, exploring, and trekking was attaining the status of Belle, symbolized by a white ribbon for purity.[24] The odd historical progression begins in colonial New England, concentrates on frontier movement west, and then concludes with an idealized image most associated with the upper-class South. This complicated process of earning one's purity through an elaborate series of steps suggests that the twentieth-century belle combined an old southern elite term with notions of rugged frontierspeople. The combination suggests that the ideal Southern Baptist Belle was devout, athletic, multifaceted and multiskilled, a bit feisty, popular among women, and ultimately, pure.

The route to becoming a Belle, significantly, involved the possibility that young women would decide to become missionaries or other reformers. Women's Missionary Unions were among the greatest organizers and proponents of camps, and missionaries consistently spoke at camp events. In 1959 organizers of the Women's Missionary Union Camp Garaywa in Mississippi were proud to announce that several missionaries, including "Miss Minnie Landrum, missionary emeritus of Brazil, will speak at Queen's Court. These 'real-live' missionaries will help your GAs realize that people in other countries are very real and that their need for Christ is our responsibility."[25] A year later, camping for teenaged girls at Camp Garaywa concluded with "a special weekend for those who have reached the Queen step or any of the steps above. There will be a banquet, a court, a tea, a candle-light service, and other features during the weekend." The next sentence complicated the notion that the ceremony was simply honoring traditional southern ideals of womanhood. "Mrs. Dewey Merritt, missionary to Nigeria, will speak on Sunday morning."[26] Campers heard stories from missionaries who had spent time throughout the world, and campers, especially female campers, had chances to meet activists they likely would not have otherwise met. For Methodists, Lake Junaluska in North Carolina was a place far outside ordinary community and congregational settings where the denomination's progressive group could encourage forms of racial desegregation. Baptist campers in the 1940s could listen to talks from African American Baptist leader Nannie Burroughs and from leftist organizer Howard Kester.[27]

Missionary work was one of the choices religiously committed young women could make that took them away from their family, church, and community. Thus, the special purity of the Belle was not just the traditional ideal of pure womanhood; for those considering life as a missionary, it also depended on trekking and exploring and pioneering for the willingness to take on new challenges. The female camper ideal, then, was complex. Sometimes the ideal went deep into history and recalled images of queens and antebellum belles. Other times the ideal opened possibilities for innovation, travel, and reform.

By contrast, and especially in the 1950s and 1960s, the ideal for the evangelical male camper was an American Indian. The appeal of a primitive outdoor life was especially pronounced in advertisements for boys' camps. As an Assemblies of God publication put it in 1967, "Camping is a magic word to the heart of a boy. Boys dream of camping out, cutting wood, building fires, cooking meals, sleeping in a tent, and hiking in the woods."[28] A Baptist publication likewise emphasized the male side of camping. "There is something in the gems of nature that pierce the innermost recesses of being. Especially is true in the case of a boy."[29] Opportunities for sports were even more extensive for boys than for girls, with some camps beginning to offer more aggressive sports like football and boxing. But the most elaborate, meaningful recreations seem to have been efforts to emulate Indians. The girls at Camp Crestridge had virtually no connections to images of Indian life, except that their villages were named after Indian nations.[30] By contrast, Indian images were everywhere in the brochures for Camp Ridgecrest for Boys. In 1954 and in every year from 1959 to 1971, the front cover of the Ridgecrest brochure featured the same stern profile of an Indian man with headdress.[31]

White Americans have a long and complicated history of projecting on American Indians both their worst fears and highest forms of respect.[32] The clearest predecessor of church camps' interest in American Indians lay in Ernest Thompson Seton's Woodcraft Indians, one of several groups that influenced and helped give birth to the Boy Scouts. Seton, a New Englander, believed American Indians fostered a harmonious relationship with nature through ritual and physical skills. He urged that American boys should emulate Indians by camping out, doing woodwork, chasing deer, and learning Indian songs and dances. The Boy Scouts were a bit more militaristic than the Woodcraft Indians, but they adopted Seton's practices of telling Indian stories at campfires and giving Indian names to successful campers.[33]

Even more important than using numerous Indian images to advertise and characterize their camps, organizers associated Indian rituals with personal transformation. They took Indians seriously, even if they seem rarely to have invited them to their camps. The director of Camp Ridgecrest from 1950 to 1955 learned enough Indian skills to gain an honorary membership in the Sioux nation, which came with a Sioux headdress and name—E-Tonchon Wambe Wachte. The director in the early 1960s signed his name with his Indian title, Skajuna. A Baptist camp in Mississippi in the 1940s invited Dan Tilden, a Baylor University student and "a fullblooded Cherokee Indian from Oklahoma" to tell stories and teach leather craft lessons. "At the campfires each night Dan told the group about strange Indian songs, customs, and ceremonies that most people know nothing about."[34] Some camping events at Ridgecrest concluded with a Tribal Banquet, not too seriously called a "Heap Big Feast," complete with "buttered tom-toms and kick-a-poo joy juice."[35] Sections of the Ridgecrest camp were named for Apaches, Choctaws, Navaho, Shawnee, and Sioux, and Ridgecrest organizers named their playground Cherokee Territory, and leaders sometimes took campers into real Cherokee territory nearby.[36]

Among Southern Baptist campers, the male equivalent of the female Council of Progress was the Council Ring. The primary ritual at Camp Ridgecrest was a step-by-step process of gaining an Indian name and rank. Beginning in 1949 and continuing into the 1970s, what the camp brochure described as "the high point of each camping season" consisted of an elaborate nighttime ceremony in which camp leaders inducted boys into an imaginary Indian nation.[37] In the Dance of the Flying Arrows, boys with painted faces, loin cloths, no shirts, and feathers tied to their arms and heads shuffled to the beat of tom-toms around the campfire to participate in what the 1958 brochure called "songs, dances, games, and other rituals of the first American outdoorsman, the Indian."[38] Boys wrestled, camp counselors told stories, and in 1960 campers could watch "Good Spirits from Wakonda Struggle with The Evil Spirit Over the Soul of An Innocent Young Warrior in the Apache Devil Dance."[39]

As at the girls' Camp Ridgecrest, boy campers moved through an elaborate series of steps, from Hunter to Warrior to Brave to Little Chief. It is unclear how campers made the progression, except that they had to learn about Indian rituals.

The highest stage of Little Chief was the climactic accomplishment that only a few campers achieved each year. Camp counselors known as Big Chiefs gave to each Little Chief a "name they keep for the rest of their lives" in "recognition for the attainment of strength of character."[40] At Ridgecrest, camp leaders counted three things—the number of campers, the number of young people who had Christian conversion experiences, and the number of new Little Chiefs. In 1956, for example, twenty-four boys became Little Chiefs. This moment of great drama involved the attainment of manly character, celebrated something close to a spiritual experience, and represented perhaps the greatest moment young Baptist boys could have except for Christian conversion.

Camp organizers in other denominations also used Indian themes in their rituals, although none approached the detailed progressions of the Baptists. At a Methodist camp in Mississippi, camp leaders dressed as Indians, started bonfires, and beat drums as one told "a wonderful story about the Native Americans teaching something wonderful about life." The storyteller ended his story by saying, "Let there be light," as his colleagues stoked the bonfire into a large flame.[41] Methodist camp counselors also told Indian stories about animals and nature. A few Church of Christ camps had Indian names. And in 1966 the Assemblies of God started a Frontiersmen Camping Fellowship, in which boys met at Royal Ranger Pow Wows, learned about tomahawks and knives, built and slept in tepees, and had to stay out all night in an initiation that demanded ingenuity and "a courageous spirit." Camp publications suggested one beginning for a powwow. "Imagine an Indian drumbeat shattering the stillness of a moonlit night, as feathered, war painted faces stand silently before majestic tepees. A flickering torch gives an amber glow to the serene countryside, and an Indian chief steps forward to pray, with hands stretched toward the starry skies."[42]

The conjunction of Christian camping and Indian manhood seems especially revealing. If the attainment of Indian maturity signified becoming a "new man" for evangelicals and if evangelical camp counselors dwelled with great affection on Indian spirituality, something dramatic seems to have been happening. Perhaps they were simply following the camping rituals established decades earlier by the Woodcraft Indians and Boy Scouts. Perhaps they were seeking in American Indian ritual a religious connection to the natural world they did not easily find in their own religious traditions. But the timing—the 1950s and 1960s—makes this fascination with Indians especially meaningful.

Studying rituals and recreation is always a slippery business, but it seems fair to speculate that this male fascination with Indians, coming in the 1950s and 1960s, had something to do with pressures white evangelical men in the South felt about their definitions of manhood in the period of the civil rights movement. As a concept, masculinity is almost always under threat and is often invoked to describe how a group of males are dealing with a challenge. When a camp's "Message to Parents" assured them that camping "is simple, virile, living,"[43] it seems clear that it was addressing people worried about failures of their understandings of manhood or failures of contemporary men to live up to them. The various traditional meanings for manhood among white southerners—meanings that could stress independence, honor, racial control, paternalism, or helluvafella—all seemed difficult to support and sustain during the civil rights years.[44] For male ideals, evangelicals reached far back into history—farther back than the women who described their ideal teenaged girls as belles—and decided that aggressively physical but also intensely spiritual American Indians stood as proper ideals.

Much of the significance of the male fascination with Indian life lies in camp organizers' almost complete neglect of African American life. In camp brochures, reports, descriptions, and advertisements, African Americans are virtually invisible. Baptists and Cumberland Presbyterians made small and generally unpublicized efforts in the early 1950s to support separate camps for African American children as part of their churches' missionary efforts.[45] The United Methodists were far more aggressive, encouraging some forms of desegregation at their Lake Junaluska Assembly earlier than the other groups. But, in general, church camping through the 1960s was for white Southerners.

The routes the Baptists' Camp Crestridge and Camp Ridgecrest took to desegregation show that evangelicals ignored the issue even more dramatically in thinking about boys than in thinking about girls. In 1970, Camp Crestridge for the first time celebrated the fact that it welcomed campers from all over the world. Two years later, the camp director's first-page message said the camp should also emphasize "dimensions of interfaith and interracial relations," and photographs in the brochure conspicuously displayed African Americans as part of the camp's ethnic diversity. By contrast, brochures for Camp Ridgecrest for Boys never mentioned international, interracial, or interfaith dimensions, although by 1973 their photographs showed occasional pictures of black campers.[46]

The most meaningful interracial experience at most camps for boys involved acting like Indians rather than meeting African Americans or people from other countries. In 1960, the camp director at Ridgecrest wrote with pride that through the Indian Lore program, "each boy has the rare opportunity to learn many fascinating things about the Redman and his way of life." At a time when white southerners were wondering about which parts of their traditions to celebrate and which parts to reject, the camp director found it relatively easy to celebrate how Baptist boys were learning "much of the great heritage left by our country's first inhabitants."[47] This turn toward embracing Indian culture seems, among other things, a form of escapism in which males unsure of changing male ideals plucked a male identity from deep in American history. And male ideals—or fantasies—about becoming Indian chiefs included nothing similar to female campers' interest in missionary work, although the occasional speaker at boys' camps did mention such work. Whereas organizers of camps for females balanced the historical image of the belle with the modern figures of activists and missionaries, male campers could choose to emulate the historical image of the Indian chief or to play a range of sports, or to do both, but their camps offered little that encouraged male campers to meet the particular challenges of their time and place.

To be sure, sending children off to church-run camps represented nothing that was particularly sinister. Evangelicals repeatedly said that camps' goals were to encourage children to become converted Christians, to help them develop a more religious understanding of the natural world, and to enjoy recreation in a safe and attractive setting. Nonetheless, the fascination with an especially Indian form of primitivism for boys looks like an attempt to rescue boys from the necessity of confronting some of the most difficult issues in southern life of their day. White evangelicals did not know what to do about the civil rights movement, and most seem to have preferred to avoid it. Should they follow many denominational leaders who called on a new activism around the concept of Christian brotherhood? Should they stay clear of politics and follow a religion that concentrated exclusively on issues of conversion? Should they make their religious lives conform to the white supremacist language they heard in discussions of politics and schools? Evangelicals who were trying not to deal with those tensions instead offered their boys images of Indian manhood that seemed ancient, in a mountaintop environment that separated them from the issues and experiences the civil rights movement was forcing most white southern adults to face.

NOTES

1. Ted Ownby, *Subduing Satan: Recreation, Religion, and Manhood in the Rural South, 1865–1920* (Chapel Hill: University of North Carolina Press, 1990).

2. See Jean E. Friedman, *The Enclosed Garden: Women and Community in the Evangelical South, 1830–1900* (Chapel Hill: University of North Carolina Press, 1985); Paul Harvey, *Redeeming the South: Religious Cultures and Racial Identities among Southern Baptists, 1865–1925* (Chapel Hill: University of North Carolina Press, 1997); John Patrick McDowell, *The Social Gospel in the South: The Woman's Home Mission Movement in the Methodist Episcopal Church South* (Baton Rouge: Louisiana State University Press, 1982).

3. Quote from George Gurganus, *Christian Camps* (Henderson, TN: self-published, 1958), 19. Other material is from Clifford Putney, *Muscular Christianity: Manhood and Sports in Protestant America, 1880–1920* (Cambridge, MA: Harvard University Press, 2001), 35–36; Floyd and Pauline Todd, *Camping for Christian Youth: A Guide to Methods and Principles for Evangelical Camps* (New York: Harper and Row, 1963); Viola Mitchell and Ida Crawford, *Camp Counseling* (Philadelphia: W. B. Saunders, 1961).

4. Putney, *Muscular Christianity;* E. Anthony Rotundo, *American Manhood: Transformations in American Masculinity from the Revolution to the Modern Age* (New York: Basic Books, 1993); Ownby, *Subduing Satan.*

5. Randall Balmer, "From Frontier Phenomenon to Victorian Institution: The Methodist Camp Meeting in Ocean Grove, New Jersey," *Methodist History* 25, no. 3 (April 1987); Troy Messenger, *Holy Leisure: Recreation and Religion in God's Square Mile* (Minneapolis: University of Minnesota Press, 1999).

6. Sally G. McMillen, *To Raise Up the South: Sunday Schools in Black and White Churches, 1865–1915* (Baton Rouge: Louisiana State University Press, 2001), 218–21.

7. On Southern Baptists, see Kenneth McAvear, *Ridgecrest: Mountain of Faith* (Nashville: Broadman Press, 1982); Robert L. Middleton, *A Dream Come True: A History of Ridgecrest Baptist Assembly, 50th Anniversary, 1907-1957* (Nashville: Convention Press, 1957). On the Cumberland Presbyterians, see Robert G. Forester, "A History of the Development of Young Camp Work in the Cumberland Presbyterian Church" (M.A. thesis, Cumberland Presbyterian Theological Seminary, 1952). On the Churches of God, see *The Continuing Generations, A History of the Church of God in Georgia* (Cleveland, TN: Pathway Press, 1986), 13; *A History of the Church of God of North Carolina, 1886–1978* (Charlotte, NC: Herb Eaton, n.d.), 37; *Tennessee Church of God History, 1886–1990* (Cleveland, TN: Pathway Press, 1990), 83.

8. *Cumberland Crusader* (Memphis) 16, no. 10 (June 1947): 41; Cumberland Presbyterian Church, General Assembly, *1958 Minutes*, 66.

9. Samuel Hill, *Southern Churches in Crisis* (New York: Holt, Rinehart, and Winston, 1967); Hill, introduction to *Religion in the Southern States*, ed. Samuel Hill (Macon: Mercer University Press, 1983); Hill, *The South and the North in American Religion* (Athens: University of Georgia Press, 1980).

10. *Gospel Advocate* (Nashville), April 21, 1966, 251.

11. Cumberland Presbyterian Church, General Assembly, *1956 Minutes*, 98.

12. *Pentecostal Gleaner* (Little Rock), August 1973, 5.

13. Gurganus, *Christian Camps*, 1958.

14. McMillen, *To Raise Up the South.*

15. Stan Schwartz, *A Practical Approach for Christian Camp Counselors* (Searcy, AR: Camp Wylde-wood, 1959), ix–x.

16. The Opry began in 1925. *I'll Take My Stand* was published in 1930.

17. Camp Ridgecrest for Boys brochure, 1938, folder 31, box 3, Ridgecrest Conference Center Collection (RCCC), AR 555, Southern Baptist Historical Library and Archive, Nashville, Tennessee.

18. Mrs. Charles Whyde, "Let's Go to Camp," *Cumberland Crusader* 15, no. 9 (June 1946): 11.

19. Schwartz, *A Practical Approach*, 42–43.

20. On John Muir and natural religion, see Catherine L. Albanese, *Nature Religion in America: From the Algonkian Indians to the New Age* (Chicago: University of Chicago Press, 1990), 93–100. See also Edwin Bernbaum, *Sacred Mountains of the World* (Berkeley and Los Angeles: University of California Press, 1997), 144–56. Also, on mountains as sacred places, see several essays in David L. Carmichael, Jane Hubert, Brian Reeves, and Audhild Schance, eds., *Sacred Sites, Sacred Places* (New York: Routledge, 1994).

21. On the expansion of church activities, Ted Ownby, "Struggling to be Old-Fashioned: Evangelical Religion in the Modern Rural South," in *The Rural South Since World War II*, ed. R. Douglas Hurt (Baton Rouge: Louisiana State University Press, 1998), 122–48; Harvey, *Redeeming the South;* McMillen, *To Raise Up the South.*

22. The term comes from Grace Elizabeth Hale, *Making Whiteness: The Culture of Segregation in the South, 1890–1940* (New York: Pantheon, 1998).

23. Camp Crestridge for Girls brochure, 1956, folder 24, RCCC.

24. The Council of Progress, the ranks from Pilgrim to Belle, and the competition for Queen Crester, continued from 1955 at least until 1973. Camp Crestridge for Girls brochures, 1956–73, folders 24–27, RCCC.

25. *Baptist Record* (Jackson, MS), May 7, 1959, 5.

26. *Baptist Record*, May 26, 1960, 5.

27. *Baptist Record*, July 25, 1940, 8; July 8, 1943, 6.

28. *Assemblies of God Men's Manual* (Springfield, MO: Gospel Publishing House, 1967), 25.

29. Camp Ridgecrest for Boys brochure, 1938, RCCC.

30. In 1962, when Camp Crestridge expanded into some new buildings, the "villages" were named after the Cherokee, Choctaw, Cheyenne, Chickasaw, and Chippewa. Camp Crestridge brochure, 1963, folder 25, RCCC.

31. Camp Ridgecrest brochures, 1954–71, folders 32–35, RCCC.

32. See, among many sources, John Demos, *The Unredeemed Captive: A Family Story from Early America* (New York: Knopf, 1994); Bernard W. Sheehan, *Savagism and Civility: Indians and Englishmen in Colonial Virginia* (Cambridge: Cambridge University Press, 1980); Mark C. Carnes, *Secret Ritual and Manhood in Victorian America* (New Haven: Yale University Press, 1989).

33. David I. Macleod, *Building Character in the American Boy: The Boy Scouts, YMCA, and Their Fore-*

runners, 1870–1920 (Madison: University of Wisconsin Press, 1983), 130–40. See also Michael Kimmel, *Manhood in America: A Cultural History* (New York: Free Press, 1996), 168–71.

34. *Baptist Record,* June 20, 1940, 8.

35. Camp Ridgecrest Silver Anniversary Tribal Banquet flyer, 1953, folder 30, RCCC.

36. Baptist Sunday School Board News Release, 1953, p. 5, folder 31; Camp Ridgecrest brochure, 1955, folder 32, RCCC.

37. Quote from Camp Ridgecrest brochure, 1957, folder 32. Other information from Camp Ridgecrest brochures, 1949–73, folders 31–35, RCCC.

38. Camp Ridgecrest brochure, 1958, folder 32, RCCC.

39. Camp Ridgecrest brochure, 1960, folder 33, RCCC.

40. Camp Ridgecrest brochure, 1957, folder 32; brochure 1949, folder 31, RCCC.

41. *Lake Stevens United Methodist Camp: A Heritage of Faith, A Future of Promise, 1946–1996* (no publishing information), Conference Assembly Grounds File, J. V. Cain Archives of Mississippi Methodism, Millsaps College, Jackson, Mississippi.

42. The quote is from *Frontiersman Camping Fellowship Handbook* (Springfield, MO: Gospel Publishing House, 1981), 114; other information, pp. 9–10. On Church of Christ camps with Native American names, such as Camp Tahkodah, see Gurganus, *Christian Camps,* 29; for Camp Ney-A-Ti, see *Gospel Advocate,* August 15, 1968, 522. For more on camps run by the Assemblies of God, see *Alabama Messenger,* July 1971, 4; *Appalachian Messenger,* July-September 1980, 6.

43. Camp Ridgecrest for Boys brochure, 1949, folder 31, RCCC.

44. This list comes from Ted Ownby, "Freedom, Manhood, and White Male Tradition in 1970s Southern Rock Music," in *Haunted Bodies: Gender and Southern Texts,* ed. Anne Goodwyn Jones and Susan V. Donaldson (Charlottesville: University Press of Virginia, 1997).

45. Cumberland Presbyterian Church, General Assembly, *1953 Minutes,* 46; Alabama Baptist State Convention, *1950 Annual,* 121.

46. Camp Crestridge for Girls brochures, 1970–73, folder 27; Camp Ridgecrest for Boys brochures, 1970–73, folder 35, RCCC.

47. Camp Ridgecrest Brochure, 1960, folder 33, RCCC.

Where the Action Is

Interstate Rest Areas, the Creation of Gay Space, and the Recovery of a Lost Narrative

BROCK THOMPSON

Public restrooms are chosen by those who want homoerotic activity . . . for a number of reasons. They are accessible, easily recognized by the initiate, and provide little public visibility. Tearooms thus offer the advantage of both public and private settings.

—LAUD HUMPHREYS

I grew up in Conway, Arkansas, and the rest area where the trouble began was only twenty miles down Interstate 40 toward Little Rock. Though I was only thirteen years old at the time, I do remember the arrests that commanded headlines across the state. The battle they began was over not only the use and misuse of a public place but also the creation and facilitation of a gay identity and space in the thick of the American South.

The interstate highway system, the great victory of the automotive lobby, began in the 1950s and soon symbolized the postwar economic boom, connecting far-flung cities and the citizens therein. It also represented the American love affair with the automobile and leisure.[1] The highway rest area, established for travelers and their families, offered services to aid them in their journey, including toilets, picnic facilities, and tourist information. The Morgan Rest Area was opened in October of 1973, at the cost of almost a half a million dollars. It sat at mile marker 146, meaning it was that many miles from the Oklahoma border to the east. From that point, it was 138 miles west to Memphis on Interstate 40, which runs coast to coast. When it opened, it was one of thirty-six rest areas in the state, offering not only public toilets but also two dozen private picnic areas and parking for recreational vehicles.[2]

On February 1, 1991, Robert Howard began his regular commute from Little Rock to Conway. He ran Self Image, Inc., a licensed massage and beauty business that offered clients in-home service. His house calls often brought him to various homes in Conway from where he lived in Little Rock, thirty or so miles away. He usually worked late, as he often accommodated clients after they finished their workdays. By the time he left his last client and began the drive to Little Rock, it was almost 11:30 p.m. Howard stopped off to use the public toilets at the Morgan rest area, sitting roughly halfway between Conway and Little Rock.

The rest area had a reputation. The fact that a great many men used the space for anonymous sexual encounters was not lost on Howard, nor was it lost on local law enforcement officers. Howard parked his car and entered the men's toilets. He had noticed a few men loitering around the building and in the woods that surrounded the rest area on one side. He paid little attention to this, though he knew of the men's intentions. Robert Howard is a gay man, but he did differ from the loitering individuals in that his intention *was* to use the toilets for their intended purpose. After he used the facilities, he was walking back to his automobile when an attractive young man in his late twenties stopped him. Howard was intrigued, though not enough to entertain the man beyond polite conversation. He felt sympathy for the young cruiser.[3] As the young man tried to make small talk, Howard told him that "cruising an interstate rest stop for sex was no way for a gay man to meet people."[4] At that point, the young cruiser's conversation turned lewd. He asked Howard to join him in his car and said that they would continue the conversation there. Howard refused and began to walk away. At this point, the young man produced a badge from under his shirt and identified himself as a Pulaski County sheriff's deputy. Robert Howard was under arrest for loitering to solicit deviant sexual activity, a misdemeanor.[5]

Howard was not the only man arrested during the two-hour sheriff's office sting that night. A total of eight men were arrested on various charges, including two for violation of the Arkansas sodomy statute. For many, especially those arrested on sodomy charges, the raid came to seem peculiarly well timed.

According to the *Arkansas Gazette,* on Thursday, January 17, 1991, Arkansas state senator Vic Snyder introduced a bill into the legislature that quickly sparked opposition from his fellow legislators as well as various religious groups. Snyder, a Democrat representing Pulaski County, introduced Senate Bill 125, aimed at removing homosexual activity from the state's sodomy statute. When the sodomy statute was enacted in March of 1977, it declared that "A person commits sodomy if such performs an act of sexual gratification involving: (1) The penetration, however slight, of the anus or the mouth of an animal or a person by the penis of a person of the same sex or an animal; or (2) The penetration, however slight, of the vagina or anus of an animal or person by any body member of a person of the same sex or an animal." Sodomy was defined as a Class A misdemeanor, punishable by a jail term of up to one year and a fine of up to $1,000.[6]

Snyder's bill would leave intact the bestiality portion of the law. Snyder, himself a Little Rock physician, noted that the law was contradictory to Arkansas' efforts to contain the AIDS virus. Snyder stated that on the one hand, the state wished to stop the spread of AIDS by encouraging homosexuals and heterosexuals to undergo blood tests and confide in their doctors, who promised confidentiality. One the other hand, Snyder argued, some of the activity that prompted the need for testing was deemed illegal by the state.[7]

Arkansas religious groups were quick to respond to Snyder's proposed legislation. Mark Lowery, executive director of the Christian Coalition of Arkansas, although he had not seen the bill, promised his organization's opposition to it. Lowery stated that Snyder's reasoning for the removal of homosexual activity from the sodomy statute was unsound, since there were no laws requiring doctors to report to the police when they discovered someone to be homosexual.[8]

Senate Bill 125 remained in the Senate Judiciary Committee, where emotions ran high. Snyder pleaded with the committee not to "incorporate one moral perspective or one religious view" when considering the bill. Opponents were quick to suggest that the state has a duty and responsibility to take a stand against homosexual behavior as destructive and unnatural. Though the committee offered no discussion on the topic, there was an invitation for citizens to testify either for or against Snyder's proposed changes to the sodomy statute. John Miles, senior pastor of St. James United Methodist Church in Little Rock offered testimony agreeing with Snyder's position that the sodomy statute might discourage gay men from being tested for AIDS. Miles added that he believed that "what goes on between two consenting adults is their private matter."[9]

In opposition to the bill, the committee heard from Larry Page, attorney for the Arkansas Baptist Association. Page stated that while he did not hate homosexuals, he abhorred homosexual behavior. He offered testimony that such "destructive" and "harmful" activity mainly occurs in public spaces such as parks and restrooms.[10] Page, himself a former Little Rock city prosecutor, said that he had never prosecuted anyone for violating the sodomy statute. He suggested that those who opposed it simply regarded it as innocuous in that it constituted no real danger to gays and lesbians in Arkansas.

Joining Page was Norman Carter of the First United Methodist Church in Conway (my home church). Carter's testimony attempted to dispute those who argued that homosexuality was a victimless crime and that the sodomy statue was unnecessary. Carter noted that there was indeed a need for the law that "puts a leash on the aggressive behavior of homosexuals toward innocent people." He added that he himself had been a victim of such behavior; though when asked, he failed to comment on how he had been victimized. During his testimony, Carter produced a copy of the *Gay Community News*. Reading from what he called the "gay credo," he said that homosexuals "will sodomize your sons" and that homosexuals' "only gods are handsome young men."[11] Carter's harsh rhetoric was joined by Lowery, who admitted that he had still not read the bill. The two offered a number of statistics indicating that gay men are more likely to incorporate minors in their "unnatural" behavior. As well as citing the danger to minors, the two men offered further statistics that gay men are more likely to have sexual relations with strangers, putting them at increased risk for sexually transmitted diseases.

After all the testimony was offered, the committee moved to vote on the resolution, hearing no discussion from its members. The day after the vote, the *Arkansas Gazette* ran a bold three-column headline: "Committee Rejects Sodomy Law Repeal." The committee had voted to strike down the measure in a rare unanimous do-not-pass motion. Snyder had had no illusions concerning the chances of House Bill 125. Nevertheless, he had felt it necessary to introduce the measure, hoping that subsequent attempts would prove successful.[12] Later, as committee members were approached by *Gazette* reporters, many stated that they were simply following the wishes of their constituents, though they may have personally agreed with Snyder. Senator Wayne Dowd of Texarkana, who made the motion to kill the bill while it remained in committee, noted that "what it comes down to is I guess I have a lack of backbone." Dowd, an attorney in Texarkana, stated that as a lawyer and lawmaker, he felt that any legal challenge to the sodomy law would most likely see it declared unconstitutional by Arkansas courts. However, Dowd noted that he "had so many communications from constituents opposed to the bill that, trying to represent the people that elected me, I voted against it."[13] So the Senate Judiciary Committee voted down Snyder's bill on Wednesday, January 30, 1991.[14]

On Friday, February 1, the day after the *Gazette* ran its front-page story, Robert Howard was on his way to Pulaski Country jail. Both in the cramped confines of the back of the state trooper patrol car and within the holding cell, Howard was bombarded with bellicose and homophobic remarks from the arresting officers, who called him "worthless" and "faggot."[15] He was released later on bond posted by his partner. To say that Howard and the seven other men arrested that night were in the wrong place at the wrong time does not begin to describe their predicament.

The raid was carried out by Sergeant Jay Campbell, who later told the *Gazette* that the sheriff's office has received a number of citizen complaints about the misuse of the Morgan rest area. Campbell noted that in their misuse of the facilities, local gay men had "gotten pretty bold," and, in his opinion, they were attempting to "take the park over." Campbell said that the rest area had become a popular gathering place for gay men looking for "one-night stands," adding, "They need to rent a motel room or something."[16] In the raid, two men were arrested for sodomy. Twenty-year-old Bryan Blystone, of Orange, California, and thirty-six-year-old Ronald Simmons of North Little Rock were arrested on sodomy charges after officers observed the two men in an act of fellatio in the backseat of Simmons's parked automobile. The other six men, not actually caught in a sexual act, were charged with loitering for the purpose of deviant sexual activity, a misdemeanor. Campbell noted that he preferred to arrest the men, rather than simply issue a citation on the scene. If arrested, the men would have to appear in court rather than simply having to pay a ticket.

The sheriff's office also revealed that two of the individuals arrested had tested positive for AIDS. As a result of this information, the sheriff's office announced their intention to ask the arraigning judge to require each of the arrested men to submit a statement during their arraignment showing that they had been tested for the AIDS virus. Campbell noted that he would ask for the AIDS test both for reasons of public health and to discourage men from coming to the rest area.

It was not long before questions arose as to the connection between the legislative debate and the raid that netted two sodomy arrests. Campbell told *Gazette* reporters that it was "merely coincidence" that the two events happened within two days of each other.[17] The Arkansas Gay and Lesbian Task Force pointed to the connection. Although small in number, they were quick to voice their outrage concerning the arrests. A small group of men and women assembled on the corner of Capitol and Main in the shadow of the state capitol building in downtown Little Rock. Jan Hodges, the head of the task force, said that the arrests were too closely linked to the debate regarding Snyder's redefinition of the sodomy statue. He condemned the Pulaski County sheriff's office, which he suggested was attempting to illustrate to the public through the raid that there was still a need for a state sodomy statute. Hodges read from a prepared statement condemning the recent sodomy arrests and the media coverage of them, which he deemed as sensational. Hodges argued to a meager assembly of local journalists that the reports concerning the Morgan rest area only perpetuated society's stereotypes concerning gay men. Hodges remarked that, in fact, "the overwhelming majority of gay male sexual activity is at home between two consenting adults." Hodges condemned the media for doing little to dispel the myths that stigmatize gays and lesbians, noting that "rarely is there something positive in the media" concerning homosexuals. Hodges noted that as a gay man, he was not embarrassed that so many were arrested at the Morgan rest area. However, he did express his sadness that "people like us are rounded up, arrested and dehumanized because anonymous sexual activity is the only way these men can keep their secret." Also, Hodges hoped that the two sodomy arrests might prove to be a good test case for removing the sodomy law through a judicial challenge.[18]

Sergeant Campbell said he had misunderstood the question asked by *Gazette* reporters after the raid. Two men had tested positive for AIDS, but those individuals had been apprehended in a separate rest area months prior, not during the raid at the Morgan rest area. Despite this misunderstanding, Pulaski County municipal judge David Hale agreed with the sheriff's office request. Upon their appearance for plea and arraignment, Hale would order that all men arrested at the rest stop submit to an AIDS test. Hale justified his decision by citing precedent in previous sex-related crimes. Hale told reporters he had followed the same procedure in a case where arresting officers had been scratched by women arrested on prostitution charges.[19]

The use of hidden cameras came to light when the sheriff's office offered different taped scenes as evidence against various men arrested at the rest area. In the early stages of the operation, the sheriff's office had installed hidden cameras inside the building that housed the public toilets. Campbell defended his use of the cameras, noting that it was his understanding that Arkansas Supreme Court rulings allowed for the use of hidden cameras in public restrooms in the course of criminal investigations. He also noted that the cameras were only in the men's restrooms and that they were only turned on when undercover officers believed someone to be breaking the law. When *Gazette* reporters approached the office of the Arkansas Attorney General, the spokesman noted that they could find neither a U.S. Supreme Court case nor an Arkansas Supreme Court case that supported the use of hidden cameras in public restrooms. However, he said that under the circumstances in which the sheriff's office was operating, courts generally would admit video surveillance as evidence. The Attorney General's Office noted that "generally, there's not an expectation of privacy in a public place."[20]

Some felt differently. Though he declined to make a motion to suppress the videotaped evidence, as his clients were not among those who were captured by the hidden cameras, Ike Allen Laws, of Russellville, disagreed with the sheriff's department. Law noted that the issue had never been appealed to the Arkansas Supreme Court, but several states had established that evidence gathered by law enforcement officers in public places where there is "an expectation of privacy," such as a toilet stall, is not admissible as evidence. Though Laws conceded that "public restrooms certainly are not the place to have sex," he did question Sergeant Campbell's extensive use of manpower and material, ostensibly to collect small fines on misdemeanor charges.[21]

It was not long before the American Civil Liberties Union (ACLU) voiced concern over the question of cameras inside the rest area. Jay Jacobson, the state director of the ACLU, noted that this was an "outrageous violation of the people's right to privacy." The case as a whole, according to Jacobson, illustrated the "bias and bigotry against homosexuals." He also argued that if the state would simply legalize sodomy, there would be no need for the sheriff's office raids. Jacobson went on to say that "if there was not a sodomy law, if homosexuals were not evicted from apartments and if they were not beaten up . . . then you wouldn't have clandestine activity because there is no place for them to meet." Attempting to defend its use of cameras, the sheriff's office stated that they were turned on only when an undercover officer thought that a violation might be in progress. Sheriff Carroll Gravett also mentioned that the cameras served a dual purpose, looking for those violating Arkansas' statutes prohibiting public sexual encounters and those using the rest area for illegal narcotics dealings.[22]

The *Arkansas Gazette* ran an editorial questioning the use of cameras by the sheriff's office. The editorial remarked that "they are called 'public restrooms' because they are installed for the public's convenience, but most people would consider what they do in a public restroom to be private." Like Laws, the editorial questions the tactics made during the sheriff's operations at the rest areas. The *Gazette* went on to say that "had the deputies quit their peeping and instead posted even one of their uniformed number where he could be seen, at the door of the restroom, say, no illegal activity would have occurred." The editorial closed by saying that "the right of privacy is real, though its boundaries are not so plainly marked as others."[23]

The cameras mounted at the rest area, and the continuing arrests that took place there, added to unwanted attention not only for the Pulaski County sheriff's office but also for the Arkansas Highway Department. After all, the rest area was ultimately the property and responsibility of the department. In October of 1992, almost a year after the raids began, the highway department announced its decision to close the rest area, with no plans to reopen it or to create a similar facility at another site. In reaching its decision to close the facilities, the highway department hardly mentioned the homosexual activity for which the space had become notorious. Instead, the highway department focused on maintenance issues and repair costs that exceeded the departmental budget. According to the highway department, an additional $300,000 would be needed over the rest area's annual budget of $84,000 to repair structural damage in the brick and concrete building that housed the public toilets. Also, the department concluded that it would cost too much to comply with the recently passed Americans with Disabilities Act, which would require modifying existing buildings, walkways, and drives to provide access to the handicapped.[24]

One employee, however, was willing to connect the closure of the rest area with the homosexual activity that had become heavily publicized in the past year. In an interview with the *Arkansas Democrat*, a state highway department employee, who wished to remain anonymous for the interview, fearing job loss, claimed that sexual encounters, along with the resulting vandalism and high maintenance cost, had become the greatest problem for the rest area. According to this employee, stalls in the men's toilets had had to be replaced, either because "glory-holes" had been cut into the metal or because they had been torn down altogether. Also, graffiti advertising willing participants for sexual activity required the restrooms to be repainted frequently.[25] The employee went on to mention that due to the high volume of the traffic through the Morgan rest area, up to ten thousand people a day in the busier summer months, the spot had become particularly attractive to gay men seeking anonymous sexual encounters.[26] Following the article's publication, the Arkansas Highway Department was quick to comment. But Randall Ort, public affairs officer for the department, simply noted that "vandalism is going to be a problem at any rest area."[27]

In October of 1992, the Arkansas Highway Department sought the approval of the Federal Highway Administration to close the rest area, effective immediately following the Thanksgiving holiday weekend, citing both the condition and the "misuse" of the facilities as the reason. The Federal Highway Department agreed but refused to fund the actual demolishing of the rest area.[28] On the morning of Monday, November 30, 1992, crews from the highway department erected barriers at the entrance of the rest area. The picnic tables were removed from beneath the family pavilions and transported to other rest areas around the state. Everything else—the charcoal grills, the restroom mirrors, the water fountains—was sold as surplus. Above the picnic and parking areas, demolition teams began razing the structure that had housed the public toilets, and so many anonymous sexual encounters.

Growing up gay in the American South is never easy. For many, it requires a duplicitous existence, constantly juggling different lives for different people—for parents, for those at church, and at school. Robert Howard likened it to walking a tightrope. I was fourteen years old when the highway department began to demolish the Morgan rest area. The story ran throughout the state's newspapers, and the work to raze the rest area was visible to all who passed by it. I remember traveling down the interstate, toward Little Rock, with my father in his oversized pickup truck, doing its share of damage to the now-ailing American interstate infrastructure. We passed the busy workmen at the rest stop. He took it upon himself to explain why the state was flattening the rest area, though I already knew. "It turned into a gay bar all the sudden," he said.

According to sociologist Laud Humphreys and his work, *Tearoom Trade: Impersonal Sex in Public Places*, the Morgan rest area would easily qualify as a tearoom. A tearoom, used here in the context of what Humphreys calls a homosexual subculture, is a place forged by reputation and facilitated by gay men seeking anonymous sexual encounters without further emotional involvement. Functioning tearooms can be found in a number of settings. Usually, they are found in spaces where the line between public and private is less distinguishable, that is, in public spaces that can afford a great deal of privacy for an individual. A space is created where one can remain for hours at a time without being asked to leave: in a dark movie theatre, deep within the stacks of a public library, or in the steamy corners of a public sauna or bathhouse.

Indeed, of all places, public toilets, particularly at roadside rest areas, are the most desirable locations for those wishing to engage in anonymous sex. They remain so for three reasons. First, in keeping with the American fascination with the automobile and the resulting drive-thru craze, public rest areas are easily accessible. The Morgan rest area, though only serving east-bound Interstate 40 traffic, was a mere twelve miles from Little Rock, the state's largest urban center. There were ample spaces for public parking, many which were connected to private picnic pavilions in remote settings throughout the grounds of the rest area. Secondly, rest areas are easily recognizable to any passing motorist. Signs are posted in numerous and highly visible locations, telling interstate travelers not only where a particular rest area is located but also how much further one can expect to travel before finding it. For those who live in close proximity to rest areas, their intended and unintended functions would be somewhat obvious. The third, and perhaps most poignant reason for the popularity of rest areas and their public toilets for private sexual encounters, is that although they are considered public space, they offer little public visibility. Cruising the tearoom offers a chance for the man to shed his known identity, to travel beyond the prying eyes of his neighbors, the watchful eyes of his family, and to find a public place that essentially affords him more privacy.[29]

The Morgan rest area was surrounded by thick woods and overgrown brush, and a few yards beyond that lies endangered wetland protected by Arkansas environmental law. This no-man's land isolated the still-accessible rest area, and indeed the tearoom forged there, from any other space. There was no chance of little leaguers wandering off from a baseball diamond, no chance of a family spotting sexual activity from an area playground. The Morgan rest area was not near any of these things.

Also worth mentioning is that the rest area was set back from the interstate an irregular distance for facilities of that type. The building that housed the public toilets was high atop a hill that overlooked the busy thoroughfare. One could observe passing automobiles whizzing by, but there was little chance of a passing motorist spotting anyone or, for that matter, recognizing any particular automobile as belonging to a neighbor or coworker.

Unbeknownst to the Arkansas Highway Department, it had constructed a space ideal for someone to engage in impersonal homoerotic activity. However, the same circumstances that led to the creation of the tearoom for those who wished to use it for sex also attracted those who wished to close it down. Given the statutes regarding sodomy and loitering for sexual purposes, the Pulaski County sheriff's office had a full range of laws with which to arrest possible offenders. Humphreys offers three possible avenues for police involvement in tearoom activity. The first is spying, used at the Morgan rest area in the form of hidden cameras. Given the unfavorable publicity surrounding their use, hidden cameras are no longer used in public toilets by either local law enforcement or the highway department. However, all rest areas in Arkansas, down from thirty-six to thirty-two, are now equipped with cameras mounted *outside* the buildings housing public toilets to monitor criminal behavior on the grounds. The second method law enforcement officers use, as Robert Howard could tell you, is decoys, that is, undercover officers. According to Humphreys, the use of decoys remains the most popular means of capturing men in the act of anonymous public sex.

Lastly, police detection seeks to hamper tearoom activity through raids. Raids, like those played out at the Morgan Rest Area, are mainly reactionary. Though the sheriff's office often stated that they had received several complaints, they failed to mention how many complaints were taken. The timing of the initial raid, especially to those arrested and local gay and lesbian rights groups, seemed peculiar at best. Following Vic Snyder's failed attempt at toppling the sodomy statute, local law enforcement agencies perhaps wished to demonstrate to the community the need for keeping a sodomy statute on the books. Perhaps more importantly, Snyder's main argument for removing the sodomy statute was not that it threatened the civil liberties for gays and lesbian Arkansans but that it hampered the state's attempt at containing HIV and AIDS.

On November 30, 1990, the *Arkansas Gazette* stated that Arkansas had jumped from ranking fortieth to twenty-eighth nationally in the number of reported AIDS cases per capita. The first reported case of AIDS in Arkansas was in 1983, but since records regarding AIDS and HIV infection began to be kept in 1985, health department officials noted that cases of AIDS had jumped 111 percent in Arkansas. In 1990, the Arkansas Department of Health had a total of 490 AIDS cases on record. Officials estimated that an additional three to five thousand Arkansans were HIV positive. In 1990, Pulaski County, the county where the Morgan rest area was located, had the highest number of cases by county, with 112 reported.[30]

Though Snyder argued that the sodomy statute worked against the state's efforts to contain the virus, perhaps many took the opposite view. It is a regrettable fact that the AIDS virus hit the gay community with particular ferocity. Though the *Gazette* in 1990 stated plainly that the majority of new cases in Arkansas were among the heterosexual population, particularly in women and children, perhaps many regarded abandoning the sodomy law as opening an opportunity for an even further dramatic rise in AIDS cases. Perhaps the raids at the Morgan rest area and the opposition to Snyder's attempt at repealing the sodomy law was a conscious (or, perhaps, unconscious) reaction to this fear. Despite the great number of deaths caused by AIDS and the social reaction to it, the virus energized gay activism and helped solidify a growing national gay identity.[31]

The sodomy statute, though considered archaic by many, was, when employed, a tool of legality and power meant to hinder the lives of individuals whose behavior a heteronormative and often racist southern society had deemed abnormal. When Vic Snyder and his allies tried dismantling the fifteen-year-old sodomy statute, no one bothered to remind the legislature of the law's rather dubious past. After all, it was not the state's first sodomy law, simply the first on the books directed towards the state's queer population. The history of Arkansas' first sodomy law is a precarious one. Fueled by racial bigotry before and during the Civil War, Arkansas legislators sought to treat the black population differently, and decidedly more severely, than whites by prescribing a penalty of death rather than imprisonment for black violators of the statute.[32] Also, as it appeared on the books, the early sodomy law was used to regulate "indecent" acts committed by anyone and made no distinction concerning same-sex behavior. For legislators, same-sex sexual activity was decidedly not as *queer* as crossracial sexual activity, a behavior worthy of regulation and, indeed, punishment by the state of Arkansas. In the late twentieth century, homosex simply replaced crossracial sex as the threatening queer behavior of the day as the southern state of Arkansas sought to redefine manhood and masculinity, once again depending on the prevailing social discourse.

Those who legislated against queer behavior made it extremely difficult for those who wished to engage in it. As for sexual encounters in public, there are certain risks to the game. Many of the men arrested at the rest area, totaling thirty-five by the time the raids finished and the rest area was demolished, lost their jobs and their families. Robert Howard was able to beat his charges. He lost very little and kept his name. Others were not as lucky. The *Arkansas Gazette* ran only the names of those men arrested for violating the sodomy statute. The *Arkansas Democrat*, its rival, was kind enough to publish the names and addresses of all the men arrested, regardless of the charges. At each man's arraignment, Hale suspended the sentence if the individual produced the results of a recent AIDS test. Those who did not provide the court with their test results were order to pay one hundred dollars in fines and serve ten days in jail.

For what it's worth, the press and the sheriff's office were perhaps unwitting accomplices in forming an Arkansas gay and lesbian identity. By arresting gay men, by running the stories, by publishing their names and addresses, the police and the press only succeeded in illustrating—to gays and lesbians all over the state, in small towns spread across a rural landscape, to people like me—that there were indeed others like us to be found. The *Gazette* and the *Democrat* not only told you who these gay men were but where you might want to go to meet them.

In his unique study of Oscar Wilde, *Who Was That Man?* queer theorist Neil Bartlett attempts to answer, through urban traces and sexual geography, to what degree his life and personal identity is connected to gay men who lived in London long before him. He explains in his introduction, "What I've done, I suppose, is to connect my life to other lives, even buildings and streets, that had an existence prior to mine. This is in itself remarkable, because for the longest time imaginable I experienced my gayness in complete isolation, just like any other gay child in a small town. And now, gradually, I've come to understand that I am connected to other men's lives . . . that's the story." Bartlett adds that "some of my of my most basic ideas about myself as a homosexual man were invented not by me, but other men, in another time, in another city."[33] Truly, these traces left behind, like those of a demolished and dilapidated rest area, are the cultural production and urban clues that one must begin to locate in order to fully document and understand queer history.[34] In this act of recovery, seeking brief and seemingly minute episodes of sexual deviance, one also places them into a proper context of broad social trends that will enable us to investigate the past as a rightful and needed intrusion into the present.[35]

I visited the Morgan Rest Area for the first time almost twelve years after the public toilets were bulldozed and the grounds closed to the public. I parked my father's dark blue pickup truck by the side of road. Ignoring signs forbidding trespassers, I scaled the concrete barricades. The roofs of the picnic pavilions were caving in, the picnic tables themselves long since carted off. Rusted parking lights, fallen trees, and overgrown brush now decorated the grounds. I made my way up to the sun-baked, brittle concrete foundation that was once the public toilets building, now punctured in places by sapling pines. I went to establish a greater connection between that space and myself than could be gained by poring over newspapers and listening to oral histories.

In preparing this essay, I had a couple of goals in mind. The first was to try to resurrect, as it were, a particular episode of Arkansas history, a certain social injustice that I saw was in danger of being forgotten. The second was to relate my growing up gay in the South with those who came before me, those I did not know, who were already living their lives as gay Arkansans while I was becoming one. What did these men have to do with me? At first glance, not much. Like Bartlett, I now live in London. At times I feel lucky to be living at such a distance, separated from the rural existence that defined a great deal of my childhood and adolescence. Other times, I feel guilty, as if I selfishly abandoned my past. The episode played out at the Morgan rest area, the gay men arrested there, the gay and lesbian Arkansans who protested them, as well as similar episodes that played out all over the South—all helped in forging the dynamics of a group to which I now count myself as belonging.

NOTES

Epigraph from Laud Humphreys, *Tearoom Trade: Impersonal Sex in Public Places* (New York: Aldine de Gruyter, 1975), 2–3. Some have criticized Humphreys's use of language and his seemingly unorthodox research methods, namely, his betrayal of research subject anonymity and personal involvement in the acts he was attempting to document. Recently, queer theorists and historians of sex and sexuality have argued the book's seminal value. See Peter M. Nardi, "Reclaiming the Importance of Laud Humphreys's *Tearoom Trade: Impersonal Sex in Public Places,*" in *Public Sex / Gay Space,* ed. William L. Leap (New York, Columbia University Press, 1999), 23–28.

1. Laud Humphreys, "Tearoom Trade: Impersonal Sex in Public Places," in Leap, *Public Sex / Gay Space,* 30–31. Also see John Howard, "The Library, the Park, and the Pervert: Public Space and Homosexual Encounter in Post–World War II Atlanta," in *Carryin' On in the Lesbian and Gay South,* ed. John Howard (New York: New York University Press, 1997), 107–31.

2. Randal Ort, Director of Public Affairs, Arkansas Highway and Transportation Department, personal interview, Little Rock, June 20, 2003. The cost of the rest stop and its construction date are from Dennis Merida, Acting Division Administrator, letter to Maurice Smith, Director of Highways and Transportation, September 28, 1992, Arkansas State Highway Commission Archives, Little Rock.

3. According to Humphreys, a cruiser is someone who seeks impersonal sex without further emotional involvement (*Tearoom Trade,* 2). For specific cruising practices in urban spaces, see Mark Turner, *Backward Glances: Cruising Queer Streets in London and New York* (London: Reaktion, 2003).

4. Robert Howard, personal interview, Little Rock, June 15, 2003.

5. Regarding loitering, the Arkansas Criminal Code reads: "(A) A person commits the offense of loitering if he or she . . . (5) Lingers or remains in a public place for the purpose of engaging or soliciting another person to engage in prostitution or deviate sexual activity. (B) Among the circumstances that may be considered in determining whether a person is loitering are that the person: (1) Takes flight upon the appearance of a law enforcement officer; or (2) Refuses to identify himself; or (3) Manifestly endeavors to conceal himself or any object." Loitering is a Class C Misdemeanor (Ark Code Ann. 5-17-213).

6. Ark. Code Ann. 5-14-122. Arkansas was the only state to repeal its sodomy law (in 1976) and then reenact it (in 1977), targeting only homosexual sex in a harsh reaction to increasing queer visibility and the religious backlash fostered by Anita Bryant. For a history of the Arkansas sodomy statute, see W. Brock Thompson, "A Crime Unfit to Be Named: Arkansas and Sodomy," *Arkansas Historical Quarterly* 61 (Autumn 2002): 255–71.

7. Mike Arbanas, "Snyder's Bills Stirs Opposition," *Arkansas Gazette,* January 18, 1991. The proposed revision of the sodomy statute was one of three bills proposed by Snyder that day.

8. Arbanas, "Snyder's Bills Stirs Opposition," 1.

9. Mark Oswald, "Committee Rejects Sodomy Law Repeal," *Arkansas Gazette,* January 31, 1991.

10. Ibid.

11. Oswald, "Committee Rejects Sodomy Law Repeal," 3. All efforts to locate a *Gay Community News* proved unsuccessful.

12. U.S. congressman Vic Snyder, personal interview, Little Rock, March 11, 2002. During his tenure as state senator, Snyder would try twice more, in 1993 and 1995, to amend or repeal the sodomy statute. Both attempts would prove unsuccessful.

13. Oswald, "Committee Rejects Sodomy Law Repeal," 1.

14. After Snyder's attempt at modifying the sodomy bill, the *Arkansas Democrat Gazette* offered his "political obituary." Editorialist John Brummett noted that Snyder's Bill 125 illustrated that Snyder "was the kind of impractical liberal more suitable for San Francisco than Arkansas." Brummett was sure that

Snyder would not survive the next election. Eric Camp, "Snyder to Run Unopposed: Survives Sodomy Repeal Effort," *Triangle Rising*, May 1992, 1. *Triangle Rising* is the official newspaper of the Arkansas Gay and Lesbian Task Force. Snyder, in fact, ran unopposed for his state senate seat in the next election. In reference to Brummett's remarks, Snyder noted that "the reports of his political death were greatly exaggerated" (Snyder, personal interview).

15. Howard, personal interview.

16. John Hoogesteger, "Deputies Acting to Remove Gays from Rest Area," *Arkansas Gazette*, February 2, 1991.

17. Peggy Harris, "Sodomy Arrests Not Tied to Debate," *Arkansas Gazette*, February 7, 1991.

18. Valerie Smith, "I-40 Sodomy Arrest Protested," *Arkansas Gazette*, February 17, 1991. There would be a legal challenge to the Arkansas sodomy statute, though not through the arrests at the Morgan Rest Area. The Arkansas sodomy statute was ruled unconstitutional in the state supreme court on July 3, 2002. See *Jegley v. Picado et. al.* 2002 Ark. LEXIS 401. Also, turning over the notorious *Bowers v. Hardwick* decision, the U.S. Supreme Court, with *Lawrence v. Texas*, ruled state sodomy laws unconstitutional on June 26, 2003; see *Lawrence v. Texas* 02-0102 United States (2003).

19. Jerry Dean, "14 Sentenced for Sex-Related Activity," *Arkansas Gazette,* March 20, 1991.

20. For a detailed account of the use of hidden cameras in public restrooms and the issues surrounding them, see Humphreys, *Tearoom Trade*, 84–86. Peggy Harris, "Sheriff's Office Defends Use of Camera," *Arkansas Gazette*, April 19, 1991.

21. Peggy Harris, "Attorney Questions Using Rest-Stop Camera," *Arkansas Gazette*, April 20, 1991.

22. Cheryl Waldrip, "ACLU Calls Camera in Rest Stop Restroom 'Outrageous,' Bigoted," *Arkansas Gazette,* April 23, 1991.

23. "No Cameras in the Restrooms," *Arkansas Gazette*, April 24, 1991.

24. Dennis L. Merida, Facilities Management, Arkansas Highway Department, to Acting Division Administrator, James C. Williams, Office of Engineering and Operations, October 20, 1992, Arkansas State Highway Commission Archives, Little Rock. The American Disabilities Act of 1990 (ADA) was introduced by Iowa senator Tom Harkin and Representative Tony Coelho of California. The act legally freed those with disabilities from discrimination due to their impairments. Section 504 of the ADA guaranteed reasonable accommodation and access to public buildings and facilities to those with disabilities. For a detailed discussion of the ADA and its social impact, see Ruth O'Brien, *Crippled Justice: The History of Modern Disability Policy in the Workplace* (Chicago: University of Chicago Press, 2001).

25. Maintenance reports found at the Arkansas Highway Department archives mention none of these things. In fact, after one inspection on August 8, 1991, Joseph Young gave satisfactory ratings to the rest area and its facilities in all thirty-one categories. In his comments, Young stated that "more attention is needed for clean up of cigarette butts. Otherwise, the park area is well maintained."

26. The traffic through the rest area was far less than ten thousand a day. During the summer months, the rest area averaged 1,025 visitors a day on the weekend and 978 during the weekday, far fewer than other rest areas in the state. Many motorists simply waited to stop in Little Rock. *Special Traffic Request*, Arkansas Highway Department.

27. John Haman, "State Worker Says Gays Cause Damage to I-40 Rest Area," *Arkansas Democrat,* February 19, 1991.

28. Permission from the Federal Highway Department was necessary in that federal funding was responsible for the construction of the rest area.

29. For a detailed theoretical look at the question of public versus private space, see George Chauncey, *Gay New York: Gender, Urban Culture, and the Making of the Gay Male World, 1890–1940* (New York: Basic, 1994), 179–206.

30. Pulaski County had the highest rates by far. The county with the second highest is Washington County with thirty-one cases, followed by Jefferson County with sixteen. The *Gazette* gave two explanations for the high AIDS rate in Pulaski County. The first, of course, is that the county is the most densely populated in the state, with a population of approximately 300,000 in 1990. The second reason is that Little Rock and Pulaski County offer numerous and affordable university hospitals, offering care to those who otherwise would not be able to afford it. Pheobe Wall Howard, "AIDS Patients Have Haven," *Arkansas Gazette*, July 9, 1990.

31. In connecting police raids and crackdowns on prostitution with public fears of disease epidemics, see Howard, *The Library, the Park, and the Pervert*, 118–19. For health department fears concerning gay cruising, see Humphreys, *Tearoom Trade*, 84, 99–101. For a complete and highly useful social history of venereal disease, see Allan M. Brandt, *No Magic Bullet: A Social History of Venereal Disease in the United States since 1880* (Oxford: Oxford University Press, 1987). For AIDS' contribution to gay activism, see Meredith Raimondo, "Dateline *Atlanta*: Place and the Social Construction of AIDS," in *Carryin' On*, 331–69. At the time of the rather notorious U.S. Supreme Court ruling in *Bowers v. Hardwick*, some were quicker to link sodomy laws to the AIDS epidemic. For this, see Raimondo, "Dateline," 344–46.

32. *A Digest of the Statutes of Arkansas Embracing All Law of a General and Permanent Character in Force at the Close of the Session of the General Assembly of One Thousand Eight Hundred and Seventy-Three* (Little Rock: Little Rock Printing and Publishing Co., 1874), 1107–8. Also see *Revised Statutes of the State of Arkansas* (Little Rock: E. H. English, 1848).

33. Neil Bartlett, *Who Was That Man? A Present of Oscar Wilde* (London: Serpent's Tail, 1988), xx, 223.

34. In this sense, *queer* is a technical term used in queer theory and studies. The word, which obviously has several definitions, is here meant as a descriptor, encompassing those who would claim to be gay and lesbian, as well as those who engage in homosexual sex but would not necessarily label themselves as gay or lesbian. For a useful treatment of the term as employed in gay and lesbian studies, see John Howard, *Men Like That: A Southern Queer History* (Chicago: University of Chicago Press, 1997) xvii–xix.

35. Social theorist Scott Bravmann notes that 'the importance of history to gay men and lesbians goes beyond the lessons to be learned from the events of the past to include the meanings generated through retellings of those events and the agency those meanings carry in the present." He adds that "lesbians and gay historical representations—queer fictions of the past—help construct, maintain, and contest identities—queer fictions of the present" (Bravmann, *Queer Fictions of the Past: History, Culture, and Difference* [Cambridge: Cambridge University Press, 1997], 4).

Political Parties

*College Social Fraternities, Manhood, and the Defense of
Southern Traditionalism, 1945–1960*

ANTHONY JAMES

At the end of World War II, numerous college social fraternities, led by members
who were returning war veterans, initiated a debate over discriminatory racial
and religious policies within their organizations. From the late 1940s into the
1950s, the *New York Times,* the *New Yorker* and *Time* magazines, educational journals, and local newspapers joined fraternities over this hotly bandied topic. Greek
chapters at several New England and Midwestern colleges, most notably Amherst
and Middlebury, admitted African American pledges in the late 1940s, often in
defiance of national fraternity policy and counsel. Fraternity integration quickly
moved students beyond the pressing civil rights issues of voting, employment, and
housing, straight to the core of what segregationists wanted to defend most, personal living arrangements, friendship, and dating, all embedded within prescribed
gender roles. College fraternities at southern schools, which balked even at the
notion of integration on campus, could not yet fathom racial equality in the more
intimate realm of Greek social life. Nevertheless, southern chapters of fraternities
faced the politics of integration at their national annual conventions when more
liberal delegates from other regions of the country proposed the elimination or
modification of racial and religious covenants.

The period from 1945 to the *Brown v. Board of Education* decision in 1954 offered a fragile bubble of opportunity and hope for the cause of racial equality. The
Double-V campaign during World War II, followed by President Truman's mod-

erate advances in racial equality, unsettled white southerners and planted seeds of white political backlash. White southern fraternity members confronted with threats of racial change mimicked their elders and peers to secure the benefits of segregation. Although most Greek members could not yet cast a ballot in local, state, or national races, they did comprise part of the campus body politic. Elections for student body president, along with other collegiate and fraternity posts, undoubtedly focused on localized issues but of necessity reflected larger social values of segregated southern life. University endorsement of mock elections of national or regional importance, combined with visits by campaigning politicians, often reinforced traditional political and racial views.

Faced with a dearth of off-campus political opportunities, college fraternities expressed their political values through other venues, primarily campus parties and entertainment. Fraternity social life offered immense opportunities for southern undergraduates to learn, practice, and implement their ideas of racial and gender roles. Under the umbrella of heterosexual frivolity, Greek-letter entertainment expressed fundamental elements of manhood, such as the pursuit of traditional sex roles and dating, but layered those with various party themes that projected segregationist ideals, from the ridiculous to the politically relevant. An examination of the Universities of Alabama, Mississippi, and North Carolina from 1945 to 1960 reveals that fraternities used casual get-togethers, formal parties, campus-sponsored events, and photographic depictions in college yearbooks to construct an identity of civilized white manhood informed and solidified by the political ideology that maintained segregation. Frequent celebrations gave fraternities a playful social space where they could not only reaffirm their privileged racial and gendered status but also flirt with the perceived weakness and decadence of black manhood.[1]

The fusion of the political with the playful gave celebrants rich understandings about how their society should be structured.[2] However, the possibility for unchecked creativity remained limited. At the University of Mississippi, administrators set guidelines for all types of campus parties, with the hope of preserving the chastity and virtue of young coeds, in addition to the reputation of the institution. Most schools recognized two broad categories of dances, the formal and the informal, with some slight variations in guidelines. At Ole Miss, for example, policies established different rules for "dignified costume parties, such as the Old South Ball" and "costume parties such as lil Abner parties." Dignified costume parties could be held both on and off campus. Perhaps to shield the high jinks of college youth from the broader public, the more informal costume parties could be held only on campus. More general rules proscribed the use of vulgar language and alcohol, "rowdyism," and "the presence of women in unchaperoned rooms." The dean of women often served as arbiter in judging the conditions of respectability.[3]

Fraternities also bestowed a civilizing influence upon young men in word, if not always in deed. Many fraternity handbooks instructed members on social rules and gave advice that ran the gamut from dating and dining etiquette to tips on personal cleanliness and proper clothing. In sum, these manuals guided fraternity members toward proper gentlemanly behavior, a key, many thought, to later social and economic success. Although not explicit in discussing race, exclusionary clauses implied that the offer was to create white gentlemen only. Pi Kappa Alpha developed a twenty-page "The Pledge as Gentleman" chapter for their manual, which reminded members of proper decorum. It was a shorter version of an earlier, separately published *Etiquette Manual* that ran to over thirty pages of very detailed suggestions. Sigma Alpha Epsilon quoted a familiar saying in their manual. "Shouting above high C, making marks with the heel on the floor, and behaving in general like a colt in pasture is more appropriate at a political convention. If you don't know the bounds of decency, it is best to play safe and stay well inside them."[4] Kappa Sigma urged their members to emulate their fraternity's birthplace, the University of Virginia, which the author recognized as a wellspring of "southern gentlemen, honor, loyalty, and rich friendships."[5] Most large fraternity residences employed a full-time housemother, who offered an additional tone of respectability and feminine advice.

The feverish round of informal parties that annually swept fraternity row undermined traditional conceptions of middle-class, respectable, southern white manhood, and created imaginary and unexpected realities.[6] In 1948, the University of Alabama's Sigma Chi fraternity hosted a party where guests revolved between heaven and hell. In heaven, costumed angels mingled amid decorations of puffy white clouds. When partygoers tired of the saintly surroundings, they descended into darkness down the hall. Here, a red pall flickered over the room, and devils served punch concoctions.[7] Similarly, the "kid party" gained popularity immediately following World War II and allowed battle-weary Greeks to reclaim shards of lost childhood innocence. In the fall of 1945, Mississippi's Pi Kappa Alpha hosted a kid party where couples wore children's clothes and enjoyed "suckers, gumdrops, pink lemonade, and ice cream cones."[8] Of course, students understood the limitations, but the shocking extremes that separated the party from everyday reality enhanced the thrill. When curfew drew near, heaven and hell transformed once again into the familiar fraternity house, and "kids," if they had really forgotten, realized they were indeed students, with tests to take, essays to write, and other collegiate responsibilities. Otherworldly behavior and childish tantrums conformed once again to expected social norms.

Other informal parties permitted fraternity members to pursue more formidable, masculine, and iconic identities. In August of 1946, Mississippi's Kappa Sigma fraternity hosted a pirate party where normally button-downed fraternity members assumed the garb of crude, salty, buccaneers. Frequent Old West theme parties also legitimized playful aggression and sexual bravado. At one saloon party, brothers dressed as cowboys, gamblers, and outlaws, while their dates masqueraded as cowgirls and milkmaids. The fraternity house became a frontier watering hole, complete with swinging doors, a bar, and a cowboy band. On another occasion "Pancho Pablo and his gang" choreographed a "raid" upon the party and "held up the women, took their purses, and gave prizes for the oddest articles found therein."[9] Such an intrusion into the secret realms of womanhood would only have been acceptable in an atmosphere where everyday rules were temporarily suspended. Alabama's Pi Kappa Alpha hosted a "Wild West Brawl" in the summer of 1947. Guests who entered the fraternity saloon encountered cow skulls, wooden horses, and even a horse thief hung from a tree.[10] The cowboy provided a familiar motif for educated and refined white men eager to express a rugged and violent masculinity. Theodore Roosevelt's late nineteenth-century adventures in the West had framed this possibility for future repressed young men. Fraternities risked a bit more when they sponsored "Apache" and other Indian-themed parties, a few of which were also held during this time period.[11] White southern men also possessed their own deep well of violent manhood, with legacies of racial murder and lynching within easy reach. Dipping into wells too close to home, however, would have unmasked the veneer of civilization and brought to a screeching halt the imaginary play.

Parties reinforced notions of Greek privilege amid the increasingly diverse postwar student body. The GI Bill welcomed an expanding number of economically marginal collegians from a kaleidoscopic range of ethnic and religious backgrounds. Although fraternity chapters absorbed some of these students, a vast financial gulf separated many Greek members from their less fortunate peers. In the fall of 1947, a sorority, Mississippi's Delta Zeta, hosted a couples "unemployment party." Dates found the classified sections of newspapers plastered to the walls and registered for employment upon arrival. Attendees wore their tackiest clothing and crowned both a king and queen of unemployment. After entertainment, guests stood in a "bread line to get hot chocolate and doughnuts." Merrymakers at Alabama's Delta Sigma Phi fraternity danced in their cast-off clothing at a "hard times" party. Prospective dates to the 1950 Ole Miss Kappa Sigma "poverty party" received invitations on old brown paper bags. Fraternity members greeted coeds on the front lawn and escorted them into the house, where every item of furnishing was tagged with a sale price.[12]

In addition to parties that spoofed penury, southern fraternity chapters enjoyed festivities that lampooned campus rivals and cast them as social inferiors. Students at flagship state universities expressed class and regional bias against fellow state colleges, usually the land grant agricultural and technical college, or less moneyed and ill-equipped teacher training colleges. The flagship universities attracted the states' better-connected, wealthy, and aggressively ambitious bunch, who used their time on campus to develop connections and test political and professional possibilities for the future. Fraternity-sponsored country hoedown parties provided a striking contrast of class symbolism. The Ole Miss mascot, Colonel Reb, connoted agrarian roots, landholding, and a prior history of slave owning; however, his version of a hoedown probably included whiskey on the moonlit piazza, not the adventures students had in mind. In December of 1952, Delta Kappa Epsilon fraternity invited dates to a "State" party, where the brothers dressed as "farm boys" and politely asked their girlfriends to "stretch their imaginations and come dressed as the typical Mississippi State co-ed."[13] In 1946, the Phi Kappa Psis at Mississippi "observed the illegal holiday of 'Hayseed Heyday.'" The party culminated when "Queen Alfalfa, ruler of the snuff dippers" was crowned with a royal headpiece of "shredded corn stalks." That same fall, Sigma Chi gave a barn party. Guests entered by sliding down an improvised chute into a pile of hay.[14] Alabama fraternity parties reviled their cross state nemesis, Alabama Polytechnic Institute. The Pi Kappa Alpha's Farmer's Ball welcomed the fall of 1947, while in 1948, Delta Chi hosted a "Down On The Farm" party and decorated various rooms in the fraternity house to correspond with areas on a farm, including a barn and chicken coop.[15]

Fraternities continued to mark social contrasts by hosting parties that incorporated the minstrel tradition and racialized entertainment. White southerners held a dual perception of African American males. On the one hand, white southerners romanticized the gentle "old darkey," who remained a loyal servant to his master after the Civil War and never fully achieved self-sufficient manhood. On the other hand, whites also imbued blacks with an excessive masculinity that preyed upon white womanhood and threatened the social control of white men. By entering into blackness in these playful spaces, white fraternity members tweaked the stereotypes in pursuit of both racial dominance and sexual license. In March of 1947 Sigma Alpha Epsilon fraternity sponsored a minstrel party on the Oxford campus. After a buffet dinner, guests enjoyed a floorshow showcased by "George Gulley's interpretation of Al Jolson's famous 'Mammy.'"[16] In the fall of 1948, North Carolina's Pi Kappa Alpha fraternity hosted a party with the Pi Phi sorority and entertained the visiting women with a minstrel show. Before the festivities began, the Pi Phis "selected their 'beaux' by choosing a chocolate drop, each of which contained the name of a PiKA wrapped up in the candy."[17] Whether or not the use of Hershey's Kisses, sometimes known in southern vernacular as *nigger tits*, was intentional, the mixture of racial and sexual imagery perhaps evoked southern white stereotypes of black sexual suggestiveness and availability. Such an insinuation of desire in the company of dates could have provided one venue to broach romantic possibilities and transgress typical dating expectations.

Traditionally, fraternities welcomed African Americans at fraternity social events only as servants, or "houseboys," and as entertainers. The first role reinforced notions of the nonthreatening, servile black male, while the second opened the door to libidinous display. Popular black bands, like the Red Tops and the Hot Nuts, traveled across the South to play the fraternity party circuit.[18] At the 1947 Phi Gamma Delta "Harlem" party in Tuscaloosa, revelers enjoyed the "party jive provided by a colored combo" amid "flop houses" and false store fronts in the background.[19] While walking down Beale Street or in Harlem may have proved too risky, fraternity house parties provided safe spaces for interracial experimentation. In 1952, the *Mississippian* social editor praised Delta Psi fraternity for its original choice of a jungle party. Not content to rest on its laurels, the fraternity created a Voodoo party for their dates at Sardis Lake one year later. In addition to decorations of "bones, zombies, drums, and horribly mutilated bodies," the Delta Psis arranged for an "intermission performance by local members of a [voodoo] cult."[20]

The presence of African Americans at social events sometimes encouraged the flouting of the racial and sexual boundaries prescribed by segregation. Black bands like the Hot Nuts, who started playing for white fraternities in Chapel Hill in 1955, often interacted with white audiences and wove them into an improvised narrative of sexually suggestive lyrics. Pete Daniel writes that at one 1950s off-campus fraternity party at Auburn, the effects of liquor produced "much fraterniz-ing among some of the boys, the house boy, and the Negro band."[21] Such mingling among fraternity members, their dates, and the entertainers would not have been unusual.

Informal parties often disguised or distorted the normal physical appearance of fraternity members and permitted uncharacteristic social behavior. While accounts of these parties provide few clues to an idealized image of fraternity life, they do offer insight into how fraternity members did *not* see themselves. Theme parties allowed fraternities to subvert the realities of everyday obligation. The fun and humor of these parties derived, in part, from the temporary escape from mundane routine. By regulating access to space (for fraternity members and dates or fraternity members and friends) and restricting the time frame of the party, fraternity members created physical and emotional zones where they freely experimented with a range of attitudes, beliefs, questions, stereotypes, and relationships. On many campuses alcohol lubricated the engines of creativity, exploration, and sometimes degeneration. While fraternities participated, usu-ally weekly, in events that allowed them to be pirates, cowboys, Indians, African Americans, poor, unemployed, or country bumpkins, the very act of poking fun at these alternative identities simultaneously reinforced the perception of Greeks as civilized white men.

In the spring of 1948, the social and political lives of many students merged in response to President Truman's proposed federal policies on race relations. The re-lease of President Truman's Civil Rights Committee report, *To Secure These Rights*, coupled with Truman's legislative package sent to Congress in February of 1948, unsettled southerners in its thorough challenge to segregation. As liberal Demo-crats gravitated toward the principle of greater equality, most white southern-ers responded by defending traditional racial segregation and supporting States' Rights.[22] The Dixiecrats met in Birmingham, Alabama, on July 17, 1948, within days of the conclusion of the Democratic National Party convention in Philadel-phia. Fifty-five students from the University of Mississippi joined with students from other southern universities and adults from around the south to campaign for the prospect of a States' Rights candidate in the oval office.[23]

The participation of Ole Miss students in the Birmingham convention resulted from prodding by the state's political leadership. Mississippi's governor, Fielding Wright, who would become the vice-presidential nominee of the Dixiecrat Party, consulted other southern political leaders to offer a response to Truman's civil rights proposal. In late April 1948, attorney Thomas J. Tubb addressed a meeting sponsored by students in the University of Mississippi law school to drum up support for the States' Rights initiative.[24] Sympathetic students on the Oxford campus met prior to the Birmingham convention and chose their own slate of delegates. The associated student body president, Mayes Hunter, presided at the meeting where a chairman, secretary, and group spokesman were elected. All three delegates and Hunter belonged to social fraternities.[25] The enthusiasm kindled at the Dixiecrat convention continued to smolder back in Oxford. One week after the convention, the student delegates assembled in the Ole Miss student union and formed a more permanent organization, the Ole Miss States' Rights Democratic Association. Students elected John "Buddy" Bowen, a Phi Delta Theta and quarterback for the Ole Miss football team, as chairman.[26] Similar student organizations coalesced elsewhere. At the University of North Carolina, a Dixiecrat organization hastily formed in support of Strom Thurmond's appearance on campus in early October 1948.[27]

Prior to the political organizing of 1948, fraternity parties had cultivated an affinity for neo-Confederate themes and the racial traditionalism the Dixiecrats represented. Kappa Alpha, more than any other southern fraternity, encapsulated these ideals. At the close of the Civil War, southern students formed Kappa Alpha Order and enshrined the ideal of chivalry by vowing to protect the virtue of southern womanhood. Kappa Alpha lauded its southern heritage, worshipped Confederate war veterans, and shrouded much of its festivity in Old South memorabilia. By the mid-1950s Kappa Alpha's memorialization of traditional ideals, including a respect for white womanhood and elders, and a romanticized vision of Old South virtue, found acceptance through chapters that stretched from Maryland to Florida and across the west to Southern California.[28]

In early April of that presidential election year, Ole Miss Kappa Alpha dramatized the formation of the Confederacy through a series of secession decrees, stunts, and parties. Kappa Alpha mailed a telegram to President Truman that read, "We aim to fight it out for 24 hours here on the campus of this wonderful . . . Southern institution." The following day the appointed KA Colonel read the secession decree before a gathered crowd at the University gymnasium.[29] A plantation theme set the tone of the formal party later that week. According to the University of Mississippi student newspaper, "two of Robert E. Lee's happy, cheerful slave servants" greeted guests and guided them through the rose arbor to the dance floor.[30]

As the States' Rights Party gained momentum in the summer of 1948, several southern fraternities offered their support to the cause. "Kappa Alpha, Kappa Sigma, S. A. E., and Phi Delta Theta fraternities have brought Confederate and Alabama state flags out of the moth balls and once more they are flapping in the warm Southern breeze," wrote Jim Harland in the University of Alabama's student newspaper, the *Crimson-White*. Two Kappa Alphas, H. Grady Tiller and George E. Mitchell, condemned recent northern aggression upon "Southern culture and ideals"—an expansive catchphrase that referred to any number of values but primarily the practice of segregation—and issued a battle cry for southern resistance. "No longer can the brothers of Alpha Beta chapter sit idly by and watch the destruction of the noble doctrine of States' Rights. Rise up, ye men of Lee! Don your colors and put asunder this menace which threatened our age-old traditions," read part of their resolution. The Kappa Alphas on campus pledged to fly their Confederate flag in defiance for an indeterminate amount of time.[31] Stubborn rebellion tapped into the longstanding southern masculine tradition of defending personal honor and rebuffing national attempts to dismantle white supremacy.

Despite the fervor for States' Rights, especially within the Deep South, limited debate on racial issues occurred on campuses before the pounding waves of massive resistance eroded dissent. At the University of Alabama, World War II veteran Morrison B. Williams ran for student body president in 1948 on a platform that favored integration.[32] At Ole Miss a contingent of twenty-six students arose in opposition to the States' Rights advocates. Led by Thomas J. Griffith, a member of Beta Theta Pi fraternity, the students wrote a letter to Democratic National Chairman, J. Howard McGrath, and asked for assistance in placing the Truman-Barkley ticket on the November ballot. The States' Rights organization at Ole Miss derided the nationalist group as a fringe element unrepresentative of the broader opinions of the students on campus.[33] At North Carolina frequent dialogue about integration stymied States' Rights zeal and created a more elastic social atmosphere. Campus religious groups, the YMCA-YWCA, the American Veterans Committee, and various political groups openly discussed integration and pressed fellow students to do likewise. The liberal leadership of former North Carolina chancellor Frank P. Graham also greatly influenced a wider campus culture of tolerance.[34]

In contrast to the informal party, most fraternities also developed formal events that fed grandiose visions of self-identity. Kappa Alpha Order, perhaps more than any other social fraternity, staged annual events that embodied culturally specific remnants of Lost Cause mythology, and imbued those events with purposeful meaning. The end of the Civil War exposed the brutalized and haggard reality of southern manhood: a lost war, physically wrecked bodies, and a ruined economic future. Ironically, the well-developed Lost Cause mythology of the post–World War II period allowed southern men to expose their weakness for the attainment of power, in the process creating a highly stylized dramatic ritual. White college men in the 1950s performed the drama from a position of dominance. They could glory in past defeat because, ultimately, they emerged victorious. White supremacy, albeit in a different form, was restored.

Following Truman's inauguration as president, Alabama's Kappa Alpha celebrated their first annual Old South weekend. This celebration in subsequent years extended to a whole week of parties that evoked class and racial tensions within southern society. Kappa Alphas began the week as Confederate soldiers at a secession ceremony, dressed the part of rednecks at an informal sharecropper's party, and became colonels and generals at the culminating formal gala. Fraternity members grew beards and wore Confederate uniforms to authenticate the recreation. The spectacle of unusual dress, parades through campus, and a round of parties created an Old South carnival.

Kappa Alpha members envisioned their fraternity as the elite of southern society, but by embodying all levels of white southern society, they consciously reflected the unified whole of segregation's power over black America. *Life* magazine photographed Old South week at Auburn University in 1950 and presented images of the secession parade along with various parties. In one curious photograph, Alpha Tau Omega fraternity members, dressed as "Klansmen," are shown burning a cross to "protest" secession. The caption notes that the Kappa Alphas broke up the ATO protest. This action protected the Old South week, yet also downplayed potentially violent manifestations of the past. Kappa Alphas wanted to be seen as civilized southerners, not the provocateurs of racial animosity.[35] By 1952 Kappa Alpha Old South weekend at the University of Mississippi held similar events. A formal colonel's tea at the fraternity house kicked off the festivities. That evening the Sharecropper's Ball witnessed dates in overalls and straw hats. The next day, following dinner on the lawn of the KA house, guests sidestepped cotton bales on a hastily constructed wharf, before passing through a replica of the Robert E. Lee riverboat and entering the Old South Ball.[36]

The reassertion of Old South traditions by the Kappa Alpha fraternity re-freshed racial divisions and reminded African Americans and more liberal white southerners of their expected roles. The utilization of well-known public and po-litical spaces, such as the capital grounds, and busy commercial thoroughfares like Fayetteville Street in Raleigh, Peachtree in Atlanta, or Main in Memphis, allowed Confederate symbolism to collide with the promises of racial change invoked by Truman's presidency. The participation of elected officials in the Kappa Alpha cer-emonies bestowed additional credibility to the reinvocation of Lost Cause ideals. North Carolina's Kappa Alpha fraternity also initiated an annual Old South ball in 1949. The UNC KAs joined fellow chapters from North Carolina State University, Wake Forest, and Duke for a weekend gala in the state's capital city. Prior to the ball, Kappa Alphas in Confederate uniforms escorted their hoop-skirted dates up Fayetteville Street in Raleigh, from the capital building to Memorial Hall, where a flag raising culminated the day's events.

Similar Old South weekends took place at other locations throughout the South. Kappa Alpha chapters from Emory, Georgia Tech, and the University of Georgia celebrated in Atlanta in late April of 1950. Georgia's last living Confeder-ate veteran, Gen. James Bush, led a procession down Peachtree Street. Behind him followed fraternity members in military attire, including one group who car-ried a casket labeled "John Brown's body." When the parade ended at the state capital, the 104-year old Bush "shot" several Yankee soldiers, portrayed by Greek members dressed in white union suits. A secession ceremony on the grounds of the state capital completed the public ritual of Old South weekend.[37] By literally and figuratively stripping the U.S. military of their uniforms, southerners perhaps projected their own vulnerability onto their "enemy." When veteran Bush shot the "Union" soldiers, it represented a concrete action to widely held emotions of animosity against the federal government. The mixture of Confederate symbol-ism in the public square served its purpose of fun but also provided political ends. Although the KAs undoubtedly enjoyed their weekend drama as a jovial escape from academic life, it also could be seen as one of the first social manifestations of white southern resistance to civil rights, a resistance that would intensify greatly following the *Brown* decision of 1954.[38]

Confederate symbolism not only found its way to the streets but also entered the printed page, as photographs of parties and celebrations appeared in college yearbooks. When the Universities of Alabama, Mississippi, and North Carolina published their first college annuals in the 1890s, fraternity members held partial, if not total, editorial control. Yearbooks contain a variety of fraternity photographs, including group shots of the whole fraternity, composite photographs of individual member portraits, and more informal images. The informal photographs often provide the greatest reflection of fraternity events. As yearbooks developed in the 1920s and 1930s, a distinct "fraternity section" emerged to showcase and highlight the individual achievements of each chapter on campus.[39]

From 1945 to 1963, the fraternity section of the University of Alabama *Corolla* included thirteen Confederate themed photographs. In most of the images, uniformed Kappa Alphas marched, stood beside hoop-skirted dates, or waved Confederate flags. The captions below the photographs affirmed southern defiance with such slogans as "The KA's will rise again," or "The South Shall Rise Again." One caption beneath the parading KAs read, "The Klan in their afternoon formals."[40] *Ole Miss,* the yearbook from the University of Mississippi, included only three Confederate-themed photographs in fraternity sections from 1945 to 1962, and these appeared in the late 1950s and 1962.[41]

At the University of North Carolina, thirteen yearbook photographs featured the Confederate battle flag. Nine of these photographs appeared between 1950 and 1954, when the flag offered a socially accepted symbol of defiance against liberal Democratic Party sentiment in Congress. Unlike in Mississippi and Alabama, the use of the Confederate battle flag drew mixed response in the Tar Heel state. The *Rocky Mount Sunday Telegram* explained that "mockery" of the flag originated when North Carolina students traveled to New York City for a Notre Dame football game in 1950. "On the day of the game Confederate flags were as common on the Gotham streets as were the lights on Broadway. New York police even had to be called out to prevent a group of overzealous Tar Heels from draping Grant's tomb with a Confederate flag."[42] College administrators swapped opposing views on the place of Confederate flags as athletic booster paraphernalia. University of North Carolina chancellor Robert B. House ascribed the flag waving to "a spirit of fun." "To attribute insidious or vicious meaning to it is—well, a lot of phooey," argued House. However, the University of Virginia's chancellor, Colgate B. Darden Jr., boiled over when he learned of his students' "improper" display of the flag. "It is part of an era that is dead. It is a symbol of a cause that was lost. It should be furled and put away," pleaded Darden.

While intersectional athletic rivalries explained part of the resurgence of the Confederate flag in southern colleges, the South's resentment of the Truman administration's racial policies accounted for most of the flag waving. The increased legal action by NAACP attorneys against school segregation also touched southern racial nerves. While most North Carolinians denied any political significance of the flag's use, at least one UNC student admitted, "many folks around here [the university] say that they [the flags] reflect rebellion against Truman Democrats." This attitude was born out when the *Charlotte News* reported an incident at the 1949 Maryland–North Carolina football game when several hundred North Carolina students planned to charge the White House and plant a Confederate flag on the lawn.[43]

Fraternity men who donned Confederate uniforms symbolized a militaristic resistance to integration and also reaffirmed southern manhood. Their photographs also appeared frequently in the University of North Carolina's fraternity sections of the *Yackety-Yack*. Of ten recorded Confederacy-related images from the late 1940s to the 1960s, nine belonged to the Kappa Alpha fraternity. The Kappa Alphas photographed marches, formations, dates, and poses in front of the university's Confederate memorial, Silent Sam. By the 1950s Kappa Alpha chapters from Tulsa, Tulane, and New Mexico featured Old South symbolism in their picture submissions to the national fraternity's illustrated *Manual*. Confederate flags prominently displayed in dining halls provided backgrounds for photographs of uniformed fraternity members and southern belles.[44]

Old South commemoration went beyond the Kappa Alpha fraternity. In 1950 the University of Mississippi observed its first annual Dixie Week. By 1954 the expanded Dixie Week included a mock assassination of President Lincoln, a formal reading of a secession proposal, an "indoctrination of Yankee students," a slave auction, and parades.[45] The 1946 Kappa Sigma Plantation Ball welcomed guests to a southern plantation home and garden. In the fall of 1949 Sigma Alpha held a showboat party.[46] During Ole Miss's 1954 Dixie Week, Phi Kappa Psi fraternity hosted its own "Old South" party, and members sported "string ties and long sideburns."[47] Kappa Alpha's Old South week and the University of Mississippi's Dixie Week assumed new importance during the 1950s. After the *Brown v. Board of Education* decision that outlawed segregation in public schools, activities once ascribed to the innocent reaffirmation of traditional southern values became yet another cultural cog in the wheel of massive resistance.[48]

Mississippi, Alabama, and North Carolina held yearly campuswide fund-raising events where fraternities and sororities publicly competed against other college organizations in performing staged skits and songs. From the late 1940s through the 1950s, the Greek skits occasionally invoked minstrelsy, offering a glimpse into the racial worldview of white students. Mississippi's stunt night raised funds for the World University Service and attracted primarily sorority and fraternity participants.[49] In the 1948 stunt night competition, Delta Gamma won the sorority talent division with the presentation, "Musical Minstrel of Magnitude." The winning members wore blackface and followed an "old-time minstrel theme" that combined songs and jokes. Although Sigma Alpha Epsilon captured the fraternity competition with a skit about the romance of an Arkansas girl, other fraternities framed their performance around racial themes. Sigma Nu took third place parodying "Uncle Tom's Cabin," with brothers acting the parts of Uncle Tom and Little Eva. Phi Delta Theta fraternity presented "The Beale Street Beauty Salon," a skit that depicted "life in a colored beauty salon on the morning after a rush day."[50] The shock of racial and gender inversion was the basis for the humor.

The 1951 stunt night again featured a persistent fascination with race. This time, sororities availed themselves of racial themes more often than their fraternity counterparts. Delta Delta Delta sorority won the competition with "Coal Black and the Seven Spades," a spoof on Snow White and the Seven Dwarfs. The Chi Omega sorority performed a minstrel show with the women in blackface.[51] At the 1953 stunt night, Sigma Nu performed a skit about several past presidents, which included a scene where John Wilkes Booth assassinated Abraham Lincoln. As he shot the president in the skit, Booth "was hailed with 'For He's a Jolly Good Fellow.'" In 1955, stunt night featured a minstrel show by the Delta Delta Delta sorority where a chorus line of girls sang "Are You From Dixie?" followed by renditions of "Dem Bones" and "Sweet Georgia Brown." The Kappa Sigmas won the fraternity competition with their interpretation of *Porgy and Bess*.[52]

Portrayals of blackface during stage minstrel shows offered an unrealistic image of African Americans. Blackface performers darkened their faces with burnt cork or cosmetics, and exaggerated their mouth and eyes. Although blackface performance originated in the 1830s as cheap entertainment for antebellum northern working-class white men, it soon gained popularity in other areas of the country. The routine became so formulaic that even African American men blackened their faces to fulfill audience expectations. As vaudeville succumbed to the technological innovations of motion pictures and television, blackface performance infiltrated the new media.[53]

It must be noted that blackface performance existed throughout all regions of the United States in the immediate post–World War II period. Alpha Sigma Phi fraternity at Ohio's Baldwin-Wallace College produced a minstrel show to raise funds for a campus service organization. The success of the event prompted the local Kiwanis Club to invite them to repeat the performance.[54] Other fraternities staged similar minstrel shows at Hillsdale College in Michigan, the University of Kansas, Gettysburg College in Pennsylvania, and Muhlenberg College in Ohio.[55] However, the minstrel performance overlaid with Civil War dramatizations, especially mock Lincoln assassinations, must have been peculiarly southern.

Photographic evidence from the *Ole Miss* captures some of the racialized distortions of blackface variety show performances at the University of Mississippi. The yearbook showed three blackface portrayals between 1945 and 1962. A picture of the 1950 annual skit night portrays fraternities and sororities entertaining an audience of peers. In one image several men perform a routine in elaborate blackface attire, with even their hands darkened.[56]

During a 1951 football weekend, a Delta Kappa Epsilon fraternity member in full blackface bent over a kettle and scrub board and acted as a black washerwoman. A sign, "We'll knock the starch out of B. C. [Boston College]," explained this homecoming tableau.[57] In the 1956 *Ole Miss*, a photograph shows "Ford and his fools," a singing troupe that included at least three blackface members, at another campus skit night.[58]

The University of North Carolina's *Yackety-Yack* offered only two blackface portrayals during the 1950s. The two photographs were taken in 1951 at the "Ugliest Man On Campus" competition. The annual contest permitted fraternities and other groups to enter their "ugly man," who received votes in the form of monetary donations, to raise funds for various charities. Theta Chi included on their yearbook fraternity page a photograph of their representative in the contest. Their "ugly man" wears the standard blackface and overdone facial features, along with an outlandish costume.[59]

Like the other two universities, Alabama also held an annual variety night, the "Jasons Jamboree." The Jasons, an honorary service organization that tapped outstanding senior men for membership, formed in 1914.[60] World War II stopped the yearly jamborees but an eager student body resumed putting on the event in 1947. The annual skit night also featured numerous blackface minstrels. Photographs of the event depict blackfaced men in band combos, dressed in tuxedoes, performing dance routines, and preaching behind pulpits. The heaviest participation in Jasons Jamboree came from campus fraternities and sororities, who prepared elaborate skits. Alpha Delta Pi sorority reenacted a "Negro revival" for their 1947 performance, while the Kappa Delta's revised biblical lessons in "Uncle Remus Says."[61] Delta Delta Delta won the 1948 sorority competition with a minstrel skit that featured "thinly-clad, black-faced lassies."[62]

Sexual inversion accompanied racial reversal as white male students not only wore blackface but dressed as black women. Mississippi Phi Delta Thetas assumed the role of black beauticians for a performance. The Delta Kappa Epsilons encouraged a member to become a black washerwoman for one night. The double inversion further heightened the disruption of normal life and simultaneously reinforced traditional forms of white manhood.[63] Sometimes the threat of overt sexuality crept too far. The Jasons Jamboree received intense administrative scrutiny due in part to what officials deemed inappropriate and suggestive acts. In 1949 the dean of women, Iona Berry, axed the "Luscious Lips" contest at the last minute.[64] Undoubtedly, blackface performance provided a cover for some of the sexual innuendo. Jasons Jamboree provided Alabama students a chance to test conventional limits and push social norms.[65] However, sexual transgression often proved a much larger concern than performances of racial inversion in the immediate postwar years.

Alabama's *Corolla*, unlike the yearbooks at Mississippi and North Carolina, included a significant number of blackface photographs involving women; particularly sorority women who staged elaborate rush programs on southern themes. From 1945 to 1963, there are twenty yearbook portrayals of women in blackface. These photographs were taken at the sorority houses during rush week and at "plantation parties," and showed "pickaninnies" with wildly ribboned hair and distorted facial features. The intended humor of the women's blackface performance occasionally alluded to the supposed savagery of black women. In a photograph from the 1950 Sigma Chi Derby Day, a woman in blackface (and body) holds a real African American child on her hip. Below the picture a mocking caption reads: "Civilization." In 1955 Delta Delta Delta sorority pictured "two African bush wuggies" in total black body paint and animalskin dresses.[66] The racial humor indulged by white women evaporated with the arrival and enrollment of Autherine Lucy at the university. In homage to Lucy's integration threat, the 1958 *Corolla* pictured two blackbodied white women who appeared to attack one another in horror-show revenge.[67] As the civil rights movement accelerated its legal progress, women may more frequently have incorporated into college yearbooks images of their participation in racial dramas to signal their growing frustration. While the tenets of segregation made white women the apex of racial purity, any dislodging of the pedestal could produce a calamitous fall indeed, bringing into question the future role of white men in the protection of white womanhood and white women's future social and economic independence.

The number of blackface photographs in the fraternity sections of the yearbooks at these three southern schools varies widely, but most of them are from the 1950s. Women were as likely, more likely in the case at Alabama, to use blackface as a source of entertainment. Southern white women who performed blackface probably elicited more shocked laughter, as their doing so transgressed normal social roles to a greater extent than did similar performances by white men. Also evident is the changing venue of blackface performance. Public displays of blackface at variety shows, stunt nights, and university parades ended after the civil rights struggle integrated campuses and towns. Blackface became a restricted and localized entertainment confined to parties at Greek houses. Similarly, sorority use of blackface, although most prolific in rush programs, moved from outside to within the sorority house. The cause of these changes is uncertain, however, an awareness of African American and broader public sentiment against the use of blackface perhaps influenced fraternities and sororities to protect their image by curtailing and limiting its use. What had at one time been a public performance for the whole white community became, after the mid-1960s, a personal expression for the immediate community of fellow Greek members.

By 1960 all three universities stood at the brink of radical change. The University of North Carolina admitted African American undergraduates in 1955, but the campus remained racially divided, and downtown Chapel Hill businesses continued the customary practice of segregation. The forces of massive resistance rallied students at Mississippi and Alabama into a frenzy of mayhem and death. Many factors, including the rhetoric of conservative southern political leadership, the formation of Citizens' Councils, and the zealous violence of the Ku Klux Klan, shaped conservative southern opinion about gender and race. Although these forces strongly influenced them, it was within their own daily activities that students more frequently worked out the interplay of manhood and race. Social fraternities used informal and formal parties, variety show skits, and campuswide celebrations, such as Old South week or Dixie week, to remind others and themselves who they were and were not. By 1960, most fraternity members in the South were well prepared, socially and politically, to defend southern segregation and traditional gender roles, if not for the whole campus then at least for themselves.

NOTES

1. Pete Daniel writes, "In a society that placed a premium on masculinity and whiteness, white men easily assumed roles that demonstrated their mastery over both women and blacks" (*Lost Revolutions: The South in the 1950s* [Chapel Hill: University of North Carolina Press, 2000], 158). Frank E. Manning, "Cosmos and Chaos: Celebration in the Modern World," in *The Celebration of Society: Perspectives on Contemporary Cultural Performance,* ed. Frank E. Manning (Bowling Green, OH: Bowling Green University Popular Press, 1983), 22, 27. See also Don Handelman, "Play and Ritual: Complementary Frames of Meta-Communication," in *It's A Funny Thing Humour: International Conference on Humour and Laughter,* ed. Antony J. Chapman and Hugh C. Foot (London: Pergamon, 1977), 185–92. For other insights into celebrations, see Victor Turner, ed., *Celebration: Studies in Festivity and Ritual* (Washington, DC: Smithsonian Institution Press, 1982), 11–30.

2. Manning, "Cosmos and Chaos," 16, 27.

3. See "Policies and Regulations Governing Social Events at the University of Mississippi," and J. D. Williams to Faculty-Student Committee on Social Affairs, August 25, 1954. Both are found in "Student Social Affairs Minutes, 1952–1953–1956–1957," in the University of Mississippi Special Collections, Oxford, Mississippi.

4. *Garnet and Gold Pledge Guide,* 1963, 38–39, in Student Archives Collection, Archives Research Center, University of Illinois, Champaign-Urbana; *Etiquette Manual* (Phi Kappa Alpha Fraternity, 1939); O. K. Quivey, *The Pledge Manual of Sigma Alpha Epsilon* (Sigma Alpha Epsilon Fraternity, 1942), 31.

5. *A Book for Kappa Sigma Pledges* (Denver: Bradford-Robinson Printing Co., 1950), 7.

6. Fraternities continued well past World War II to invoke an understanding of society (that at times assumed racial and class characteristics) based on the polarity of civilization versus barbarism. These terms first characterized fraternity and nonfraternity members in the late 1800s. See Gail Bederman, *Manliness and Civilization: A Cultural History of Gender and Race in the United States, 1880–1917* (Chicago: University of Chicago Press, 1995); Stephen Kantrowitz, *Ben Tillman and the Reconstruction of White Supremacy* (Chapel Hill: University of North Carolina Press, 2000).

7. "Sigma Chi to Give 'Heaven and Hell' Dance on Saturday," *Crimson-White,* April 5, 1948.

8. "Pikes to Stage Kid Party Tonight," *Mississippian,* October 19, 1945; "Kid Party Given by Sigma Chi," *Crimson-White,* April 16, 1946. For kid parties at another school, see "Colorado," in Alpha Tau Omega's *Palm* 69 (June 1949): 38.

9. "Shades of John Silver Kappa Sigs Play Pirate," *Mississippian*, August 9, 1946; "Kappa Sigs Give Gala Saloon Party," *Mississippian*, May 10, 1946. A similar harvest party at North Carolina sponsored a costume contest. See Violet LaRue, "Parties, Dance Spark Coed Plan," *Daily Tar Heel*, November 14, 1948.

10. "Pike Party Has 'Wild West' Theme," *Crimson-White*, July 15, 1947.

11. "Zetas Horse Up Party at House," *Mississippian*, March 21, 1947; "Kappa Alpha Clan Will Present Costume Party, Apache Style," *Mississippian*, December 2, 1949. See also "Oregon Staters Look Brave at Pow-Wow," ATO's *Palm* 67 (March 1947): 34.

12. "Delta Zetas Invite Unemployed to Work," *Mississippian*, November 7, 1947; "Hard Times Party to Be Presented by Delta Sig Men," *Crimson-White*, February 4, 1947; "Kappa Sigma Party Proves Great Success; No Funds, Lots of Fun," *Mississippian*, March 17, 1950. Oklahoma A&M's Lambda Chi Alpha fraternity hosted a "hobo" party in 1947, complete with a shack, clothesline, and pictures of hobo scenes to decorate the walls. See "Model T Ford Leads Grand March in Lambda Chi Hobo Dance at Oklahoma A&M," *Cross and Crescent* 34 (May 1947): 35; "Auburn Taus Have Hay-Day At Annual Hobo Party," *Palm* 69 (June 1949): 35.

13. "Deke House Will Play Cow College Tonight When Members, Dates Enjoy 'State' Party," *Mississippian*, December 12, 1952.

14. "Hayseed Heyday Observed at Phi Kappa Psi House," *Mississippian*, November 18, 1946; "Sigma Chi Actives Give Barn Party for Pledges," *Mississippian*, November 15, 1946.

15. "Pi Kap Hold Farmers' Ball," *Crimson-White*, November 10, 1947; "'Down on the Farm' Is Delta Chi Theme as Dates Hop Wagon," *Crimson-White*, May 25, 1948. The foil of rural life was also used by Emory's Alpha Tau Omega. See "Crud Brothers Entertain Emory Brothers and Rushees," *Palm* 68 (December 1948): 34.

16. "Minstrels Invade Gala SAE Social," *Mississippian*, March 14, 1947.

17. Violet LaRue, "Parties, Dance Spark Coed Plan," *Daily Tar Heel*, November 14, 1948.

18. Willie Morris, *North toward Home* (Oxford: Yoknapatawpha Press, 1982), 127–28; Frank Deford, *Everybody's All-American* (New York: Viking, 1981), 36; Daniel, *Lost Revolutions*, 169.

19. "Fijis Punch-Party In 'Harlem' Style," *Crimson-White*, July 20, 1947.

20. Granthan Brigance, "The Jungle Ball . . ." *Mississippian*, April 11, 1952; "Delta Psis Will Use Eerie 'Voodoo,'" *Mississippian*, May 15, 1953.

21. Daniel, *Lost Revolutions*, 172; see also a brief history of Doug Clark and the Hot Nuts at www .ibiblio.org/hotnuts/history.html (accessed November 10, 2004).

22. Kari Frederickson, *The Dixiecrat Revolt and the End of the Solid South, 1932–1968* (Chapel Hill: University of North Carolina Press, 2001), 76–86.

23. Robert A. Garson, *The Democratic Party and the Politics of Sectionalism, 1941–1948* (Baton Rouge: Louisiana State University Press, 1974), 232–314; Numan V. Bartley, *The Rise of Massive Resistance: Race and Politics in the South During the 1950s* (Baton Rouge: Louisiana State University Press, 1969): 28–46; Sarah McCulloh Lemmon, "The Ideology of the 'Dixiecrat' Movement," *Social Forces* 30 (December 1951): 162–71; Robert H. Ferrell, "The Last Hurrah," *Wilson Quarterly* 12 (Spring 1988): 66–82; William D. Barnard, *Dixiecrats and Democrats: Alabama Politics, 1942–1950* (Tuscaloosa, Alabama: University of Alabama Press, 1974), 113–15; William F. Winter, "New Directions in Politics, 1948–1956," in *A History*

of Mississippi, vol. 2, ed. Richard Aubrey McLemore (Hattiesburg: University and College Press of Mississippi, 1973), 140–44; Dean DuBois, "Fifty-Five Ole Miss Students Attend States' Rights Meeting," *Mississippian,* July 22, 1948.

24. Winter, "New Directions," 142. Several weeks after President Truman urged Congress to pass the civil rights proposals, opposition in Mississippi developed in earnest, led by the speaker of the House of Representatives, Walter Spillers. State meetings to discuss the crisis occurred in February of 1948 and were followed by a meeting of States' Rights supporters from ten states in Jackson on May 10, 1948. "Tubbs Gives Address on States' Rights to Ole Miss Students," *Mississippian,* April 30, 1948.

25. DuBois, "Fifty-Five Ole Miss Students." Mayes Hunter belonged to Kappa Alpha fraternity. The delegates elected at the meeting included David Whitaker, a Kappa Sigma, John C. Murray, a Kappa Alpha, and Noah "Soggy" Sweat, a Sigma Chi. All three elected delegates were also first- or second-year students in the law school. For information on students, see *Ole Miss* (Nashville: Benson Printing Co., 1948).

26. "Campus States' Righters Elect Bowen as Leader," *Mississippian,* July 29, 1948. The other three elected officers were enrolled in the law school, and at least two of the three belonged to social fraternities.

27. Jim Dickinson, "States' Rights Organization Will Be Formed on Campus," *Daily Tar Heel,* October 1, 1948; Sam McKeel, "Dixiecrat Candidate Strom Thurmond to Speak Tonight in Memorial Hall," *Daily Tar Heel,* October 5, 1948; Sam McKeel, "Thurmond Repeats Truman Debate Challenge; Says He Will Even Argue in Missouri," *Daily Tar Heel,* October 6, 1948; Frederickson, *The Dixiecrat Revolt,* 144.

28. Gary T. Scott, "The Kappa Alpha Order, 1865–1897, How It Came to Be and How It Came to Be Southern," M.A. thesis, University of North Carolina at Chapel Hill, 1968. A competing paradigm in the African American community is noted in celebrations such as Texas's Juneteenth. See W. Fitzhugh Brundage, *The Southern Past: A Clash of Race and Memory* (Cambridge: Harvard University Press, 2005).

29. Dean Dubois, "Kappa Alpha Plans Secession: To Join Confederate Army," *Mississippian,* April 2, 1948.

30. "Formals Hit Peak At KA, DZ, Delta Psi, ROTC Balls," *Mississippian,* April 9, 1948.

31. Jim Harland, "Confederate Flags Fly Again on Capstone Fraternity Houses," *Crimson-White,* July 20, 1948, 1.

32. Williams's father, Aubrey Williams, edited the *Southern Farmer* newspaper and came out in support of Jim Folsom and Henry Wallace. See "Presidential Hopeful Williams Favors Civil Rights at Bama," *Crimson-White,* April 7, 1948; "Civil Righters Fight Campus Segregation," *Crimson-White,* May 11, 1948; "Politics," *Rammer-Jammer* 23 (April 1948): 3–4. Despite Morrison's campaign, Alabama students overwhelmingly favored segregation. See Sue B. Ray, "Survey Shows Students Oppose Civil Rights, Admission of Negroes," *Crimson-White,* August 17, 1948.

33. "Students Write McGrath Asking for Truman Electors," *Mississippian,* August 12, 1948. The leader of the anti–States' Rights petition was also a fraternity man. Although in his second year of law school at Ole Miss, Thomas served as president of Beta Theta Pi. Of thirteen other signers listed in the *Mississippian,* three belonged to fraternities and seven were enrolled in the law school. Sarah Lemmon characterized leaders within the States' Rights movement as middle or upper class, well educated, from

traditional southern families, participants in numerous social clubs, and affiliated with social fraternities during their college years. How effectively some States' Rights leaders utilized alumni networks within their fraternities to promote their cause remains unclear. See Lemmon, "The Ideology of the Dixiecrat Movement," 169.

34. "Negro Students Are Concerned in AVC Motion," *Daily Tar Heel*, October 28, 1948; Junius Scales and Richard Nickson, *Cause at Heart: A Former Communist Remembers* (Athens: University of Georgia Press, 1987); Warren Ashby, *Frank Porter Graham: A Southern Liberal* (Winston-Salem, NC: John F. Blair, 1980), 224–39; Julian M. Pleasants and Augustus M. Burns, III, *Frank Porter Graham and the 1950 Senate Race in North Carolina* (Chapel Hill: University of North Carolina Press, 1990). Graham served on Truman's Civil Rights Commission, and although he agreed with all of the objectives of the report, he hesitated on supporting governmental means to obtain them.

35. "Life Goes to the Old South Ball," *Life* 28 (May 22, 1950): 167.

36. "KA Gentlemen Dust Off Confederate Full Dress for a Real Taste of Ole Southern Hospitality," *Mississippian*, May 9, 1952.

37. "State's Last Man in Gray To Parade," *Atlanta Constitution*, April 15, 1950; "Rebel-Yelling Grays Seize City, State in Mock Rites," *Atlanta Constitution*, April 16, 1950; "Georgia 'Secedes' from Union, Tells Truman by Pigeon; 'Dixie' Is Played," *Daily Tar Heel*, April 23, 1950. For details of Old South weekend in Memphis in the 1960s, see "KA," *Press-Scimitar* folder #60524, University of Memphis Special Collections, Memphis, Tennessee.

38. On the public nature of these celebration rituals, see Don Handelman, *Models and Mirrors: Towards an Anthropology of Public Events* (Cambridge: Cambridge University Press, 1990), 3–21.

39. This essay draws on an examination of all of the photographs represented in the fraternity sections of Alabama's *Corolla*, Mississippi's *Ole Miss*, and North Carolina's *Yackety-Yack* from 1945–1980. The composite is a formal individualized portrait that offers little information for this study. The group photo, which came into vogue in the 1960s, and the candid, which portrays various aspects of informal fraternity life, offer a great deal more information about daily activities and the type of image fraternity men sought to portray. The yearbook photographs are of interest because they are self-selected and posed by the fraternity men for an audience beyond themselves. They present a clear picture of what activities and ideals the fraternity wanted to show to the larger student body and general public. For useful information on reading and interpreting photographs, see Alan Trachtenberg, "Introduction: Photographs As Symbolic History," in *The American Image: Photographs from the National Archives, 1860–1960* (New York: Random House, 1979), xxvi; David L. Jacobs, "Domestic Snapshots: Toward a Grammar of Motives," *Journal of American Culture* 4 (Spring 1981): 93–105; Marsha Peters and Bernard Mergen, "'Doing the Rest': The Uses of Photographs in American Studies," *American Quarterly* 29 (1977): 280–303; Thomas J. Schlereth, *Artifacts and the American Past* (Nashville: American Association for State and Local History, 1980), 11–47; James Borchert, "Historical Photo-analysis: A Research Method," *Historical Methods* 15 (Spring 1982): 35–44; Neal Slavin, *When Two or More Are Gathered Together* (New York: Farrar, Straus and Giroux, 1974); Graham King, *Say 'Cheese'! The Snapshot as Art and Social History* (London: Collins, 1986), 1–14, 114–30.

40. The captions come from the following years: *Corolla* (Tuscaloosa: Students of the University of Alabama, 1952), 66; *Corolla* (1957), 110; *Corolla* (1959), 46. The photographs come from the following

years: *Corolla* (1949), 296; *Corolla* (1951), unnumbered introduction; *Corolla* (1952), 66; *Corolla* (1953), 238; *Corolla* (1954), 63, 254; *Corolla* (1957), 110, 293; *Corolla* (1959), 46; *Corolla* (1960), 294; *Corolla* (1961), 272; *Corolla* (1963), 276.

41. *Ole Miss* (Nashville: Benson Printing Company, 1958), 149; *Ole Miss* (1959), no page number; *Ole Miss* (1962), 9.

42. "Commercializing the Stars and Bars," *Rocky Mount Sunday Telegram*, November 11, 1951, in the North Carolina Clipping File, 969, North Carolina Collection, Wilson Library, Chapel Hill. On the surging popularity of the Confederate flag, see also Fletcher M. Green, "Resurgent Southern Sectionalism, 1933–1955," *North Carolina Historical Review* 33 (April 1956): 227; John M. Coski, "The Confederate Battle Flag in American History and Culture," *Southern Cultures* 2 (Winter 1996): 195–231.

43. Edward T. Folliard, "Dixie Rides Again, Flying Its Battle Flag of the Confederacy," *Washington Post*, November 13, 1951; Roy Parker Jr., "Students Back Team to Limit with Cheering," *Daily Tar Heel*, November 13, 1949, 1; "Things Aren't the Same on the Hill," *Charlotte News*, November 26, 1951, found in the North Carolina Clipping File, 971, North Carolina Collection, Wilson Library.

44. Ransom H. Bassett, ed., *Kappa Alpha Illustrated Manual* (1951), 31–48; *Illustrated Manual* (1954), unnumbered pages; *Illustrated Manual* (1962), 27.

45. Ann Flautt, "Secession from Union, Slave Auction, Ku Klux Klan to Highlight Dixie Week," *Mississippian*, November 5, 1954; Kevin Pierce Thornton, "Symbolism at Ole Miss and the Crisis of Southern Identity," *South Atlantic Quarterly* 86 (Summer 1987): 254–68. See the secession proclamation from 1953 in "Let There Be Dixie," *Mississippian*, October 9, 1953.

46. "Plantation Ball Given by Kappa Sigma in Gym," *Mississippian*, December 6, 1946; "Sig Alphs Present Showboat Party with Music by Vicksburg Rebops," *Mississippian*, November 11, 1949.

47. "Phi Kappa Psi Has 'Old South' Party at House Tonight," *Mississippian*, November 12, 1954, 2.

48. Neil McMillan, *The Citizens' Council: Organized Resistance to the Second Reconstruction, 1954–1964* (Urbana: University of Illinois Press, 1971); Bartley, *The Rise of Massive Resistance*.

49. "Attend Stunt Night," *Mississippian*, April 29, 1955.

50. "Delta Gamma, SAE Skits Win Stunt Night Trophies," *Mississippian*, April 2, 1948; "Annual Stunt Night Provides 2 Hours of Laughs, Fun," *Mississippian*, April 9, 1948.

51. Sara Murphey, "Tri-Delts, Sigma Pis Snag Prizes in Stunt Night," *Mississippian*, April 25, 1952.

52. Josephine Barner, "Sigma Pi, Chi O Win Stunt Trophies with Perfume Shop, Dragnet Skills," *Mississippian*, May 1, 1953; "Delta Gamma, Kappa Sigs Present Best Skits," *Mississippian*, May 6, 1955; Elmo Povall, "Kappa Delta, Sigma Nu Win Trophies in Annual Stunt Night Competition," *Mississippian*, April 13, 1956.

53. There are numerous works on blackface minstrelsy. See Eric Lott, *Love and Theft: Blackface Minstrelsy and the American Working Class* (New York: Oxford University Press, 1993); Joseph Boskin, *Sambo: The Rise and Demise of an American Jester* (New York: Oxford University Press, 1986); Robert Toll, *Blackening Up: The Minstrel Show in Nineteenth-Century America* (New York: Oxford University Press, 1974); Melvin Patrick Ely, *The Adventures of Amos 'n' Andy: A Social History of an American Phenomenon* (New York: Free Press, 1991).

54. Ed Hard, "Beards Flourish at Baldwin-Wallace," *Tomahawk of Alpha Sigma Phi* 46 (June 1949): 105–6. Even in Vermont, minstrelsy attracted some appeal among locals. See Franklin T. Laskin, "Minstrel Show Hits Lebanon, Ends Famine of Local Talent," *Dartmouth*, November 8, 1948.

55. "Blackfeet in Blackface at Hillsdale," *Palm* 68 (June 1948): 33; "Well, Shut My Mouf," *Palm* 68 (December 1948): 38; "Middle Man," *Palm* 70 (March 1950): 21; *Magazine of Sigma Chi* (July/August 1949): 84–85; *Cross and Crescent* 37 (Early Summer 1950): inside cover.

56. *Ole Miss* (1950), 198.

57. *Ole Miss* (1951), 248.

58. *Ole Miss* (1956), 148.

59. *Yackety-Yack* (Charlotte: Lassiter Corporation, 1951), 353.

60. See *Jason's Directory,* University of Alabama, 1974, in W. S. Hoole Special Collections, University of Alabama, Tuscaloosa; "Jasons and Honors Day" file, in W. S. Hoole Special Collections, University of Alabama, Tuscaloosa.

61. For fraternity men in blackface, see *Corolla* (1952), 71; *Corolla* (1953), 76; *Corolla* (1954), 76; *Corolla* (1957), 73; Cherie Chandler, "Chi Phi Men Dance to Top Rating in Jason Jamboree Presentation; Alpha Chi Omegas Come in 2nd," *Crimson-White,* January 28, 1947.

62. "Lamar Falkner, "Tri Deltas' Minstrel Wins Jasons Cup," *Crimson-White,* March 2, 1948; "Jammed-Up Jamboree," *Crimson-White,* March 2, 1948.

63. For examples from the yearbooks, see *Ole Miss* (1951), 248; *Corolla* (1957), 73. Similar experiences can be found outside of the South. John Harris, an ATO at Union College in Schenectady, New York, "brought down the house" and won first place for the second straight year with his "Sweet Georgia Brown" Stunt Night performance. See "Sweet Georgia Brown," *Palm* 70 (March 1950): 38.

64. "Alpha Chi, Theta Chi Take Top Places in '49 Jamboree," *Crimson-White,* March 1, 1949.

65. Some skits appeared to intertwine relatively accepted racial themes with more problematic sexual overtures. In 1952 Delta Zeta sorority presented a skit called "Orgy and Mess" that parodied *Porgy and Bess.* See "Delts Cop 3rd Jamboree in Row; Kappas, Marilyn Tate Win," *Crimson-White,* April 1, 1952.

66. *Corolla* (1950), 71; *Corolla* (1955), 316.

67. *Corolla* (1958), 130.

A Real Man's Place

Attitudes and Environment at a Southern Deer Camp

ADAM WATTS

It is the humidity, not the heat—so the cliché goes—that makes summers in the Deep South so famously oppressive. But when August's dog days and autumn's pleasant weather are gone, the region's moist climate is also responsible for wet, uncomfortable winters. The fields and forests, framed by flat gray skies and seemingly ceaseless rains, are muted, no longer thick with riotous vegetation and the hum of cicadas. Even when temperatures are well above freezing, this "wet cold" can make July seem appealing again. Standing in the chill air of a cut-over southwest Mississippi pine plantation, one might wonder why so many people choose to spend so much time outdoors in the region's most miserable weather. But for thousands of white southern men, the deep baying of a pack of hounds, the reverberating concussion of a shotgun, and the pursuit of whitetail deer (*Odocoileus virginianus*) mark an essential, natural rhythm of the year. "The guns, the bedding, the dogs, the food, the whiskey," wrote Faulkner in "Delta Autumn," providing a succinct description of the seasonal southern malady known as "buck fever," "the keen heart-lifting anticipation of hunting."[1]

Place your thumb over any blank, unlabeled portion of a map of the southeastern United States, and there is a fair chance that you have found the location of a hunting camp (often better known in the South as a deer camp). On maps or aerial photographs, and generally in the minds of the uninitiated, the deer camp is merely a speck, lost in the woods. However, to those people—mostly white men—who leave home, family, and work to spend hours or days ostensibly in pursuit of whitetail deer, the deer camp is a cultural institution, in fact if not in name. Mention "hunting camp," and one might think of stereotypical images of mule-drawn wagons and furnished bunkhouses (as in Faulkner's "The Bear," for instance) or the even more well-appointed trappings found in North Woods Maine hunting lodges of the rich. Instead, the vast majority of southern deer camps these days consist of a small group of shacks, trailers, second- or third-hand mobile homes, or even school buses that function as shelter at the end of a cold, soggy day.

Since my early adolescence, I have spent many winter afternoons and evenings at the Clear Run Hunting (and Social) Club in southwest Mississippi. Having exchanged shotgun for camera, I photographed the camp, its members, and the natural environment of the area in the years 2001 and 2002. This essay and selection of photographs meditate on the role of the deer camp as an institution of southern masculinity through which masculine values are preserved and passed on—that is to say, where southern boys become southern men. Only one camp is represented in these images; also, I chose to approach this analysis of the relationship between the institution of the deer camp and southern masculinity from behind the lens of a camera and as a native participant, rather than as an academic. I intended the images to evoke the common experiences many southern boys and men have at the deer camp, just as Clear Run is representative of thousands of small southern deer camps.[2]

The land leased by Clear Run, like that owned or hunted by most deer camps, was the home of whitetail deer long before European and African settlement. One hundred years ago Clear Run was part of the vast southeastern belt of longleaf pine (*Pinus palustris*), a variety prized by timber companies for its high quality and, in the late nineteenth and early twentieth centuries, for the tremendous trees still to be found in this relatively uncut area. But by World War I, the vast longleaf pine forests of southwest Mississippi fell before the axe and the saw and were replaced by thousands of acres of row-planted loblolly pines, called "plantations" or "tree farms." The wide-ranging, hearty loblolly pine (*Pinus taeda*) tolerates the partial shade found in recovering cut-over areas better than longleaf pine and, more important to timber companies, is particularly fast growing. Today, that land which is not under intense industrial cultivation for paper pulp is in its third- or fourth-generation growth of mixed pine and hardwood forest, either recovering from or awaiting another round of clear-cutting to feed the paper, chip, and lumber mills that provide jobs and revenue to the region. The variety of pine tree has changed, but the whitetail deer remain.

Although whitetail deer find few herbaceous plants to eat under the dense canopies of pine saplings, they find many food plants in the so-called edge habitats produced by the fragmentation of forest ecosystems. In fact, despite a precipitous population decline throughout the South in the nineteenth and early twentieth centuries (primarily due to unrestrained hunting), the whitetail has rebounded to become abundant in recent decades.[3] Ironically, the same human development that destroys and fragments habitat for many other wildlife species is largely favorable to the whitetail because of the edge habitat that is created adjacent to our homes and transportation corridors. (In another ironic and also dangerous juxtaposition of human civilization and wildlife, state departments of transportation expend great effort to maintain grass pastures, highly sought by deer, on highway shoulders and medians.) As rural Mississippi has become more suburbanized, humans have become the surrogates for the now-extirpated population of animal predators (primarily panthers, wolves, and bears) in the hunting of southwest Mississippi's whitetail deer populations. Thus people have come full circle, once again taking up the biological role of top predator in at least one forest food chain.

Clear Run currently leases approximately 2,400 acres of land from timber companies like Georgia-Pacific and International Paper—together, by far the largest private landowners in the region—and the local school district. (In each township in the state of Mississippi, the sixteenth section of land—a 640-acre block one-mile square—belongs to school districts, which often use it to generate income through forestry and hunting leases.) Clear Run's center of semipermanent structures—its "headquarters"—lies near the borders of Lincoln and Franklin Counties, approximately twenty miles southwest of the town of Brookhaven and fifty miles east of the river town of Natchez. Roads linking Natchez and Brookhaven were once heavily traveled by wagons carrying cotton to the river, but the outlying landscape remained largely forested until logging railroads proliferated in the late nineteenth century.[4]

At Clear Run there is, of course, far more to the deer camp than pine timber, whitetail deer, and an aggregation of shacks and camping trailers in varying states of disrepair. There is more, too, than the friendship of the members or their enthusiasm for the sport—indeed, some members rarely hunt. What makes this institution special (even sacred, some might say, considering the number of hunters to be found sitting around a fire on any given Sunday morning)[5] seems to be something like a collective sense of place where the roots of members—and, some might say, of a particular cast of white southern masculinity—remain firmly planted.

As a formal club, Clear Run has existed for almost twenty years. During its existence, the membership has usually numbered between twenty and thirty men. Today, the membership consists almost exclusively of middle-aged white men and their sons. Thus there is a distinct gap in the ages of members, with no current members in their thirties. The bulk of the men are in their fifties, with a handful in their sixties and seventies; their sons range in age from adolescence to their mid-twenties. A few of the men hunt with their spouses or daughters, but the presence of women is a rare exception to the rule at Clear Run, as at many other southern deer camps. Current members of Clear Run hold both blue- and white-collar jobs. Few would claim the label *working-class*, although all proudly claim to be "working men," taking care to distinguish themselves from government employees, college professors, and others whose work is perceived to involve relatively little sweat or danger, and whose masculinity seems somewhat in doubt by local "good ol' boy" standards. The most common employers for members are the offshore oil industry, the timber industry, and the telephone company (BellSouth, in this area). There are also a few other tradesmen, a few farmers, an owner of a clothing store, and a pharmacist. Around the camp and campfire, manners are rough and egalitarian, indicating the suspension of at least one set of sociocultural barriers—income and occupation—in favor of a social order in which those traditionally espoused masculine values of hard work and toughness, age and experience, are given greater value.

Members of Clear Run, like thousands of other white southern men, view the pursuit of whitetail deer as a natural, even necessary, reason for white southern boys and men—increasingly urban or suburban, with predominantly indoor lifestyles and careers—to enjoy the outdoors.[6] As the cultural center of hunting and related social activities, the deer camp provides both opportunity and context for experiencing and understanding the natural environment. Younger members learn from older ones the techniques of hunting, cooking, and shooting, as well as rudiments of natural history, albeit a version that denigrates self-described environmentalists. Although such modern lessons in campcraft are a far cry from the traditional ecological knowledge shared around campfires in many other cultures, a subtle wilderness ethic is taught at Clear Run as well. In the best of cases, a young hunter learns to be humane and not to abuse the environment that supports his quarry.

Waking well before dawn to sit still for hours in drenching rain and bitter cold, to smell mud and hounds, and to experience the thrill of the kill are all sacraments of white manhood in much of the rural and small-town South today. The men and boys who pass on this ethic at Clear Run and thousands of other deer camps in the Deep South seem engaged in particularly self-conscious rituals of manhood and masculinity. Boys who kill their first deer, for example, have the animal's blood smeared on their faces, and during camp "work days," members who enjoy seniority in the camp are assigned enviable tasks compared to those given to young or new members, who clean dog pens or clear briars from the approaches to tree stands. During social events, younger members sometimes undergo other rites of initiation, not unlike the "hazing" seen in some university fraternities.[7] The indoctrination a young member of a deer camp receives is also quite explicitly meant to foster toughness and encourage self-reliance, qualities camp members associate with a perceived older and heartier America.

The intentional self-removal, from a world containing women and a controlled work environment to a place where social rules of engagement are altered, facilitates the cultivation of certain discomforts and difficulties, of course. Such an environment serves well as the framework for the construction of man-versus-nature conflicts that—when seen from the context of disciplines such as ecofeminism, in which nature is viewed as feminine—may smack of entrenched misogyny. What appears on the surface to be the relatively harmless pursuit of an escapist fantasy of a wild, idealized past of masculine control, then, may have more sinister implications in its encouragement of subjugation and control, of violence toward nature and the feminine. Although no members of Clear Run or most other deer camps would admit that such themes emerge in the process of growing up as a member of a deer camp, they certainly play a role in the socialization of southern men and, no doubt, exist on some level here.

Regardless of location, the number of members, or whether the quarry is deer or ducks or fox, the deer camp encourages its members to adopt, at least temporarily, a separate and traditional (if perhaps somewhat contrived) social order emphasizing masculine characteristics. Boys are taught something of a wilderness ethic, with older members passing on their knowledge of traditional masculine skills such as campcraft, hunting, and shooting. They also undergo rites of passage unique to southern boys and to the deer camp, which help to form their own masculine identity as they experience them and administer them later in life to the next generation. Perhaps most important, the deer camp and deer hunting provide an annual, renewable assertion of male values held in common, as well as a physical space apart from "work and women" where those gendered values may be performed and perpetuated.

NOTES

1. William Faulkner, "Delta Autumn," in *Go Down, Moses*, in *Novels, 1942–1954* (New York: Library of America, 1994), 247.

2. For a collection of deer camp photographs chronicling an earlier era, see Alan Huffman, *Ten Point: Deer Camp in the Mississippi Delta* (Jackson: University Press of Mississippi, 1997).

3. Phillip Thomas provides a brief description of the importance of several wildlife species to the southern landscape in "Animals," in *Encyclopedia of Southern Culture*, ed. Charles Reagan Wilson et al. (Chapel Hill: University of North Carolina Press, 1989), 323–26.

4. See James Fickle, *Mississippi Forests and Forestry* (Jackson: University Press of Mississippi, 2001); Nollie Hickman, *Mississippi Harvest: Lumbering in the Longleaf Pine Belt, 1840–1915* (Jackson: University of Mississippi, 1962); and Gilbert H. Hoffman, *Dummy Lines through the Longleaf: A History of the Sawmills and Logging Railroads of Southwest Mississippi* (Oxford, MS: Center for the Study of Southern Culture, 1992).

5. In his *Encyclopedia of Southern Culture* entry, Stuart Marks indicates that for planters in the Old South, at least, hunting fulfilled a role also played by religion; it "enabled them to understand nature and man's place in the world" ("Hunting," 1228).

6. The question of why people hunt has been examined by numerous authors: see, for example, Stuart Marks, *Southern Hunting in Black and White: Nature, History, and Ritual in a Carolina Community* (Princeton: Princeton University Press, 1991); and Simon Bronner, "This Is Why We Hunt: Social-Psychological Meanings of the Traditions and Rituals of Deer Camp," *Western Folklore* 63 (Winter 2004): 11–50. Answers include economic reasons, ritual, and, for some men, the desire to "drink beer, shoot at inoffensive animals, and talk about pussy." See Roy Blount Jr., *Crackers: This Whole Many-Angled Thing of Jimmy, More Carters, Ominous Little Animals, Sad-Singing Women, My Daddy and Me* (New York: Knopf, 1980); quoted in Matt Cartmill, *A View to a Death in the Morning* (Cambridge: Harvard University Press, 1993).

7. Bronner remarks dryly, "Ritual in deer camp is enlivened by an air of play," and goes on to list the some activities at camp: "teasing, joking, swearing, playful insulting . . . drinking, joke telling, and looking at pornographic and outdoor magazines" ("This Is Why We Hunt").

A successful end to a day of hunting at Clear Run Hunting Club. Dwayne Roberts displays a buck taken with the help of the camp dogs' keen noses. Photographs of the hunter with his (or her) vanquished quarry are common in photo albums and newspapers throughout the South.

The Clear Run Hunting Club is a "real man's place," as one of the members told me, where men can join their friends in escaping from the constraints and obligations of family and work. No matter whether a man's occupation is blue- or white-collar, here he is judged by clearly defined standards for manhood, including the ability to withstand miserable weather, a high tolerance for alcohol, and skill at hunting.

Back at the camp, hunters warm themselves by the fire. The campfire is the epicenter of social activity after dark, when remaining sober enough to hunt or drive safely in no longer a concern.

Although there are clearly if informally defined standards for manhood here, miles of pine woods and meandering roads effectively separate this place from the nearest town and lend a sense of wildness to the surroundings. One of the results of this isolation is a certain level of distaste for rules, even the camp's own rules, when members are "out here." Even a prohibition on loaded guns around the campfire, enacted following an accident involving an assault rifle and a drum of aviation fuel, has its objectors.

The independent spirit inspired by the camp's wild location is often carried beyond the camp grounds during hunts. Driving or hunting under the influence of alcohol may result from the members' tendency to view the rural areas where they hunt as a place apart from family and community, a place where a man does as he pleases and where legal or domestic authority has no jurisdiction.

Sometimes legal authority will intrude upon the insular and autonomous social order of the deer camp, in this case manifested by game wardens. Franklin and Lincoln counties are "dry," and game warden Lynn Oglesby (second from left) observes as hunters dispose of contraband.

The space around the camp is cluttered with shacks, trailers, and buses, which members have converted into shelters. Furniture, appliances, and building materials that might otherwise have been discarded are put to use. The ability to scavenge such items from one's own workplace is considered a valuable skill.

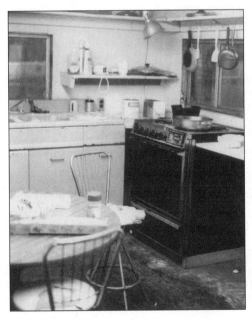

Men at Clear Run often say that they are simply trying to get away from the stresses and pressures of everyday life. The camp's kitchen may represent a more domestic and refined space than many members seek at the deer camp. This kitchen's appearance reflects both the relatively small amount of time spent here and the hunters' lack of interest in making it anything more than a place to warm the food previously cooked on the grill.

For those who want to get away from it all without leaving all of the comforts of home, some of the larger deer stands at Clear Run come equipped with chairs, heaters, and even makeshift latrines.

Hunting dogs are ubiquitous at the deer camp. Large pens house dozens of dogs of several breeds, used by the hunters to track and chase deer. Often the most exciting activity of the day's hunt consists of finding dogs that were let out hours earlier and had followed a scent into the next county. The task of rounding up the dogs is more appealing to some hunters than the hunt itself because it is a more social and fast-paced activity.

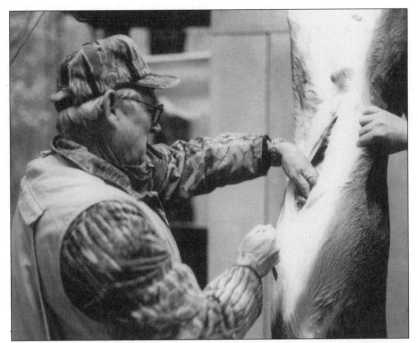

Camp president "Cap'n" Bob begins the process of preparing this buck for the table. After gutting, skinning, and butchering are finished, members will enjoy the fruits of their labor. The venison is truly free range and hormone and antibiotic free, but given the hunters' expenditure on arms, ammunition, specialized clothing, and other equipment, the price per pound is hardly cheap.

A Question of Honor
Masculinity and Massive Resistance to Integration

STEVE ESTES

Howard University professor Roosevelt Williams gripped the podium with both hands as he addressed the Mississippi NAACP audience in December 1954. Williams began by paying his respects to the black Mississippians who helped to pave the way for the Supreme Court's *Brown v. Board of Education* decision, which overturned racial segregation. He then lauded the efforts of African American soldiers in World War II and Korea, noting, "Our people have fearlessly fought and died in the front lines while the white soldiers crouched in the back areas," proving once again that "the negro is the white man's superior." As he moved on to the heart of his speech, a discussion of relations between white women and black men, Williams leaned toward the audience as if he were divulging a secret. He explained that southern white women supported black equality because they "have been subjected to the same persecution that we have," but he believed that there was a deeper reason why "millions of southern white women" fought for integration. Black men, Williams claimed, "have long known that the white woman is violently dissatisfied with the white man and we know of the millions of clandestine meetings sought by the white woman. They, along with us, demand the right to win and love the negro man of their choice and shout to the world, 'This is my man and he is a man in every respect.'"[1]

Roosevelt Williams never gave this speech to the NAACP in Mississippi. In fact, Roosevelt Williams existed only in the minds of southern white men, the Citizens' Council leaders who drafted, recorded, and distributed this speech to state legislatures and opponents of integration all over the South.[2] National

NAACP president Roy Wilkins dubbed the speech "an obvious fake," pointing out that Howard University did not employ a Roosevelt Williams and that no such person belonged to the NAACP. Robert "Tut" Patterson, executive secretary of the Citizens' Council, could only respond by saying that the council had "never claimed [the speech] to be authentic."[3] As a figment of the council's imagination, the fake NAACP speech provides stark evidence of the fears about race, sex, and gender that animated the campaign of massive resistance to integration throughout the Deep South.

In the 1950s southern white men faced a stiff challenge for control of a social order they had dominated for centuries. The "race mixers" in the NAACP and Supreme Court seemed hell-bent on overturning a gender and racial hierarchy that rested on the solid foundations of black disfranchisement and segregation.[4] The Williams speech called into question white women's loyalty and white men's performances on the battlefield and in the bedroom. Rather than revealing the secret desires of black men and white women, this speech illustrates the anxieties about manhood that spurred massive resistance to integration. It also shows the lengths to which segregationists would go to band white men together in defense of their race and region, their women and children, and their status as white men.

A careful analysis of the gendered debate between the Citizens' Councils and their opponents reveals intersections between the segregationists' rhetoric of manhood and themes of southern honor, historical memory, social control, and racial violence.[5] Massive resistance was not a "crisis of masculinity," but it was a struggle for power often expressed in gendered terms. Segregation gave elite white men control of black workers in white homes, shops, fields, and factories, and it kept wages low for working-class blacks *and* whites. To retain their economic and social authority, white southern leaders in the Citizens' Councils demonized black men's sexuality and galvanized southern white men with ideals of whiteness, honor, and manhood. This gendered rhetoric was not simply a mask that hid race and class conflict, however. It was a reflection of male insecurities in the larger society of 1950s America and a response to assaults on southern society by a new integrationist mass culture and an increasingly interventionist federal government. While the reliance on honor and masculinist rhetoric did help the Citizens' Councils mobilize white men and women for massive resistance campaigns, this strategy backfired on the segregationists. By demonizing black manhood and appealing to antiquated conceptions of manhood and honor, the Councils created

hysteria in the South which encouraged vigilante violence in defense of segregation. The violent extremism inspired by such masculinist rhetoric eventually gave
civil rights officials and the federal government the moral authority to dismantle
legal segregation.

Racial separation had been the rule in southern society since the Supreme Court
upheld segregation in its *Plessy v. Ferguson* decision in 1896. Segregation defined
the region's educational system, worship patterns, recreational activities, and
sexual mores. Wealthy white men manipulated the sense of racial loyalty inherent
in segregation to undercut class solidarity between black and white workers, and
all white men could use segregation to protect and control "their" women. Ideals
of chivalry and honor had been used to justify protection and control of white
women in the South since the antebellum period, and such mores were also preva-
lent in the European societies from which many white southerners traced their
roots. Yet the rhetoric of racial and sexual fear wielded by elites in constructing
the segregated social order brought protection of white womanhood to the fore-
front of southern consciousness during the Jim Crow era. Segregation offered no
such protection for black women, however, for under the cover of darkness and
even during the light of day, white men reserved the "right" to rape black women
with impunity. Certainly, not all white men took advantage of this "right," but
many did, and segregation buttressed the social structure that made such atrocities possible. In short, segregation supported a system that gave elite white men
control over southern society, while it guaranteed the allegiance of working-class
white men by offering them a sense of psychological superiority over their black
neighbors and coworkers.[6]

Segregation's high walls also confined black men. For them, any transgression in the white world might lead to lynching for supposed sexual impropri-
eties. When around whites, especially white women, black men had to cloak their
sexuality and mask their manhood for fear of trespassing on the race and gender
prerogatives of white men. The African American writer Ralph Ellison captured
this dilemma in his novel *Invisible Man*. In the face of virulent racism, the novel's
black male protagonist disappears from view altogether, hiding underground until
a day when he can reemerge and confront racial discrimination. The system of
segregation forced all black men in the South to hide their manhood, in effect,
rendering them invisible.[7]

Black men who fought in World War II briefly stepped out of this system. Although they fought in segregated units, black GIs experienced a world outside of the South and the United States where racial segregation was not embedded in the very fabric of society. These men returned from the war and victory over oppression abroad with a new sense of the possibilities for victory against racism at home. NAACP membership and activism grew by leaps and bounds in the post-war years as black people across the South organized in protest of segregation. The NAACP Legal Defense Fund harnessed the energy of these local struggles and focused it in a successful challenge to segregation in the *Brown v. Board of Education* Supreme Court decision of 1954. This decision and local black activism threatened the dominant position of white men in the South. Groups such as the Citizens' Councils sprang up across the region to combat this threat.[8]

For nights after he learned of the impending *Brown* decision at a school board meeting in Indianola, Mississippi, Robert Patterson, the future executive secretary of the Citizens' Councils of America, lay awake in his home, worrying about sending his daughter to first grade in an integrated school. Finally, he rose from bed and wrote a letter of protest calling for other men to join him in defense of segregation. "I, for one," he vowed, "would gladly lay down my life to prevent mongrelization . . . There is no greater cause." While some southern whites resigned themselves to accepting the court's decision, Patterson, a World War II paratrooper, Mississippi State football hero, and manager of a 1,585 acre plantation in LeFlore County, was not the sort of man to give up the fight that easily. In July 1954 he met with thirteen like-minded businessmen and politicians from Indianola and formed the first Citizens' Council to battle the integrationists. Looking back on that first meeting two years later, Patterson recalled that he had had "no idea that such a small beginning would, in a few months time, expand miraculously into a virile and potent organization." The majority of new recruits to this "virile and potent organization" were middle-class white men. By the summer of 1956 the councils claimed to have over 80,000 members in Mississippi alone. Though there were chapters in sixty-five out of the state's eighty-two counties, membership was highest in Delta counties where the majority of the state's black population lived and worked for a white minority.[9]

The Citizens' Councils quickly spread from Mississippi to other Deep South states. In December of 1954, six months after the first council meeting in Mississippi, segregationists from the Magnolia State were invited to lead a revival-style meeting in western Alabama. As dusk settled on the sleepy town of 1,300, pickup trucks and large sedans cruised up to the county courthouse. "When they parked," one observer recalled, "only men—white men—emerged and all walked silently" to the meeting. A local state senator warmed up the crowd, preaching, "This is a white man's county. It always was and always will be if the white men will unite to keep it so." The speakers hammered on one theme over and over again. School integration, they argued, would inevitably lead to sexual relations between black men and white women. In other words, one councilor warned, "The door to the school room is the door to the bedroom." To slam those doors shut, southern white men felt that they must band together and squash the movement for integration. Although the potential for violent reprisals against civil rights activism was discussed, economic pressure was the preferred method of "persuasion" for the council leaders. They urged bankers, for instance, not to lend money to black and white "trouble makers" and encouraged business owners to fire employees who showed any interest in or attended meetings of civil rights organizations. At the conclusion of the meeting, most of the four hundred men present anted up the three-dollar annual dues to join the Citizens' Council.[10]

Though they used much the same recruiting approach, council organizers in the Upper South were not as successful as those in Alabama and Mississippi. In the border states of the old Confederacy, politicians who held fast to massive resistance vied with business leaders who sought to project a "progressive" image of race relations in order to attract outside investment in the boom years of the 1950s.[11] Virginia and North Carolina may not have witnessed the level of grassroots organizing that Mississippi and Alabama did, but segregationists in the Upper South were just as worried about "miscegenation" and "race mixing" as their Deep South counterparts. Dr. Wesley Critz George, a professor of anatomy at the University of North Carolina at Chapel Hill, responded to the *Brown* decision by lending his scientific credentials to the defense of segregation. George theorized that integration allowed for "the illicit and illegitimate crossing of blood" between the two races which would inevitably lead to a "lowering of the quality of our race and [destruction] of our civilization." He helped found the Patriots of North Carolina, a group with approximately 20,000 members affiliated with the Citizens' Councils of America.[12]

Hundreds of white men and women from all over North Carolina admired George's courageous defiance of integration. Supporters hailed him as a paragon of southern white manhood, revealing that rank and file segregationists as well as their leaders understood the fight in gendered terms. Working-class white men like Eugene Hood, a staunch segregationist from Greensboro, praised George for leading the "common folk." "It is difficult to see how a man can retain his 'own self-respect' unless he also maintains his pride in his race . . . It is to men of the type of Dr. W. C. George, of the faculty of the University of North Carolina, to whom we are largely indebted for the maintenance of segregation . . . [and] for some of us being able to maintain our 'own self-respect' and possibly our racial integrity and 'pride in race' by providing leadership for us common folk." If George and other segregationist leaders helped working-class white men regain their self-respect, they served an equally important role for some southern white women. North Carolina women thanked George for protecting their children from integration, echoing the masculinist organizing rhetoric used by leading segregationists. "I sure do wish we had some more men just like you," wrote Mrs. J. P. Thornton. "This is the saddest thing that has ever faced the mothers of the South."[13]

Black North Carolinians reacted to segregationists quite differently than their white neighbors. Dr. F. W. Avant was one of the few black North Carolinians to write to George, targeting the segregationist's assumptions about "race mixing" in his response. "The disgusting thing that has been such a problem to thinking Negroes all of the time," Avant observed, "has been how to keep the white man out of our back yards, debauching our Negro women, and crossing the races in this diabolical, dishonorable, disgusting manner." Avant then went on to argue that rather than leading to a destruction of American civilization, "the crossings of the human beings here in America have produced a very . . . sturdy specimen of manhood and womanhood."[14]

In a strange twist of fate, segregationists in North Carolina actually turned to black men for support (at least rhetorically) when their organization began to falter in the late 1950s. The North Carolina Patriots folded in 1958, in part, because local governments had co-opted their agenda. By then, education policymakers had formulated plans to forestall real integration by accepting a few black students into white schools. Unwilling to let even one black child attend school with their sons and daughters, diehard Tar Heel segregationists resorted to desperate measures, even attempting to muster a *biracial* coalition of men to combat integration. The charter for the North Carolina Defenders of State's Rights, which succeeded the Patriots, called for all men "who have pride in their race, whether they be white or Negro . . . to show it. Let honorable men take their stand for their inalienable rights, their race, and their country." Evidently, no black men answered the call.[15]

The clearest statement of the council's ideology during its early years was the call to arms written by Judge Tom P. Brady in Brookhaven, Mississippi, on July 23, 1954. Brady's *Black Monday* provided a history of "racial amalgamation," a censure of the Supreme Court decision, and a call for grassroots political organizations to defend segregation through nonviolent, legal means. In the segregationist tract, Brady elaborated on his paternalistic vision of race and gender relations in the South. He argued that the court should not meddle in the social affairs of the South until it "knew the Negro" as southern white men supposedly did: "If you have a negro man and his wife and children live and work with you on your place; if he has worked your crops . . . and performed other obligations; if his wife has cooked your meals, cleaned your home and watched over your children; and you in turn have fed and clothed all of them and protected them . . . THEN you are beginning to know the Negro." Brady also reconstructed the Old South pedestal for "the loveliest and purest of God's creatures, . . . the well-bred, cultured Southern white woman or her blue-eyed, golden-haired little girl." Brady's book implicitly acknowledged that segregation restricted not only the social position of black women and men but the sexuality and social mobility of white women as well. He gently latched the door of segregation's gilded cage, arguing that the "peaceful and harmonious relationship" between blacks and whites in the South rested on the "inviolability of Southern Womanhood." Although he carefully emphasized that only a nonviolent organization could successfully defend segregation, Brady warned ominously that "trouble" would inevitably come to Mississippi if a "supercilious glib young negro who has sojourned in Chicago or New York" ever performed "an obscene act or [made] an obscene remark, or a vile overture or assault upon some white girl." Brady concluded his book with a strident appeal to white southern manhood: "No true, loyal, Southern man will ever agree to [integration] or permit it. It shall not be!"[16]

Brady's warning proved prophetic. A year after the publication of *Black Monday*, two white men named Roy Bryant and J. W. Milam lynched Emmett Till, a black youth from Chicago who supposedly whistled at a white woman in Money, Mississippi. Although Bryant and Milam were acquitted in the Till murder trial by an all-white jury, they later told a journalist their story. When they picked up

Till, Bryant and Milam had only intended to scare him. But after Till supposedly boasted of having a white girlfriend back in Chicago, the white men decided to make an example of him. "Well, when he told me about this white girl he had," Milam told the reporter, "my friend, that's what this war's about down here, now. That's what we got to fight to protect. And I just looked at him and I said, 'Boy, you ain't never going to see the sun come up again.'"[17] Citizens' Council spokesmen offered little comment on the Till case, except to say that it was "regrettable" and to deny responsibility. The NAACP saw things differently. They argued that the councils should have been held accountable for Till's death because the group had fomented intense racial animosity in Mississippi and all but called for such vigilantism in Brady's *Black Monday*. As Milam's belated admission of guilt revealed, calls for the protection of white womanhood and defense of white manhood led directly to vigilante violence against black men.[18]

The national media spotlight focused on the Mississippi Delta during the Till murder trial, and white Mississippians were angered by what they viewed as the "biased" nature of the press reports. To combat this coverage of the struggle, the Citizens' Council began publishing a monthly newspaper. The first issue rushed off the Jackson press in October 1955. William J. Simmons, the son of a prominent Jackson banker, edited and wrote most of the articles for the paper and eventually supplanted Patterson as the leading spokesperson for the organization. In the *Citizens' Council*, Simmons kept Mississippians and, ultimately, over 40,000 subscribers across the South, apprised of the status of the organization and the results of integration in northern cities.[19]

Nearly every month in the first several years of publication, the *Citizens' Council* "documented" the inevitable sexual repercussions of racial integration in schools, calling on white men to do their paternal duty by protecting their children from this menace. Headlines shocked readers with stories of "Rape [and] Assault in New York Schools," "Sex Atrocities in Massachusetts: Blacks Rape White Girl Repeatedly," and "Brotherly Love Stained in Philadelphia." The specter of rape and miscegenation struck a chord with white readers. The segregationist paper published an open letter to President Dwight Eisenhower from a former Air Force officer explaining why he, as a father, had to fight against integration: "Do you think any American father with any red blood in his veins is going to allow his dear, little girl to be insulted, possibly sexually molested and exposed to disease" through integration? Such sentiment actually found a sympathetic ear in the White House. "These [segregationists] are not bad people," President Eisenhower confided to Supreme

Court chief justice Earl Warren. "All they are concerned about is to see that their sweet little girls are not required to sit in school alongside some big overgrown Negroes." Positioning themselves as loyal husbands and fathers, Council leaders won at least tacit support from the president and other white men by arguing that they were simply protecting the flower of southern womanhood from black men who supposedly could not control their "animalistic" passions.[20]

Southern editors and politicians also described the Supreme Court's "attack" on southern society with language that further illustrates the gendered nature of this overtly racial conflict. The *Richmond News Leader* denounced the *Brown* decision as a "rape of the Constitution" in its call for "a valiant effort to halt the evil."[21] Senator Strom Thurmond of South Carolina observed, "The court has flung a challenge of integration directly into the South's face . . . This means as much as a demand for surrender."[22] The Richmond editor's equation of the court decision with rape dipped into a deep well of racial animosity by linking the integration of schools to sexual violence and miscegenation. Strom Thurmond's mixture of the metaphor of the duel with allusions to the South's surrender in the Civil War tapped into yet another historical reservoir of ideals of southern white manhood.[23]

Southerners had lost and found the cause of the Civil War many times since 1865, and these calls still resonated in the hearts of many southern white men. Arguments based on historical obligations and protection of white womanhood represented self-conscious resurrection and reinterpretation of regional "traditions" that gave the fight for segregation and white male supremacy a powerful but false sense of timelessness. Although they borrowed from the language and symbols of earlier southern struggles, these arguments must be viewed in the specific context of the 1950s and 1960s, during a time when southern white men's status as leaders of their society was being challenged by black activists and the federal judiciary. Nowhere was the resurrection and reinterpretation of southern traditions more apparent than in the campaign to raise the Confederate battle flag over southern state houses in the late 1950s and early 1960s. Claiming that the flags simply commemorated the Civil War centennial, state politicians recognized the unifying value of such militaristic icons as symbols of manly independence and resistance to the federal government. At the same time that they hoisted the rebel flag, segregationist leaders unfurled a highly purposeful heritage of hatred and honor to bring white southerners together.[24]

Segregationists hoped that a combination of honor and shame would galvanize white community consensus against integration. Historically, honor denoted the respect and esteem that the members of a community conferred upon an individual, usually a man, who was willing to stand up and often fight for his ideas. In the first half of the nineteenth century, a challenge to a southern white man's honor was a challenge to his manhood, and such slights often necessitated dueling. This rather brutal form of conflict resolution faded from southern society after the Civil War, but the concept of honor endured, retaining its association with militarism. Honor's salience in southern society seemed to ebb during relatively stable periods of race and gender relations and flow during challenges to white male authority and identity. During the late 1950s, southern white opponents of integration consciously resurrected this code of judgment by community and regional consensus to forge a "Solid South," in which staunch segregationists would be held in high esteem, while "moderates" would be dishonored and ostracized.[25]

Framing the integration debate in terms of honor and manhood, the segregationist leadership left little space for women in their ranks. In the first few years after the *Brown* decision, many prosegregation groups restricted their membership to men only.[26] The names of these groups suggested their gender exclusivity: White Men, Inc.; White Brotherhood; and Southern Gentlemen.[27] Many councilmen did not originally believe that women's participation in the organization was necessary or appropriate. "Women will not be allowed to join," announced one Alabama organizer late in 1954, "because we feel that it is a job for men."[28]

By the end of 1956, council leaders had begun to acknowledge the need for women's activism and voting power in the segregationist crusade. "Special attention should be given to bringing ladies into active, working membership in your Council," William Simmons wrote. "Determined ladies will put backbone in some of your timid men." Women in the segregation struggle believed they could do more than stiffen the flagging fealty of their men, however. Council member Janice Neill wrote, "We women have an opportunity to do a job that is peculiarly ours: [teach] the children . . . Men of the present generation can fight a delaying action, but if we women do our job we can play a part in attaining victory in the next generation."[29] Another self-styled "Southern Lady" asked women to use their vote to elect prosegregation candidates. In a telling (if implicit) admission that women might be tempted to join the campaign against white male supremacy, she also warned her white sisters to avoid integrationist organizations that were "part of the shrewd, premeditated campaign to enlist the sympathies of inexperienced women."[30]

Most women who joined the councils were relegated to low-profile positions, but Sara McCorkle, director of the Councils' Youth Activities Division, led the charge in the battle over education. Arguing that "women must fight along side of men in this war," McCorkle coordinated a high school essay contest about the advantages of racial segregation.[31] The *Citizens' Council* supplemented McCorkle's efforts in the field of youth education by publishing a serial primer for white children that told the "true" story of American history and race relations. "Our country is very big," one installment of this "Manual for Southerners" began. "And white men built it all . . . Did you know our country will grow weak if we mix our races? It will . . . We do not want our country to grow weak. White men worked hard to build our country."[32] The councils' defense of segregated schooling and alternate lesson plans for southern youth would eventually fuel the private school movement in the South during the 1960s. In the 1950s, the obsession with protecting the racially divided pubic school system revealed fears that the younger generation would be easily swayed by integrationist propaganda and ideas. "For although to most persons today the idea of mixed mating is disagreeable or even repugnant," one council spokesman warned, "this would not be true of the new generation brought up in mixed schools."[33]

Nowhere was the issue of "mixed schools" more explosive than in Little Rock, Arkansas, where President Eisenhower grudgingly enforced racial integration with the presence of the National Guard in 1957.[34] "Remember Little Rock" became a rallying cry for Citizens' Councils, and council leaders blamed the defeat of segregation in Arkansas on southern white moderates, who had exposed cracks in the "Solid South." Segregationists responded to moderate men's heretical positions with attacks that depicted them as women, for in the eyes of Citizens' Councilors, no true southern white man would ever question Jim Crow. After Harry Ashmore, editor of the *Arkansas Gazette,* won two Pulitzer Prizes for his critical assessments of Governor Orval Faubus's segregationist stance, one *Citizens' Council* cartoonist portrayed Ashmore as an old woman named "Mrs. Pussyfoot" who won prizes for her articles in the "Carpetbag Chronicle." William Simmons challenged the morality of moderate editors like Ashmore and Mississippi's own Hodding Carter, calling them "recognition-starved printing-press prostitutes."[35]

Southern journalists like Ashmore and Carter did not view themselves as radicals or integrationists because they too hewed to the concept of honor, remaining loyal southern men even as they rewrote what that identity meant. Describing a 1948 broadcast of the ABC radio and television program *Town Hall on the Air,* Ashmore remembered that Walter White, then president of the NAACP, was demanding desegregation and "Hodding and I were defending the honor of the South."[36] Even though Carter defended segregation in the Greenville (Mississippi) *Delta Democrat-Times* throughout the 1950s, he had to withstand boycotts and threats of violence for his condemnation of council tactics. "Any white who didn't agree with the white majority was more than a dissenter," Carter remembered. "He was a traitor, and was to be treated as a traitor would be treated in war time."[37] Moderate southern editors like Hodding Carter and Atlanta's Ralph McGill abhorred the strategies of arch-segregationist groups, but social and personal mores made them reluctant to advocate immediate integration. Straddling the fence on racial issues, these moderates garnered scathing criticism from both segregationists and civil rights activists. A master of dark humor, the black comedian Dick Gregory joked that the southern moderate was "a cat who'll lynch you from a low tree." Moderate southern whites may have seemed no different from arch-segregationists in the eyes of movement activists, but their acceptance of gradual reform served as a harbinger of future change. Explaining the ambivalent regional allegiances of newsmen like Ashmore, McGill, and her husband, Betty Carter said, "You see they never wanted to be anything but loyal sons of the South. But the South wasn't going to be what they wanted [it] to be. So they struggled to make the South be what they wanted."[38]

Southern moderates represented one threat to the councils' goal of regional hegemony, but violent supporters of segregation represented an even more dangerous problem because their actions ran the risk of provoking federal intervention. From the very beginning, most council spokesmen publicly distanced themselves from other white supremacist organizations like the Ku Klux Klan by denouncing their proclivity for violence. In one early council address, Judge Tom Brady surveyed his audience and surmised, "None of you men look like Ku Kluxers to me. I wouldn't join a Ku Klux [Klan] . . . because they hid their faces; because they did things you and I wouldn't approve of." However, realizing that it might be politically expedient to soften criticism of the Klan in Mississippi, Brady continued, "I'm not going to find fault with anyone who did [join the Klan]. Every man looks at the proposition not in the same way."[39] Although officially nonviolent, the councils issued mixed messages about the uses of violent tactics by supporters of segregation, just as their masculinist discourse and rhetoric of honor carried the implication that if pushed, the only honorable course of action for white southern men might be to "defend" their communities by force. Violent acts committed by noncouncil members also allowed council leaders to claim that their defense of segregation offered a peaceful solution to the region's racial tensions, but members who openly used violent tactics undercut these claims.

One council member who "looked at the proposition" of violence and Klan membership in a slightly different way was Asa "Ace" Carter, executive secretary of the North Alabama Citizens' Councils. Unlike most of the Mississippi Delta Councils, which were dominated by leading businessmen and planters, the North Alabama Citizens' Council consisted mainly of laborers and union men. Carter's working-class roots, propensity for violence, outspoken anti-Semitism, and direct connection to the "Original Ku Klux Klan of the Confederacy" proved too much for white-collar council leaders, who refused to recognize the North Alabama chapter. Despite this rejection from the official state organization, Carter continued to agitate openly for segregation until members of his klavern were arrested and convicted for castrating a black man in an initiation ceremony in 1957.[40] Castration of black men, a more common occurrence during the nadir of race relations around the turn of the century, continued through the 1960s, clearly underlining the salience of masculinity and sexual control in the struggle for civil rights.[41] The Birmingham castration incident damaged Carter's public position in the segregationist movement, but he continued to work behind the scenes and would later become a speechwriter for Alabama governor George Wallace. National council leaders nonetheless distanced themselves from Carter in the late 1950s. "Ace Carter is an Alabama problem," William Simmons observed. "He has no standing with our group . . . However, it might be added that the NAACP never feels it necessary to apologize for every Nigger rapist or for the Commies who help their cause."[42]

The councils' harangues against communism and integration echoed the gendered discourse of national debates concerning America's response to the cold war. As historian K. A. Cuordileone has argued, politicians of this era attempted to position themselves not only as staunch anticommunists, but also as "hard," manly cold warriors who were imminently more capable of defending America than their "soft," sometimes "queer" or "effete" opponents. Senators Strom Thurmond, James Eastland, and Richard Russell were leading segregationists and national political figures who aligned themselves with the "hard" cold warriors, brooking no quarter for communist "subversives" or liberals who were "soft" on communism. Leander H.

Perez, a powerful Louisiana politician and Citizens' Council leader, likened the national Democratic platform in 1960 to the Communist Manifesto because of its moderate support for civil rights. "How can we preserve *our* constitutional rights, *our* liberty and freedom under law, *our* status as first class citizens, *our* self-respect and manhood," Perez demanded, "IF we continue to run from the negroes" and bow to "the worldwide Communist conspiracy." Despite certain ideological inconsistencies, these leading southerners wielded masculinist discourse both to defend democracy abroad and to deny it at home.[43]

Shifts in American society and popular culture reinforced and reflected the gender anxieties that were rife in the political arena. As men and women settled down to domestic bliss in the cookie-cutter suburban subdivisions that sprang up across the country in the 1950s, some husbands began to wonder if they controlled their domains and their destinies to the same extent that their fathers had. Films of the era, such as *The Man in the Gray Flannel Suit,* depicted men grappling with the insecurities that accompanied domesticity and conformity, but no picture was more emblematic of this male angst than *Rebel without a Cause.* At the heart of the story is a dysfunctional relationship between a father and son. James Dean is the archetypal rebellious son who cannot understand why his father, played by Jim Backus, has exchanged his manhood for domestic servility. In one especially telling scene, the effete father, wearing a striking full-length, flower-print apron, futilely attempts to bond with the troubled teen. The son flees from the house and rushes to defend his honor in a game of chicken. With his smoldering intensity, Dean's character eventually teaches his father to be a strong man who stands up for himself and his son. One moral of the story is clearly that men must be careful not to become too domesticated or feminized in the rush to conjugal bliss. By the late 1950s and early 1960s, pop culture paeans to the patriarchal, nuclear family such as *Leave It to Beaver* and *Father Knows Best* reassured American men that they were still masters of their domains. Yet the reassurances may have seemed hollow to southern white men who struggled to shield their families from integration.[44]

Rock and roll music, television shows, and major motion pictures "invaded" homes and hamlets throughout the South in the late 1950s, challenging the basic tenets of segregation with interracial casts and integrationist themes. The Citizens' Councils railed against what they saw as the insidious tendency toward integration in American popular culture. When Asa Carter defended six members of the North Alabama Council who assaulted Nat "King" Cole in 1956, he called Cole a "vicious agitator for integration." If Cole and other popular black artists threatened segregation by attracting black and white fans to their concerts, Elvis Presley, Jerry Lee Lewis, and the white rockers of the 1950s seemed even more dangerous. They personally embodied integration. Unabashedly mingling black rhythm and blues with white country music, Elvis was the undisputed "king" of the white rockers who gained popularity by embracing black music, clothes, and dance styles. Elvis blurred gender lines as well. Dressed to the nines in meticulous outfits with bold pink accents or done up in the eye shadow that he liked to wear for shows, Elvis tapped into a tender masculinity that made girls swoon without letting go of the motorcycle machismo that inspired boys to rock. Like other rockers broadcast by radio to even the most remote areas of the South, Elvis presented a serious problem for segregationists bent on defending a traditional ideal of southern manhood and keeping white culture "pure" of black influences. The airwaves crackled with more than the insidious sounds of R&B and rock and roll on the radio; they carried the images of television programs, which also seemed tainted by integration. Robert Patterson referred to the abominable influence of "Hellavision" on impressionable southern children, who might see "white men hugging Eartha Kitt or Pearl Bailey or some other form of interracial brainwash." And William Simmons frequently worried about the implications of television programs like Ed Sullivan's "mixed entertainment."[45]

Hollywood similarly shocked segregationist sensibilities in the 1950s, daring to depict interracial relationships on the silver screen. *Island in the Sun* (1957) revolved around an interracial relationship between a black man (Harry Belafonte) and a white woman (Joan Fontaine). Belafonte's character ultimately decides against interracial marriage, explaining that a white wife "would only mean snubs and misery. Besides, the girl would forget herself one day and call me a nigger." In a subplot, however, a white British officer does successfully woo an Afro-Caribbean woman. Despite the fact that the interracial couples are never seen kissing in the film, *Jet* dubbed *Island in the Sun* "the most frank portrayal of interracial love ever to hit the screen." Segregationists called for whites to picket theaters that screened the film. In fact, a posse of Citizens' Councilors cut the power and blocked the entrance to one rural Alabama drive-in that dared to show it. The angry councilors even assaulted a journalist sent from the state capital to photograph the protest and then boasted, "Niggers may run wild in Montgomery, but Elmore County is going to take care of itself."[46] To segregationists, *Island in the Sun* was only the beginning. Don Whelply, a council member from Atlanta, responded to Hollywood's purported slander against the southern white men and women in a *Citizens' Council* article entitled "What They Say About Dixie." He decried what he saw as celluloid caricatures of "the spineless Southern male [and] the sickly simpering belle," noting that "overnight, the southern gentleman vanished. In his place stood the beefy bigot, with blacksnake whip poised over the poor 'kneegrow.'" For Whelply, the last straw was the 1957 film *Band of Angels*, which cast Yvonne DeCarlo, a "luscious, very Anglo-Saxon young starlet as a Negress." Writers like Erskine Caldwell and Tennessee Williams, whose novels and plays became movies in the 1950s, also fell under Whelply's caustic critique for their gothic depictions "of the masses' strange doings in the land of cotton."[47]

If Citizens' Council members felt besieged by popular national culture during the 1950s, they were horrified when some politicians in their own region took stock of the shifting political winds and adjusted their course accordingly. By the late 1950s, national sentiment and the federal government opposed southern segregationists and favored at least gradual school integration. Politicians in the border states were beginning to view token integration as an acceptable alternative to federal intervention. When Governor J. Lindsay Almond of Virginia "surrendered" to the opponents of segregation by agreeing to token integration in Virginia schools, one Tennessee paper suggested that the governor had "emerged with the honor that is due wisdom and courage and good citizenship." As a spokesman for the Citizens' Councils, William Simmons vehemently disagreed, noting that "the only 'honor' Almond emerged with is that accorded by others of like persuasion of whom, mercifully, there are but few in the deep South." Simmons termed Almond's action a "massive betrayal," and he felt certain that white Virginians had "enough pride and honor to make certain that [this] never happens again." Moderate southern whites in border states had begun to redefine the "honorable" position in the integration crisis, as massive resistance lost its already tenuous hold on the Upper South.[48]

Meanwhile, in the Deep South, Mississippi segregationists were about to elect one of their own to the highest office in the state. In his 1959 campaign for governor of Mississippi, Ross Barnett made it crystal clear that no other candidate could offer a stronger defense of segregation than he could. A long-time member of the Citizens' Councils, Barnett's election as governor represented the political high water mark for the organization. At a council dinner to commemorate his election, Barnett hammered away at racial moderates with a masculinist rhetoric that had become the staple of segregationists. "Physical courage is a trait sadly lacking in altogether too many of the South's so-called leaders," Barnett said. "We must separate the men from the boys. We must identify the traitors in our midst. We must eliminate the cowards from the front lines."[49]

Ross Barnett's outspoken opposition to integration set him on a collision course with the federal government, which by 1962 was no longer willing to forestall the integration of the University of Mississippi. In that year, President John F. Kennedy and his brother, Attorney General Robert Kennedy, pressured Governor Barnett to accept court-ordered integration of Ole Miss. Publicly, Barnett had vowed never to permit integration, but privately he cut a deal with the Kennedy brothers that would allow him to save face as he allowed James Meredith, a black Mississippian, to register at Ole Miss. Barnett made the attorney general promise that Meredith would be led onto campus by a phalanx of federal marshals, who would all draw their guns as they forced the governor to step aside. In Barnett's mind, this choreographed showdown would be the only way to convince Mississippians that he had done his manly duty and acted honorably to defend them against integration.[50]

Even the governor realized that this hollow performance of manliness would not be enough to rationalize surrender in the eyes of Mississippians whipped into a frenzy by his own demagoguery. At the last minute, Barnett reneged on the deal, and the federal marshals assigned to ensure order as Meredith integrated Ole Miss were left facing a mob of angry students and armed vigilantes with little state protection. A massive riot erupted on the campus in the wake of Meredith's enrollment. Unaware of the violence in Mississippi, Kennedy delivered a nationally televised speech concerning the integration of Ole Miss just as the marshals began to exchange salvos of teargas canisters for snipers' bullets coming from the mob. In his speech, Kennedy co-opted white Mississippian's own conceptions of manhood and honor as he asked Ole Miss students to accept Meredith, saying, "You have a great tradition to uphold, a tradition of honor and courage, won on the battlefield and the gridiron, as well as the university campus . . . I am certain the great majority of the students will uphold that honor." In the riot that followed Meredith's entrance into the university, thirty-five marshals were shot and two people were killed.[51]

Vigilante violence was a direct result of the masculinist demagoguery used by segregationists in calls for white southern men to defend their honor and their positions of power in the racial and gender hierarchy of the Jim Crow South. The circumstances and rhetoric that inspired the 1955 lynching of Emmett Till, the 1962 riots at Ole Miss, and countless other acts of violence (primarily directed against black men) underline this point. Segregation had constituted a solid foundation for white male supremacy in the South. Understanding this, the Citizens' Council recruited thousands of southern white men into the fight against integration with antiquated ideals of manhood and honor. The council's manipulation of honor and a hateful heritage of militant white male supremacy led directly to violence against black citizens, civil rights activists, and federal officials. Once the struggle against integration became a question of honor, violence became the only recourse for militant white supremacists when political and legal actions failed. Rather than cowing African Americans, this violence inspired more activism for integration and voting rights. Nonviolent civil rights protests would brilliantly caricature the violent tactics and macho posturing of the segregationists, forcing the South to dismantle the legal vestiges of Jim Crow once and for all.

NOTES

1. A transcript of this speech is included in the correspondence files of former UNC professor Wesley C. George, series 1.2, folder 11, box 2, Wesley George Papers, Southern Historical Collection (SHC), Wilson Library, University of North Carolina, Chapel Hill.

2. For an alternate version of this speech, see "It is claimed that white people secretly wired the building and recorded the speech as follows," a broadside in the NAACP folder, 1956–1964, Segregation and Integration Miscellaneous Collection, Special Collections, Mitchell Memorial Library, Mississippi State University (hereafter, MSU Special Collections),

3. Neil R. McMillen, *The Citizens' Council: Organized Resistance to the Second Reconstruction, 1954–1964* (Urbana: University of Illinois Press, 1994), 36; Hodding Carter III, *The South Strikes Back* (New York: Doubleday and Co., 1959), 137–38.

4. For examinations of the gendered nature of Reconstruction and the rise of Jim Crow, see Laura Edwards, *Gendered Strife and Confusion: The Politics and Culture of Reconstruction* (Urbana: University of Illinois Press, 1997); Glenda Gilmore, *Gender and Jim Crow: Women and the Politics of White Supremacy in North Carolina, 1896–1920* (Chapel Hill: University of North Carolina Press, 1996); and Stephen Kantrowitz, *Ben Tillman and the Reconstruction of White Supremacy* (Chapel Hill: University of North Carolina Press, 2000).

5. Numan V. Bartley, *The Rise of Massive Resistance: Race and Politics in the South During the 1950s*

(Baton Rouge: Louisiana State University Press, 1969). Bartley's more recent work *The New South, 1945–1980* (Baton Rouge: Louisiana State University Press, 1995) places massive resistance in the broader context of the postwar period. Bartley and McMillen (in *The Citizens' Council*) deftly depict the political rise of the segregationist movement. Although they touch on the gender and sexual dynamics of the struggle, they do not scrutinize these aspects closely.

6. See Lillian Smith, *Killers of the Dream* (New York: W. W. Norton, 1949, 1961), for a southern critique of segregation that highlights issues of sex and gender. See also John Dollard, *Caste and Class in a Southern Town* (New York: Harper, 1949), and Neil R. McMillen, *Dark Journey: Black Mississippians in the Age of Jim Crow* (Urbana: University of Illinois Press, 1989). For a deeper history of gender roles and sexual mores in the South, see Bertram Wyatt-Brown, *Southern Honor: Ethics and Behavior in the Old South* (Oxford: Oxford University Press, 1982).

7. Ralph Ellison, *Invisible Man* (New York: Random House, 1952).

8. John Dittmer, *Local People: The Struggle for Civil Rights in Mississippi* (Urbana: University of Illinois Press, 1994), 1–40. James Hicks, a leading black journalist in the post–World War II period, remembered that "when the black veterans of World War II returned home, they were . . . activists and they had been trained, and of course when they said, 'No more of this Jim Crow' or what have you, the people, that is black people picked it up." Henry Hampton, Steve Frasier, Sarah Flynn, eds., *Voices of Freedom: An Oral History of the Civil Rights Movement, From the 1950s through the 1980s* (New York: Bantam, 1990).

9. John Barlow Martin, *The Deep South Says Never* (New York, Ballantine, 1957), 1–4; Howell Raines, *My Soul Is Rested: Movement Days in the Deep South Remembered* (New York: Penguin, 1983), 297–303; Robert Patterson, *Second Annual Report: August 1956* (Winona: Association of the Citizens' Councils of Mississippi, 1956), Southern Pamphlet Folio 6860, Rare Book Collection (RBC), Wilson Library, University of North Carolina, Chapel Hill.

10. Anonymous, "How the White Citizens' Councils Came to Alabama," *New South* (December 1955): 9–12, folder 4, box 1-A, Cox Papers, MSU Special Collections. The author hid the location of the meeting and his own identity for fear of council retaliation. By 1956, the Alabama Councils claimed a statewide membership of 40,000 people. See article in the *Birmingham News*, February 19, 1956. For an examination of the Louisiana Citizen's Council activities, see William McFerrin Stowe Jr., "Willie Rainach and the Defense of Segregation in Louisiana," Ph.D. diss., Texas Christian University, 1989.

11. For an analysis of this struggle between business leaders and older state politicians, see Bartley, *The Rise of Massive Resistance*, 17–24; and William Chafe, *Civilities and Civil Rights: Greensboro, North Carolina, and the Black Struggle for Freedom* (Oxford: Oxford University Press, 1980).

12. George stated his position in a letter to "Mr. French" in December 1954, folder 11, box 2, George Papers; McMillen, *The Citizens' Council*, 113–14.

13. Hood to George, February 2, 1955, folder 15; Thornton to George, November 29, 1954, folder 10, box 2, George Papers.

14. Avant to George, November 29, 1954, folder 10, box 2, George Papers. George eventually furnished the state of Alabama with a "scientific" treatise on the disastrous consequences of integration entitled "Biology of the Race Problem."

15. North Carolina Defenders of State's Rights charter quoted in the *Citizens' Council,* December 1958. For more on how local government in North Carolina thwarted desegregation mandates, see Chafe, *Civilities and Civil Rights,* 64–67.

16. Tom P. Brady, *Black Monday* (Winona, MS: Association of Citizens' Councils, 1955), 45, 47, 63, 87. See also Austin Earl Burges, *What Price Integration?* (Dallas: American Guild Press, 1956).

17. Hampton, Frasier, and Flynn, *Voices of Freedom,* 12–14.

18. "M is for Mississippi and Murder" (New York: NAACP, 1956), folder 19, box 2, Citizens' Councils / Civil Rights Collection (1954–1977), Manuscript Collection of the McCain Library and Archives at the University of Southern Mississippi (USM Archives); McMillen, *The Citizens' Council,* 217–18. See Stephen J. Whitfield, *A Death in the Delta: The Story of Emmett Till* (New York: Free Press, 1988).

19. McMillen, *The Citizens' Council,* 37, 123.

20. *Citizens' Council,* November 1956, August and November 1957; Earl Warren, *The Memoirs of Earl Warren* (New York: Doubleday, 1977): 291–92.

21. Numan Bartley, *The New South, 1945–1980* (Baton Rouge: Louisiana State University Press, 1996), 188.

22. *Citizens' Council,* December 1958.

23. The councils also drew on the rhetoric of the Lost Cause to spur men to defend segregation. See, e.g., the poem "The Ghost of Robert E. Lee" in the *Citizens' Council,* February 1957. James J. Kilpatrick, the editor of the *Richmond News Leader,* later commended Simmons on the Councils' work. See letter from Kilpatrick to Simmons, April 19, 1963, in the Mississippi State Sovereignty Commission files, document # 9-11-1-106-2-1-1, housed at the State Department of Archives and History.

24. For more on the political and cultural meanings of the Civil War, see David W. Blight, *Race and Reunion: The Civil War in American Memory* (Cambridge, MA: Harvard University Press, 2001).

25. Bertram Wyatt-Brown, *Southern Honor,* xv, xvii, 14, and 34. Although Wyatt-Brown argues that the southern code of honor began to decline after the Civil War, he suggests that it might be fruitful to study the concept even into the 1950s. See also Edward L. Ayers, *Vengeance and Justice: Crime and Punishment in the 19th Century American South* (New York: Oxford University Press, 1984), and Richard E. Nisbett and Dov Cohen, *Culture of Honor: The Psychology of Violence in the South* (Boulder: Westview, 1996).

26. See, e.g., an Alabama Citizens' Council constitution, which expressly limited membership to "adult white male citizens" in the mid-1950s (folder 13, box 1, Citizen's Council / Civil Rights Collection).

27. McMillen, *The Citizens' Councils,* 11.

28. Bartley, *The New South,* 201. Few rosters of local Citizens' Councils remain, but a typical example would be the 1956 membership rolls from the chapter in Forest, Mississippi, which included only 15 women out of 190 total members folder 46, box 2, McIlhenny Papers, MSU Special Collections.

29. *Citizens' Council,* November 1956.

30. Ibid., February 1957. See also a report from the Texas Councils in August 1957, which said, "In many of our Councils the men are doing more than the women. We are making a great mistake if we do not enlist the patriotic services of these women."

31. Memo from Robert Patterson, December 30, 1957; and "Women's Aid Sought in Segregation

Fight" *Jackson Daily News,* January 3, 1958, folder "Assoc. of Citizens' Councils of Miss.: Women's Activities," Citizens' Council Collection, MSU Special Collections; McMillen, *The Citizens' Council,* 241–42.

32. *Citizens' Council,* February 1957.

33. Herbert Ravenel Sass, "Mixed Schools and Mixed Blood" (Citizens' Councils of America, 1956), Southern Pamphlet #1632, RBC.

34. Neil McMillen, "White Citizens' Council and Resistance to School Desegregation in Arkansas," *Arkansas Historical Quarterly* 30, no. 2 (1971): 106; Daisy Bates interviewed by Elizabeth Jacoway, October 11, 1976, Southern Oral History Program (SOHP), Collection 4007, series G-009, SHC.

35. *Citizens' Council,* June 1958.

36. Harry Ashmore interviewed by John Egerton, June 16, 1990, #4007, SOHP Series A: 3553, 10–11.

37. Hodding Carter interviewed by Jack Bass, April 1, 1974, #4007, SOHP Series A: 100, 29.

38. Dick Gregory quoted in Sally Belfrage, *Freedom Summer* (Charlottesville: University of Virginia Press, 1965). Betty Carter interviewed by John Egerton, September 6, 1990, #4007, SOHP Series A: 350.

39. Tom Brady, "A Review of 'Black Monday,'" an address to the Indianola Citizens' Councils, October 28, 1954, p. 14, Southern Pamphlet #811, RBC.

40. For a detailed account of this assault and a full biographical sketch of Ace Carter, see Glenn T. Eskew, *But for Birmingham: The Local and National Movements in the Civil Rights Struggle* (Chapel Hill: University of North Carolina Press, 1997): 107–18. Quotes from McMillen, *The Citizens' Councils,* 47–55; and Bartley, *The Rise of Massive Resistance,* 201–8.

41. Jacquelyn Dowd Hall, "The Mind That Burns in Each Body: Women, Rape, and Racial Violence," *Southern Exposure* 12, no. 6 (1984): 61–71.

42. Carter, *The South Strikes Back,* 201–2.

43. K. A. Cuordileone, "'Politics in an Age of Anxiety': Cold War Political Culture and the Crisis in American Masculinity, 1949–1960," *Journal of American History* 87, no. 2 (2000): 515–45. See also Robert D. Dean, "Masculinity as Ideology: John F. Kennedy and the Domestic Politics of Foreign Policy," *Diplomatic History* 22 (Winter 1998): 29–62. Perez quote from "The Challenge to the South and How It Must Be Met," a speech to the Louisiana Citizens' Councils (July 21, 1960), folder 12, box 3, Citizens' Council Collection.

44. Steven Cohan, *Masked Men: Masculinity and the Movies in the Fifties* (Bloomington: Indiana University Press, 1997); Barbara Ehrenreich, *The Hearts of Men: American Dreams and the Flight from Commitment* (Garden City: Anchor, 1983); Michael Kimmel, *Manhood in America: A Cultural History* (New York: Free Press, 1996): 249–58. See also Joanne Meyerowitz, ed., *Not June Cleaver: Women and Gender in Postwar America, 1945–1960* (Philadelphia: Temple University Press, 1994). Peter Filene discusses what he calls the "domestic mystique" for middle-class American men that arose in the 1950s and produced an anxiety about domesticity leading to emasculation. For more on this, see Filene, *Him/Her/Self: Sex Roles in Modern America* (Baltimore: Johns Hopkins University Press, 1974): 169–76.

45. For a detailed analysis of race, class, and gender in the southern musical culture of the 1950s, see Pete Daniel, *Lost Revolutions: The South in the 1950s* (Chapel Hill, NC: University of North Carolina Press and the Smithsonian National Museum of American History, 2000): 121–74. Daniel observes,

"Rock 'n' roll unlocked women's emotions, but it also threatened white men's control." Patterson to George, Jan. 25, 1955, folder 11, box 2, George Papers; Carter, *The South Strikes Back*, 160; *Citizens' Council*, February 1957.

46. For several reviews, see the "Moving Pictures—*Island in the Sun*" folder, Clippings File, Schomburg Research Center, New York Public Library. For the call for pickets, see *Citizens' Council*, January and February 1957. For protestor quote and description of drive-in protest, see Daniel, *Lost Revolutions*, 165. Klan members picketed a showing of the film in Jacksonville, Florida. See Charles Reagan Wilson et al., eds., *Encyclopedia of Southern Culture* (Chapel Hill: University of North Carolina Press, 1989) 915–16, 924–27.

47. *Citizens' Council*, August 1958. Caldwell's *Tobacco Road* and many of Williams's plays were turned into feature films in the late 1950s and early 1960s. For a full description of southern images in popular culture, see Jack Temple Kirby's *Media-Made Dixie: The South in the American Imagination* (Athens: University of Georgia Press, 1986).

48. *Citizens' Council*, February 1959.

49. *Citizens' Council*, September 1959. See also Barnett's speeches, folder 38, box 2, McIlhenny Papers, MSU Special Collections.

50. Transcripts of the phone conversations between the Kennedy brothers and Barnett are printed verbatim in Victor S. Navasky, *Kennedy Justice* (New York: Atheneum, 1971): 189–90, 208–11. See also George Leonard, George Harris, and Christopher Wren, "How a Secret Deal Prevented a Massacre at Ole Miss" *Look*, December 31, 1962, 19–36.

51. Ibid. Kennedy quoted in Taylor Branch, *Parting the Waters: America in the King Years, 1954–63* (New York: Simon and Schuster, 1988), 665. For the full speech transcript, see "Radio and Television Report to the Nation on the Situation at the University of Mississippi (September 30, 1962)," *Public Papers of the Presidents: John F. Kennedy, 1962* (Washington, DC: U.S. Government Printing Office, 1963): 726–28.

The Boycotting of Coach Rutter

Manhood, Race, and Authority in Post-1970 Mississippi

TRENT WATTS

John Grisham's novel *Bleachers* (2003) reminds us just how seriously some Mississippians take their football. The novel centers on the reconciliatory funeral of long-time Messina High School football coach Eddie Rake, a hated but beloved figure whose legendary tenure ended after a particularly intense practice killed a player. Coach Rake led the Spartans to a Harlem Globetrotter–like streak of eighty-four straight wins, along with another dozen or so undefeated regular seasons, for an enviable if improbable overall record of 418 wins and 62 losses, with thirteen state titles thrown in. The novel's vague southernness allows its setting to seem like anybody's old hometown. For instance, high school players consider whether to attend "Tech" or "State." Grisham's market-driven ambiguity suggests that coaches, football, and the life lessons they teach work pretty much the same way everywhere. More significant, Rake single-handedly makes school integration work, ends racial segregation in public facilities, and provides former Spartans with the right stuff that they need to survive Vietnam firefights, state prison, broken hearts, and general angst and anomie. "[Coach Rake] said he didn't care what color we were," recalls one man. "All his players wore green." He concludes: "We are all one in Christ. And in this wonderful little town, we are one in Eddie Rake."[1]

High school football has long been recognized as a ritual of great import in the Deep South.[2] Observers in Mississippi's small-town cafes as well as public school central offices agree that the Friday night game is invested with a potent "shadow behind the act," as the late Mississippi writer Willie Morris put it. In the 1970s and early 1980s, Morris and others saw in high school football the power to salve racial tensions in the newly integrated public schools, as well as to transmit what most Mississippians unambiguously viewed as traditional masculine values of hard work, toughness, and teamwork.[3] Of the movement away from Jim Crow in Columbia, Mississippi, one reporter wrote recently: "The school's highly successful football team—about half black and half white—showed the way." A white former athlete agreed: "We weren't even thinking about color . . . we just thought about doing what it took to win . . . We were like *Remember the Titans.*"[4] The film *Remember the Titans* (2000), featuring Denzel Washington as the first African American coach at a previously all-white Alexandria, Virginia, high school, represents a common southern view of football: that the sport establishes a powerful male bond across racial and class lines; the coach holds this bond in place.[5]

In the years since school integration, most small-town white Mississippians have pointed to integrated sports teams as *ipso facto* evidence that integration and indeed the broader civil rights movement have worked and have left little unfinished business. Thus, most of the time and indeed without much conscious effort, white Mississippians subordinate questions of race to those of masculine character-building in thinking and talking about the football played at these integrated high schools. Few white Mississippians publicly acknowledge that race and sports have anything much to do with each other any more, certainly not in any way that supports white power and privilege.[6] Football, then, typically performs its work of encouraging racial bonhomie quietly, while both black and white Mississippians continue to view the game as a significant masculine ritual of passage. Yet, since integration, the head football coach at the typical Mississippi public high school has been white, a fact that seems natural and unremarkable to most white Mississippians. The coach's authority, derived much less obviously from his race than from his masculinity, is usually rewarded with loyalty so long as his "color blindness" seems to remain intact—so long as he, too, seems to subordinate race to the masculinity manifested in athletic performance.

The coach, then, stands as the most prominent representative of masculine authority in most Mississippi towns, seemingly because of an interracial respect for the coach's work with adolescent males. But the situation is more complicated than this dream of colorblindness might suggest. It is difficult to say where the coach's male authority ends and his racial authority begins. Historically, masculinity in the South has been so deeply racialized that the white coach carries resonances of the Jim Crow years along with his whistle and clipboard, whether he likes it or not. Consider, for instance, the racial paternalism evidenced in Ole Miss coach Billy Brewer's 1984 statement: "I understand the Southern black."[7] The coach does not cease being white just because he is coach. And while whites in the integrated public schools of 1970s and 1980s Mississippi may have preferred not to point out that the culture's most visible public symbol of masculine authority was white, black Mississippians were increasingly well aware of the fact.

In 1988, there was an incident in a small Mississippi town where public high school football exacerbated rather than muted racial tensions. The boycotting of Coach Hollis Rutter in Brookhaven demonstrates what happened when one coach's color-blindness—his public commitment to the racial equity necessary to the smooth functioning of integrated public schools—was challenged and placed in doubt. Along with a black boycott of white-owned businesses, a black student walkout from classes, a disruption of the high school and junior high basketball season, and a general souring of race relations, the event also called into question the reassuring stories white Brookhavenites told themselves about the elevating effects of sports and the benevolence of (white male) authority. Black Brookhaven's rejection of Rutter thus compromised the quiet fiction that football, both before and especially after school integration, had nothing fundamentally to do with race or politics but was rather a tried and trusted device for turning boys into men. From Brookhaven's coaches, Assistant Superintendent Dorothy Logan-Alexander explained recently, "the [white and black] community expects 'win and blend.'"[8] Hollis Rutter never got the opportunity to do either one.

Brookhaven shows little evidence of the stereotypical Old South and not much of the New South, if by New South one means either political progressivism or industry in the manner of Tupelo, Mississippi, say, or the Gulf Coast. Indeed, it is hard to put one's finger on what is "southern" about Brookhaven, if one is looking for Civil War or civil rights–era battlefields. Like the city of Picayune in literary scholar Noel Polk's excellent memoir, Brookhaven is a town that does not fit satisfyingly within conventional southern myths.[9] The courthouse monument honors the town's twentieth-century war dead, not the Lost Cause. The antebellum past has never been a cottage (or rather, mansion) industry there, as in Natchez. But outside the Super 8 Motel room where I stayed while researching this essay, one can easily see geographical, social, and economic elements that tie Brookhaven into other familiar southern stories. For instance, there is interstate highway I-55, with its J. B. Hunt and Wal-Mart trucks going by, evidence of the recent South's bracing but uneven economic development; the highway suggests as well a longer history of white and black migration out of and back into the region. And looking across the parking lot, one can see a picturesque if stereotypical reminder of the area's ruralness: a rusted barbed wire fence nearly obscured by honeysuckle, ripe blackberries, and Johnson grass.

The town lies on the southwestern edge of Mississippi's pine timber belt. Brookhaven was settled before the Civil War but was not the seat of large cotton plantations, nor was the war a particularly scarring experience, physically or culturally, despite the town's lying at the apex of a triangle completed by Natchez to the West and Vicksburg to the Northwest. Lincoln County, created in 1870, was populated by white farmers and a class of merchants made prosperous by the railroad and the area's rich stand of longleaf pine timber, some of which can still be seen in the heart-pine floors of the town's handsome houses along Railroad Avenue. By the turn of the twentieth century, Brookhaven had grown to 2,678 residents; since World War II, the town's population has peaked and shrunk gradually from around 10,700 in 1970 to approximately 9,800 in 2000. The percentage of white population was a constant 62 percent in 1960 and 1970, but the population has since evened out to approximately 51 percent white and 47 percent black.[10]

There was slavery here, and cotton, too, recently enough so that one's parents or grandparents, white or black, might have picked it. And like most Mississippi towns, Brookhaven operated a separate but unequal system of public education. In 1956 the city built a handsome brick structure for Alexander High School (formerly Alexander Colored School); as in many communities, Brookhaven's apparent generosity was an attempt to mute black discontent as the white South began its strategy of massive resistance to the integration of public education.[11] Still, Brookhaven does not carry the same civil rights–era resonances as Oxford or McComb or Neshoba County, among other places.[12] But that is not to say that the town does not hold its own deep history of race.

At the height of massive resistance, Brookhaven's most famous resident was certainly Thomas P. Brady, the Yale-educated jurist and author of *Black Monday* (1955), the semiofficial handbook of the Citizens' Council. Brady's segregationist tract essays a racialist history of mankind, attacks the communistic impulses behind the Brown decision, and outlines a white southern political strategy for preserving states' rights and segregation. Brady's arguments were once staples of

Mississippi political discourse. Mississippians black and white were aware that the Brookhavenite cut a real figure in the controversies of the day. In her memoir *For Us, the Living*, Myrlie Evers remembered that after Lamar Smith, a black registered voter, was shot to death in front of the Lincoln County courthouse in August 1955, "few Negroes heard the news without recalling that Brookhaven was the home of Judge Tom Brady."[13] In Brookhaven in the 1970s and 1980s, Judge Brady had faded from public view, if not from memory, and the Brady family name was (and still is) one to conjure with.

By the 1980s, however, *Black Monday*, massive resistance, and the murder of Lamar Smith had disappeared from Brookhaven's public discourse, at least from white public discourse, and arguments about race and power rarely disturbed the front page of the local paper. The most common public complaints about Brookhaven High School had little to do with race but pointed instead to the football team's failure to win games. Coaching football at Brookhaven High in the 1980s presented distinct challenges. One of the smaller schools in Mississippi's Class 5A, Brookhaven struggled perennially against division powers Hattiesburg, Warren Central, and McComb. From 1985 to 1987 the team limped to a nine and twenty-two record, going winless the last year. Brookhaven High's glory days of the 1950s, with graceful receiver and future National Football League Hall of Fame member Lance Alworth and Big Eight championships, seemed far away. But through those fat years and the lean of the 1970s and 1980s, the black and white players had won or lost together, albeit always under a white head coach. With the ending of the dual system of education in Brookhaven in 1970, the team was meaningfully racially integrated, with a white majority until the mid-1980s but with a black starting quarterback as early as 1971.[14] The integration of the schools seemed to most white Brookhavenites a problem that had been confronted when the time finally came, and that had been managed adequately by the town fathers, as people called them, accurately (in terms of gender and power) and without apparent irony.

In the winter of 1987, the school board went looking for a man to revive Brookhaven's football fortunes. Hollis Rutter seemed a good fit. A 1947 graduate of Brookhaven High, the sixty-one-year-old Rutter had enjoyed a successful twenty-nine-year career, winning championships in four divisions. Instead of inspiring dreams of a winning season, however, the next months brought bitter racial conflict to the town. While Rutter had enjoyed a successful career at several

Mississippi public high schools before and after racial integration, he had also, before taking the job at Brookhaven, coached at two of the state's segregation academies, Greenwood's Pillow Academy, founded in 1966, and Brookhaven Academy, founded in 1970. This association with noxious institutions caused practically all black Brookhavenites to perceive Rutter as at least a tacit supporter of segregation. In their eyes, his authority as coach and his privilege to mold young men was fatally compromised; what masculinity gave, race (or rather, black perceptions of his racism) took away.

Indeed, black distaste for Rutter's association with these segregated institutions manifested itself occasionally in dismissals of his masculinity. "He was an old white man," one school administrator told me. "Rutter was too old," said another. Both statements are revealing. At first, they seem simply to attack his age, perhaps with the added implication that Rutter's age implicated him in the racialist politics of the 1960s. But both statements should be understood as attacks on Rutter's manhood as well as his age. Turning boys into men requires vigor and virility; the implication here is that Rutter no longer had enough of either quality. Both statements say essentially that in their eyes, Rutter was not man enough for the job, about as damning a judgment as can be delivered on any small-town Mississippi man.

Rutter never coached a game at Brookhaven High. Instead, he accepted a central office administrative position and quietly retired two years later. Only Rutter's removal as head coach satisfied black Brookhaven's insistence that the coach—a figure who embodied overt and widely shared views about manhood—not embody overt and divisive messages about race. White business and civic leaders in Brookhaven were prepared to sacrifice Rutter, a gesture that kept public order without shaking white male control of the city. The use of the economic boycott by black Brookhavenites to register their dissatisfaction with Rutter's hiring proved particularly unsettling to whites, recalling as it did the civil rights movement, which had similarly rejected claims of benevolent white authority.

The boycott tells us just how contingent and fragile small-town narratives of placid, equitable race relations really are. Other school activities in Brookhaven, such as homecoming dances, class reunions, and the prom were segregated. In many small Mississippi towns in the 1970s and 1980s, such division seemed natural and went largely unremarked. Sports, however, provided an arena in which blacks and whites worked in close physical proximity and achieved what appeared from the stands to be color-blind teamwork. The success of integrated team sports required that racial division be bridged or even ignored in the interests of an apparently seamless, natural masculinity. Furthermore, the authority of coaches (who often double as teachers and administrators, especially in small schools) lends credence to their words off the football field as well as on it. During the boycott, one of Coach Rutter's defenders voiced a common view of the southern coach's cultural work: his job was "to turn boys into men." The phenomenon is not confined to south Mississippi. Recent scholars of education point to signs that school management itself has become suffused with a "'competitive, point-scoring, over-confident, sporting, career and status conscious' version of masculinity."[15]

Football coaches in Mississippi do occupy real public positions of authority, one of the few models of masculine respectability to cross racial lines. In small towns such as Brookhaven, ministers and elected officials (an overwhelmingly male group) typically are seen by blacks and whites to represent racially exclusive constituencies. The coach is an exception. In Brookhaven, two former head coaches became successful businessmen in the 1970s, selling men's clothing and sporting goods. One later served as Brookhaven mayor, the other as a school board member. Both continued to be called "Coach" many years after their last game. The coach is expected not only to win games but to mold character. Even if few people outside the Deep South take that rhetoric seriously any longer, many Mississippians still do. Former Brookhaven coach James McCullom, architect of 1987's zero-and-ten season, remarked: "I hope to influence these kids in positive ways. Someday the Lord is going to ask them, 'What did you do besides football?'"[16] A deacon in his church and advocate of the Fellowship of Christian athletes, McCollum reminds us of the tenacity of turn-of-the-century conceptions of muscular Christianity in the Deep South.[17] In Lincoln County, the coach occasionally wears multiple hats of male authority. Ronald Greer, a 1983 graduate of Brookhaven High School, and the head football coach, athletic director, and principal of Wesson High School, announced in the spring of 2004 that he would resign his head coaching position to concentrate more heavily on his Christian ministry: "I know the impact my coaches had on me . . . I took the opportunity to talk to the kids about the Lord. I have heard some of the sweetest prayers from these guys."[18]

"There's certainly more to life than football," wrote the Brookhaven newspaper's sports editor shortly before the Rutter controversy.[19] But sometimes in Mississippi, it seems difficult to say for sure. The salary of more than $36,000 that Rutter was to have drawn as coach and athletic director was equal to that of the high school principal. But as the newspaper pointed out in familiar idiom, "Coach earns it . . . It's a tough row to hoe . . . The football team is the focal point of the community."[20] Another Brookhavenite agreed, "I don't care how many books you read. You may become a very prominent person through them, but there isn't a single book on earth that can give you [what] school sports do."[21]

Schools everywhere elicit proprietary feelings, of course, especially in communities like Brookhaven, where racial division is palpable, if usually unspoken.[22] The crux of the Rutter problem was that he had recently coached at the all-white academy outside of town. Brookhaven Academy was little different from other private schools organized in the state in the late 1960s and early 1970s. After the federal courts made it clear in early 1970 that "never" had finally come, many concerned white parents set about preserving lily-white education. No one spoke in those years of the merits of home schooling; few identified the public schools they themselves had attended with creeping secular humanism. Instead, the purposes of Brookhaven Academy were clear then and later to most Brookhavenites. While the school now features a rare nonwhite face or two, a Brookhaven public school administrator recently told me: "If they are integrated, it's just to receive federal funds."[23] No official policy prohibited the school board from hiring teachers who had taught at Brookhaven Academy. It happened commonly in the 1970s and 1980s.[24] Why then did the hiring of Coach Rutter turn out so disastrously? Former Brookhaven superintendent of education George Brumfield told me, "If Hollis Rutter had been an algebra or a history teacher, none of this would have happened."[25]

At their January 21, 1988, meeting, the school board voted "after a lengthy discussion" to hire Rutter as high school football coach and athletic director: three members for, one against, and one abstention.[26] The split decision foreshadowed difficulties that lay ahead. Rutter's advocates stressed his ties to Brookhaven and his winning of championships at Eupora, Morton, Jackson Provine, and Greenwood. Capping Rutter's 225–118–9 record was his induction into the Mississippi Coaches Association Hall of Fame in 1984. Most important, he had the administrative experience that would make him capable of handling the athletic department's budget of more than $100,000.[27] Jessie Buie, the only black member of the school board and the only dissenting vote, emerged as a chief critic of Rutter. "We plan to protest," he announced, "but have yet to work out the details." Buie continued: "We feel the hiring of Coach Rutter from an academy was a deep insult. The board and the superintendent were warned that this was not an acceptable action."[28]

Signs of black dissatisfaction with Rutter's hiring appeared immediately. The day following the school board's announcement, the Brookhaven High Lady Panthers played for the Big Eight Conference basketball championship. The coach had to persuade several black players to start the game against their parents' wishes. The following Tuesday night about 400 people met with local NAACP officials, while two black starters on the girls' basketball team sat out a game the Lady Panthers lost badly. The father of one of the players expressed what became a common view among black Brookhavenites: "I don't feel it is right for a private school coach to coach black kids. He was in public schools but gave it up in favor in private schools. It isn't right." School board member Jesse Buie added: "It's past time for black youngsters to have role models to look up to. If they always see the black man as assistant coach and the white man as the head coach, it's almost ingrained on them that that's the way it is."[29]

Two local ministers, Julius Bass and O. D. Evans, emerged as the public face of black protest. "This is not a black and white issue," insisted Bass. The problem, both men argued, was that Rutter was an outsider, brought into the community from an institution hostile to the interests of Brookhaven's public schools. The protest exposed fracture lines between white and black definitions of community in Brookhaven. White Brookhavenites were puzzled by this reaction to Rutter. An alumnus of Brookhaven High wrote to the newspaper, "When I played ball at BHS, I played for my coach, my teammates, and my school."[30] One of the functions of sports is to create this sort of easily identifiable "we." Without a moment of disjunction like the Rutter hiring, the asserted "we" in sports and in public schools themselves can go conveniently undefined.

Black dissatisfaction with the Rutter hire quickly grew into a broad boycott of extracurricular activities. The basketball walkout continued. With the boys' team reduced from twenty-four to eight players, and the girls' team missing its starters, the Panthers dropped key conference games. Student protest reached the junior high as well. The remainder of the ninth-grade team's season was cancelled because there was no team left. "There are definitely some outside factions leading the kids," argued the boys' coach.[31] Identifying those "factions" and their motivations remained difficult for white Brookhavenites, who throughout the controversy seemed unable to accept that the hiring of Hollis Rutter could be a source of legitimate grievance to local blacks.

"We will not let our kids play under a private school person," insisted Rev. Julius Bass on February 2. Bass rightly pointed out that with black students constituting more than 70 percent of the school district's athletes, a boycott could effectively end the basketball and track seasons. While black protestors continued to speak succinctly of the unacceptability of a coach moving from a private to a public school, a few people elaborated on precisely why that move was so significant. Rev. O. D. Evans, minister of the Macedonia Missionary Baptist Church, stressed that "it is important for all children to have a role model."[32]

Racial difference was a subject not much discussed in the Brookhaven public schools in the 1970s and 1980s.[33] Few teachers or administrators wished students to believe that there were "black" issues and "white" issues to divide the schools or students. Initially, indeed, the survival of the schools seemed to demand the absence of such conversations. But the old habit of not speaking publicly of the town's recent past and of the social and economic problems that remained was a difficult habit to break. As one black correspondent to the Brookhaven newspaper put it, "the time has come for these and other issues [to] be addressed . . . or [will it be, as always]: this isn't the time to talk about it?" By the 1980s, many black Brookhavenites began questioning the cost of school integration. Brookhaven High had never had a black principal, football coach, or band director, all prominent figures of masculine authority at the old black Alexander High.[34] The pattern in Brookhaven was common across the state of Mississippi in the 1970s and 1980s. Writing in 1971, Willie Morris notes that "practically without exception in the state, all the black principals have been demoted to assistant . . . In Canton, the black football coach became 'assistant principal for discipline' in the new high school and a white coach took over the predominately black team."[35]

From the beginning, Superintendent George Brumfield was determined to stand by his man. "It flabbergasts me," said Brumfield. "We were not aware that his appointment would upset anyone." Two long-time Brookhaven public school administrators told me that Brumfield simply did not consult the lone black member of the school board or any of the black administrators in the Brookhaven schools' central office before deciding to recommend Rutter to the school board. Dorothy Alexander, Brumfield's assistant superintendent, said succinctly: "He never asked." Carl Holloway, a long-time Brookhaven resident and himself a former coach, then served as the central office's attendance coordinator. According to Holloway, Brumfield informed him of his decision to recommend Rutter shortly before the school board meeting. Holloway replied: "I know it's going to be a problem."[36] Brumfield's apparent decision not to seek broader counsel about the likely reaction of black Brookhavenites to the hiring of Brookhaven Academy's coach is curious, given his years in integrated public schools and his reputation as a racial moderate.

In the habit of most small-town newspaper editors, the *Daily Leader's* William Jacobs asserted that all was well in Brookhaven, and that there was somewhere a golden mean on which all reasonable people could agree. The protest seemed at times to become an argument over who had the best interests of the kids at stake, with white Brookhavenites adopting unfamiliar postures of solicitude toward the welfare of young blacks. "Emotion and prejudice," wrote the editor, "threaten to tear down everything that has been built over the years." Insisting, as had generations of white Mississippians, that all was potentially well if agitation ceased, the newspaper held up as the model of reason a black basketball player who refused to participate in the boycott, that is, not to worry about the racial implications of a former segregated school coach at Brookhaven High. Another white Brookhavenite offered, "All authority is by the will of God . . . That means not undermining decisions already made."[37]

White and black Brookhavenites peppered the newspaper with commentary. Some writers showed a peculiar sense of the law: "I do believe," wrote one man assuredly, "that it states in the U.S. Constitution that prejudice towards any race shall not be tolerated, does it not?" One white man advised: "Just look at yourself as neither black or white, Catholic or Jew or Baptist, Russian or American, cripple or retarded. I think I'm gray!"[38] Others were clearer, if less amusing, "This is one time the minority will have to go by the wishes of the majority (I'm sure you know what I mean by that)."[39]

The protest moved onto a wider stage on February 9, when opponents of the Rutter hiring announced an economic boycott of most white-owned businesses to force Rutter's resignation. The protestors declared, "The boycott is in effect . . . The battle lines have been drawn." On February 17, some seventy-five people set up a picket line outside Superintendent Brumfield's office. "We are ready to hold out as long as it takes," said Rev. Evans. The boycott was selective but not racially targeted, leaders insisted. All doctors, dentists, drugstores, and automobile dealerships were exempt, as were a handful of grocery, gasoline, and department stores. The rhetoric grew heated and ugly, with whites liberally using the epithet *ignorant* and worse, while NAACP education director Morris Kinsey apocalyptically mischaracterized Rutter's hiring as "apartheid." Within a week, two white men were arrested for threatening protestors, one for pointing a gun at a group of them.[40] In the meantime, black Brookhavenites were aware that their dollars counted. "The eagle flies on the first of the month," said Rev. Percy Dixon, "but she will only fly where we let her fly."[41] The Chamber of Commerce was concerned enough to consider buying out Rutter's contract, a legally and practically questionable move; Rutter himself had been publicly silent since his hiring.

As the protest moved into its seventh week, more complications surfaced, but few solutions seemed at hand. Black leaders announced that 90 percent of the black teachers in the district had signed a letter in support of their cause. Potentially more inflammatory, white supremacist Richard Barrett and his Nationalist Movement road show filed a request to march and rally in Brookhaven, a request that the mayor and board of alderman granted, then withdrew, then renewed.[42] Black ministers planned a counterdemonstration, calling on supporters of the boycott to attend. "I want to find out how many men we have in Brookhaven," challenged Rev. Evans, in a statement that reminds us that the Rutter affair carried clear gender as well as racial implications. In the meantime, Brookhaven police had also begun to file charges against demonstrators, some of whom were using threats and intimidation against would-be patrons of boycotted businesses. Throughout the protest and in later years, white Brookhavenites remained convinced that the boycott was conjured up and controlled by a small group of shadowy black conspirators. In fact, the boycott seems to have been a real grassroots movement aimed at real and broad racial grievance, despite white Brookhaven's insistence that black consumers and students were being misled or duped.

On Tuesday, April 19, almost two hundred students in the district walked out of classes. To the cheers of adult protestors, Brookhaven High students left class at 2:30 and removed the state flag from the school's flagpole. Meeting swiftly in executive session, members of the school board prepared to suspend the students. By that point, however, the ten-week boycott was nearly over. "I knew then that something had to be done," former Superintendent George Brumfield told me. "The kids' safety was now at risk."[43] Brumfield met secretly with black protest leaders on the night of April 20 to signal his intention to withdraw support from Rutter.

At a school board meeting on April 21, Brumfield announced that Rutter would be reassigned to a noncoaching position as administrative assistant to the superintendent. "[Rutter] thought that when the protest started," Brumfield said in a prepared statement, "It would not cause the disruption of the school system and the community—but this proved to be incorrect."[44] Thirty-three-year-old white defensive coordinator Don Coleman was named interim coach, and the economic boycott quietly ended. Nevertheless, Richard Barrett's Nationalist Movement made good on its threat to come to town to "march for freedom," as Barrett put it. Characterizing the reassignment of Rutter as "a day that will live in infamy," Barrett charged that the school board had made "a covenant with hell." Despite the rancorous rhetoric, the rally and parade occurred without incident, drawing only a small crowd of sixty supporters. It inflamed few and changed nothing.[45]

Was the black boycott triggered by the hiring of Hollis Rutter a success? Economically, Brookhaven and Lincoln County appear not to have suffered significant overall loss of revenue from the boycott. Indeed, for the period from 1986 to 1990, Lincoln County's $246,303,795 in sales tax receipts for 1988 stands as the five-year high.[46] For one thing, the boycott was not complete; various categories of businesses were exempt. Also, the boycott did not last for many months as had more famous boycotts, such as Montgomery's bus boycott. But on another level, the boycott achieved its aims. Rutter never coached. White Brookhaven backed down in the face of organized black pressure. And "the boycott" is still remembered by black and white Brookhavenites as a black "victory."

The largest apparent puzzle about the Rutter incident is why members of the administration and white Brookhavenites generally did not anticipate the black reaction to Rutter's association with Brookhaven Academy. There is no doubt that Rutter was a coach of real achievement and that he had acquitted himself well in the 1960s in Greenwood. When "many students, teachers and coaches left the public schools for private academies," wrote a former Greenwood High student, "Coach Rutter . . . stood fast."[47]

But coaching at a racially integrated high school and years of distinguished public high school coaching did not provide Hollis Rutter with life-long immunity from charges of racial insensitivity or worse. In the eyes of his critics, he had blundered by taking jobs at two of the state's segregation academies. Most white Brookhaven did not seem to know or did not care to imagine what such an association would mean to most blacks in town. Black Brookhavenites did not demand a black coach. They simply refused to accept one who had coached the year before at the school built by whites who refused to let their children go to school with blacks. As every old coach can tell you, the job is about more than football. Like whites, black Brookhavenites believed in the masculine authority of the coach; they too believed that his work was more important than that of a math or reading teacher, or at least that he had greater responsibility than those teachers did for inculcating fundamental, gendered behavior in adolescent boys. From black Brookhaven's perspective, Rutter's association with Brookhaven Academy represented an ethical lapse unacceptable in a man whose appearance of color-blindness needed to be beyond question.

The controversy reveals the complex nature of contact between black and white Brookhaven residents. Going to school together each day, working together as teachers and administrators, asserting that all wanted the best for "the kids" did not lead white Brookhaven to anticipate the depth of feeling that black Brookhaven had against the academy, especially when it was associated with the most unambiguous masculine authority figure in town. "What is the purpose of the Academy?" asked one black student. "Why are there nothing but whites there?"[48] White Brookhavenites, on the other hand, had a great deal invested in assuring themselves that all was well. During the boycott, the editor of the Daily Leader wrote in language reminiscent of earlier denunciations of outside agitators: "Brookhaven has long enjoyed unusually good racial harmony. During the . . . sixties and seventies . . . black leaders literally ran off professional troublemakers who hoped to profit from discord in Brookhaven."[49]

What of the aftermath of the boycotting of Coach Rutter? Immediately, students and teachers noticed a much-chilled racial atmosphere. One student said, "We have grown up with each other since first grade . . . now we fight and argue."[50] Hollis Rutter never coached again. "It was tough personally," he said, "tough to ride down the streets and see your name on signs saying 'Rutter Go Home.'"[51] A white teacher recently told me, "It's as racist here as it's ever been, if not more so. There's no common ground, no effort to find common ground."[52] Former superintendent George Brumfield speaks of his career with a mixture of melancholy and pride. After twenty-five years guiding Mississippi public schools through some of their most challenging times, Brumfield retired after the Rutter controversy. "Of course I'm disappointed," he told me. "I'm an idealist. My challenge over the years was in keeping the middle of the road people in the community interested in supporting public education." From another perspective, Brumfield's challenge was to keep the public schools running in ways that did not upset the prevailing consensus of Brookhaven as a town of placid race relations. Two black Brookhavenites told me in almost precisely the same words that after the boycott the "[white] men who run things" lost confidence in Brumfield's ability to "handle" the schools and thus the school board signaled to him that it was time for him to retire.

Hollis Rutter's tenure as Brookhaven High's coach and athletic director followed a simple narrative structure; it is a story with traditional and readily apparent elements. Rutter was hired, lines within the community were drawn or became apparent, and the resulting tensions rose toward a climax and soon achieved a seemingly neat resolution or closure. Like John Grisham's *Bleachers* or the film *Mississippi Burning* or countless other representations of race and racism in Mississippi, this story can be read through a lens of familiar cultural stereotypes. Rutter is a coach's coach, a color-blind leader skilled at turning boys into men, or a crypto-racist, a reminder of years of white male privilege in Mississippi; how he appears depends upon how one wants the story told. George Brumfield is a well-intentioned but badly miscalculating man (the version in my telling of the story) or a weak man who refused to stand by his friend and who conducted public business out of sight—conspiratorially, as it were. The cast of supporting characters is full and satisfying, too. There are black preachers, community leaders in the eyes of most blacks but race-obsessed troublemakers to most whites; to blacks and whites with sufficiently long memory, the spectacle of black preachers leading a protest carries unmistakable resonances of the civil rights movement. In the Brookhaven story there is a racist buffoon (Richard Barrett) but not the crowd of violent white massive resisters that people other Mississippi stories about race relations. There are black schoolchildren, too, who serve—as reporters since David Halberstam have realized—as harmed innocents or as young citizens awakening to their sense of power, community, and rights.

At a deeper level, the Coach Rutter controversy highlights the hard feelings and mutual suspicions caused by years of failure in Mississippi to acknowledge the true cost of the Jim Crow years. Today, white eighteen to forty year olds say that they have no memories of those years, yet feel blamed for wrongs of a past generation. Black Mississippians young and old live in certainty that all is not yet well, though the villains are not as clearly discernable as they were thirty or forty years ago. What we have today in Mississippi, then, is a failure to craft a post–Jim Crow public culture, a post–Jim Crow sense of community. And despite nearly thirty-five years of integrated schools in Mississippi, high school football and other sports have not proved a panacea to the state's inherited woes. Black and white players may win or lose together, but the communities in which they live give poignant testimony to the economic inequalities, racial miscommunications, and insufficiently examined notions of gender and power handed us from the past.

One black Brookhavenite, a long-time public employee, told me in the summer of 2004, "There is real tension here, and unresolved injustices." Why, I asked, did Brookhaven not have a more visible, aggressive civil rights movement? She answered that in the 1960s and early 1970s, "people, white and black, but whites especially, did not want bad publicity for Brookhaven." Whites wanted to control the pace, direction, and extent of change. And according to her, they largely succeeded. "They didn't care if someone threw a rock, as long as nobody saw who threw it." They looked for blacks with whom they could work and pronounced them leaders of the black community, in a pattern familiar in other small southern towns. She politely but firmly deflected my attempts to characterize race relations in Brookhaven as pretty good, suggesting instead that lack of strife did not mean peace.

To appreciate Brookhaven's vehement reaction to the Coach Rutter affair, it is essential to understand the tensions inherent in race relations and children's education in the years just before and after school integration. School integration in Brookhaven began quietly in the mid-1960s with the state's adoption of "freedom of choice," that era's school choice plan, in which black parents were disingenuously given the right to choose to send their children into the white schools and into the teeth of white hostility and backlash. Full-scale integration, the folding of the two school systems into one, came in 1970. Growing up in Brookhaven in the 1970s and 1980s, as my friends and I did, signs of race and southernness were everywhere, but not in the same way they had been just a decade before. The birthdays of Jefferson Davis and Robert E. Lee, for instance, were state holidays, though not Martin Luther King's or Medgar Evers's. Many of us attended one of the (whites only, but no one mentioned it) Southern Baptist churches in town. Middle-class coffee tables held copies of the ubiquitous *Southern Living* magazine, with its normative vision of tidy white consumerism. Bumper stickers with representations of grizzled Confederate veterans spat, "Ferget, Hell." Businesses, boys' baseball leagues, and grocery store products were labeled "Dixie." And adults in unguarded moments spoke with no irony or humor of Yankees and their ways.

But it was also easy not to ask many questions about race, especially in the racially integrated public schools of the early 1970s that most of us attended. We learned nothing of events from the state's recent past such as freedom rides, the summer of 1964, burned churches, or the founding of segregation "academies." We were, however, seated and lined up for games in an alternating white/black pattern—or "salt/pepper," as the teachers always said—to prevent the self-segregation that most children adopted.

In the years before the hiring and boycotting of Hollis Rutter, it was easy, for white Brookhavenites at least, to forget that Brookhaven's history had much to do with race, or more important, that the integration of the public schools had cost white Brookhaven more than a principle ("Never!") that they had once been unprepared to concede. For most black Brookhavenites, though, the integration of the schools and the relative calm of the 1960s and 1970s had come at a real price. One black long-time teacher and administrator told me: "With the integration of the schools, we lost the ability to make direct decisions about our children's education, and we gave up leadership positions. But things here never got to the boiling point. Most people's attitude was 'let's make this work.'" The story of race and power that most black Brookhavenites told among themselves, then, was one that few whites were positioned to hear. It was a story in which blacks had compromised and in which legitimate black political and economic aspirations were checked by a white racism that may have been polite but that was definitely firm. Whites may not have noticed (or if they noticed, certainly did not object to) the absence of a black professional class (other than teachers) in the town. Doctor's offices, banks, law firms, and the old-line businesses along Monticello Street and Railroad Avenue were preserves of white power, in fact, if not in name. Black Brookhaven's reaction to the hiring of Rutter thus puzzled and angered most of white Brookhaven. "It was a way of saying [to whites] that things are not going as well as you think they are."[53]

The Coach Rutter controversy highlights the absence of public figures of black masculine authority in post-1970 Mississippi. In small towns like Brookhaven, beyond ministers and one or two school board or city council members, there are certainly fewer black men in visible positions of authority than there were in 1970. Brookhaven has never had a significant black business district, and downtown today remains a bastion of white-owned businesses. In 1970, however, black Brookhaven had its own schools, however underfunded, with black male principals, teachers, coaches, and administrators. Such an observation should not be read as nostalgia for Mississippi in the era of Jim Crow. Assertions of black masculinity authority or independence in the 1950s and 1960s were likely to be met by whites with violence, not applause for providing worthy models for black youth. Still, as Brookhaven and other small southern towns become increasingly integrated in the workplace and schools and government, the relative absence of figures of black masculine authority is conspicuous.

The Hollis Rutter affair also demonstrates the cultural hold of sports in small southern towns. It seems almost clichéd to suggest that the football coach is a respected male icon in the South. But if, as Flannery O'Connor suggested, the South is a Christ-haunted landscape, it is surely a football-haunted landscape as well. One can be cynical or even mock the Friday night and Saturday afternoon holy days, but the culture is suffused with reminders of the seriousness with which most of the region's residents take the game. As a handbook for high school coaches puts it, "To most aspiring young athletes, the high school football coach is a God-figure, a highly visible link between the boundaries of the home and community and the limitless possibilities that are football."[54] Coaches insist and most southerners believe that the game is intimately connected with questions of character—indeed, that the game is character building. Consider, for instance, that in 2003, a coach in Louisville, Mississippi, insisted upon removing photos of former football players from the school's hall of fame when the players were convicted of felonies. An administrator insisted that the photos be replaced; the coach held his ground, arguing that the former stars' conduct now overshadowed their accomplishments on the playing field. The coach was fired, allegedly for defying the administrator.[55]

The contest in Brookhaven was not primarily a matter of football, of course. It does not explain the Hollis Rutter controversy to say that it was "about race." First, it is difficult to find any cultural practice in Mississippi, whether hairstyles, food, zoning laws, or the building of the Nissan plant near Canton, that is not somehow "about race." We have known for years that Mississippi is a racialized, racially conscious society. The Rutter incident was perhaps just as much about the complex interworkings of masculine authority and public culture in Mississippi. The white fathers of the town were pitted against the black fathers of the churches. Black children saw the authority of coach pitted against the authority of preacher. The association of Coach Rutter with racialist practices compromised his authority and, ultimately, his job. The hiring and boycotting of Coach Rutter makes sense only when read as a story also grounded in Brookhavenites' assumptions about manhood and authority, about who should be charged with turning boys into men.

All five members of the school board, the black ministers who were the public face of the boycott, the football players, Coach Hollis Rutter, rejected head coaching aspirant Levander German, and Richard Barrett, would-be rouser of white ire in Brookhaven: all were male. Even in the Deep South, it is striking that no woman sat on the school board, nor had any woman sat on the school board since the racial integration of the schools. Indeed, the only woman whose name came up at all as I interviewed black and white Brookhavenites was that of long-time Assistant Superintendent Dorothy Alexander. "She was behind all this," one white businessman told me. "She's a snake," said another. "Why do so many white people here dislike Dorothy Alexander?" I asked a retired (white) teacher. "Because she came to town and tried to act white," she told me matter-of-factly. These white Brookhavenites' vicious reactions to Alexander, an African American woman, suggest just how viscerally some white Mississippians react to blacks, especially black women, who hold positions of power once reserved for white men.

Brookhaven was and remains a city in which white men wield authority quite visibly but without much public comment. Brookhaven's white men have a stranglehold on the city's business and economic life, a near-complete domination of its politics, and still essentially a veto power over anything having to do with public education that can be controlled at the local level. Not all white men are wealthy and powerful, of course; there are many middling and poor whites in Lincoln County. But the mayor's office, the superintendent's office, and the pulpits of the white churches are filled by white men, and practically all the business owners and civic leaders are white men, even though blacks now make up a slight majority of the town's population.[56] This white male control seems to most white Brookhavenites to be natural (or biblically sanctioned) or unworthy of comment. In the years since school integration, many white Mississippians speak in public as if race in the state no longer matters. When blacks notice race, they are accused of "playing the race card" or "bringing race into everything." If anything, gender is even less remarked upon, considered by most blacks and whites as vitally important but as self-evident as the summer heat.

For good or ill, high school football and other high school sports continue to command great respect in small southern towns. The coach remains a figure of masculine authority to adolescent (and postadolescent) males. Currently, there are signs that sports might play a critical role in forging community in post–Jim Crow Mississippi. After a battle in the spring of 2001, the Mississippi Private School Association agreed to allow member schools to play teams from the public Mississippi High School Activities Association.[57] The first of these interassociational football games took place on September 14 when George County defeated Jackson Prep twenty-seven to fourteen. Players and other members of the community will watch closely to see what coaches make of these developments. Newspaper accounts suggest that a new, color-blind era is dawning in Mississippi. Such talk is premature. The need for identity, for belonging, for a sense of place, will not end. But what contemporary Mississippi needs is *more* rather than *less* talk about race, and the past and its discontents, even from the coach. Too often the rhetoric of sports suggests color-blindness as a model. This way of thinking and speaking ultimately limits the role sports might play in contemporary southern culture. Players walk off the field into a deeply racialized society in which traditional models of manhood and womanhood still command much respect. To pretend otherwise is naive, and one suspects that adolescent males know this. As long as we insist that silence about the complex and interwoven history of race and gender is a useful model for states like Mississippi with their complex past and present, we invite only anger, resentment, and the boycotting of future Coach Rutters, and preclude real reconciliation and healing.

NOTES

1. John Grisham, *Bleachers* (New York: Doubleday, 2003), 45, 152, 154. The book carries a dedication to Grisham's son, the boys his son played football with, "their superb coach; and the memories of two state titles." The dust jacket reads: "John Grisham played (at times) quarterback for the Chargers of Southaven High School, Southaven, Mississippi. He was not an All-American."

2. The intensity of southern football mania, especially its centrality to southern boyhood and manhood, disguises its recent vintage. "Up to mid-century," suggests Ted Ownby, "no sport attracted much attention from people trying to define southern culture . . . It seems likely that if a similar body of literature in the late 1990s tried to explain what it means to be a southerner, white men would see sports as much more significant than they did at mid-century" (106, 107). See Ownby, "Manhood, Memory and White Men's Sports in the Recent South," *International Journal of the History of Sport* 15 (August 1998): 103–18. For a classic account of Odessa, Texas, high school football in the late 1980s, see H. G. Bissinger, *Friday Night Lights: A Town, a Team, and a Dream* (1990; reprint, Cambridge, MA: Da Capo, 2000). Larry Goodwyn, former editor of the *Texas Observer*, argued that "the Friday night

high school football game was a civic celebration, a rite of passage not merely for the male teenagers on the field or the female cheerleaders on the sidelines, but for the whole society" (42). See Goodwyn, "Wonder and Glory in Another Century," *Southern Exposure* 7 (Fall 1979): 42–47. For a provocative recent study that integrates sports history with social and cultural history, see Pamela Grundy, *Learning to Win: Sports, Education and Social Change in Twentieth-Century North Carolina* (Chapel Hill: University of North Carolina Press, 2001).

3. Willie Morris, *The Courting of Marcus Dupree* (1983; reprint, Jackson: University Press of Mississippi, 1992), 33. Morris sees public school sports of the 1970s and 1980s as essential to fostering integrated communities. Still, writes Morris, "the further one got away from the aegis of the public schools, the more some things reverted to the older patterns" (142). Many Americans had long argued that football had some larger social utility. By the 1890s, writes Gail Bederman, "college football had become a national craze; and commentators like Theodore Roosevelt argued that football's ability to foster virility was worth even an occasional death on the playing field" (15). See Bederman, *Manliness and Civilization: A Cultural History of Race and Gender in the United States, 1880–1917* (Chicago: University of Chicago Press, 1995).

4. See Rick Cleveland, "Sports Cleared the Way for Ease from Segregation," *Clarion-Ledger,* May 16, 2004.

5. *Remember the Titans,* dir. Boaz Yakin (Walt Disney Productions, 2000). Set in Alexandria, Virginia, in the early 1970s, the film stars Denzel Washington as the coach of the first racially integrated high school football team in the city. The coach's benevolence and quiet masculine authority overcome racial prejudice.

6. Even by southern standards, Mississippi was late in ending the dual system of segregated schools. See Charles Bolton, "The Last Stand of Massive Resistance: Mississippi Public School Integration, 1970," *Journal of Mississippi History* 61 (Winter 1999): 329–50.

7. Don Whitten, *The Dog Comes Home: Ole Miss Football in 1983* (Oxford, MS: Yoknapatawpha Press, 1984), viii. The book contains a foreword by Willie Morris, who writes of Brewer: "He arrives with a reputation for recruiting blacks and for getting along well with them, a father figure of sorts" (viii).

8. Interview with Dr. Dorothy Logan-Alexander, Brookhaven, Mississippi, June 3, 2004. Dr. Logan-Alexander has served twenty-three years in the Brookhaven public schools and is currently assistant superintendent.

9. See Noel Polk, *Outside the Southern Myth* (Jackson: University Press of Mississippi, 1997).

10. Census data from 2000 drawn from www.city-data.com/city/Brookhaven-Mississippi.html (accessed June 11, 2004). Census data from 1960 and 1970 drawn from Comprehensive Development Plan, Brookhaven, Mississippi, July 1978, copy in author's possession.

11. As in many towns, after integration Brookhaven used both school systems' buildings. Of the formerly white schools, Brookhaven High housed grades ten through twelve, Lipsey School (formerly Lipsey Junior High) housed grades six and seven, Mamie Martin School (formerly an elementary school) housed grades two and three, and Brookhaven Elementary housed the first grade. Of the formerly African American schools, Alexander Junior High (formerly Alexander High) housed grades eight and nine, Fannie Mullins (formerly a junior high) housed grades four and five, and Eva Harris (formerly an elementary school) was put to multiple uses, including a vocational educational center

and a school for special needs children. This arrangement continued through the 1970s and 1980s. Two points are worth noting here: the black schools were clearly "demoted" in the new order of things, although it is hard to imagine white Brookhavenites accepting any other arrangement. Second, white students did not enter formerly black schools, located in an essentially all-black section of town, until grade four, and all students finished their education at what white Brookhavenites unproblematically called "the high school," Brookhaven High.

12. Brookhaven and Lincoln County are not mentioned in either John Dittmer's *Local People: The Struggle for Civil Rights in Mississippi* or Charles M. Payne's *I've Got the Light of Freedom: The Organizing Tradition and the Mississippi Freedom Struggle* (Berkeley: University of California Press, 1995), both standard histories of the civil rights movement in Mississippi.

13. Myrlie Evers, *For Us, the Living* (1967; reprint, Jackson: University Press of Mississippi, 1996), 169.

14. That quarterback, Johnny C. Wilcher, was later murdered in Brookhaven on July 2, 1987. See *Daily Leader,* July 3, 1987. The front-page account of Wilcher's shooting noted that he was "the first black quarterback to play for the Brookhaven High School Panthers."

15. Nancy Lesko, "Preparing to Coach: Tracking the Gendered Relations of Dominance, On and Off the Football Field," 189, in *Masculinities at School,* ed. Nancy Lesko (Thousand Oaks, CA: Sage, 2000): 187–212.

16. McCollum resigned after his team's zero-and-ten campaign; Board of Trustees of the Brookhaven School District, Meeting Minutes, December 17, 1987, 658 (hereafter called School Board Minutes).

17. *Daily Leader,* December 24, 1987. One study suggests that black athletes tend to see the coach as a figure of even greater authority than white athletes do. This authority extends beyond the football field, with the black athletes in one sample including the coach along with God, luck, and fate as significant factors shaping the course their lives will take. See Chick Bryan Farha, "The Relationship of Race to the Locus of Control among Collegiate and High School Football Players," Ed.D. thesis, University of Tulsa, 1985.

18. *Daily Leader,* April 30, 2004.

19. *Daily Leader,* December 24, 1987.

20. *Daily Leader,* December 31, 1987. For a broader view, see Jesse Randall Hale, "Significance of a High School Football Program to School Culture, Community Development, and School-Community Connections in Rural Settings," Ed.D. thesis, Peabody College for Teachers, Vanderbilt University, 1999.

21. *Daily Leader,* February 15, 1988. Much of the scholarship on high school football is celebratory. "As long as the game exists," writes Ty Cashion, "coaches will continue to imprint upon their players the traditional values of hard work, sacrifice, physical courage, and teamwork." See Cashion, *Pigskin Pulpit: A Social History of Texas High School Football Coaches* (Austin: Texas States Historical Association, 1998), 2.

22. There are no extended scholarly treatments of education in Brookhaven and Lincoln County. See [Rita Rich?], "History of Brookhaven Public Schools," Brookhaven School District, Central Office. The document is an eight-page typewritten account of black and white public education in Brookhaven from the late nineteenth century through the 1980s. Copy in author's possession.

23. Interview with Dr. Dorothy Logan-Alexander, Brookhaven, Mississippi, June 3 2004.

24. Interview with George Brumfield, Brookhaven, Mississippi, December 22, 2000; interview with Donald Paterson, Brookhaven, June 12, 2001; interview with Rita Watts, Brookhaven, June 12, 2001. Paterson has taught in the Brookhaven public schools for over twenty-five years. Watts retired with twenty-five years of service in the Brookhaven public schools; she is my mother.

25. Interview with George Brumfield, December 22, 2000.

26. Under Mississippi's complicated formula for school administration, Brookhaven's distribution of students within the school district meant that the school board consisted of five members, three appointed by the mayor and board of aldermen, and two elected at large. Interview with George Brumfield, December 22, 2000. At the beginning of the Rutter controversy, the school board consisted of the following members: John W. Sproles, Jerry T. Rudman, Jack A. Williams, Jesse Buie, and George H. Edmonson. School Board Minutes, December 1, 1987, 655. Beginning with the March 17 meeting, Les Bumgarner, a businessman and former high school football coach, replaced Sproles as one of the appointed members. Brookhaven operates under a mayor / city council form of government. The city is regularly redistricted; just as regularly, the redistricting plans are the subject of lawsuits. The school district lines, on the other hand, have been stable since the end of the dual school system. For a map of the school district, which extends beyond the Brookhaven city limits, see Lincoln County School District Map, Brookhaven School District, Central Office; copy in author's possession. The decision to combine the position of head coach and athletic director was made at the December 17, 1987 meeting of the School Board, the same meeting that accepted former coach James McCollum's letter of resignation. See School Board Minutes, December 17, 1987, 658. The board voted unanimously to combine the positions. See School Board Minutes, January 21, 1988, 661.

27. Superintendent George Brumfield presented the school board with a twenty-six point description of the athletic director / head coaching position. See "Brookhaven School District, Job Description, Statement of Responsibilities (Component One)," [January 21, 1988?], Brookhaven School District, Central Office. Brumfield also presented the school board with a four-page, twelve-point recommendation of Hollis Rutter for the job. Brumfield cited Rutter's "vastly superior knowledge of football," his "16 years experience managing an athletic budget as large or larger than the budget of this district," his "vast experience in working with parents and students of both races," and his "high moral character." See [George Brumfield], "Recommendation for Head Football Coach at Brookhaven High School and Athletic Director for the Brookhaven School District," [January 21, 1988?], Brookhaven School District, Central Office.

28. *Daily Leader,* January 28, 1988; *Clarion-Ledger* (Jackson, Mississippi) February 2, 1988.

29. *Clarion-Ledger,* February 4, 1988.

30. *Daily Leader,* February 2, 1988.

31. *Daily Leader,* February 1, 1988.

32. *Daily Leader,* February 3, 1988.

33. On the early years of black education in Brookhaven, see Dana Brumfield, "Progress and Prejudice: Black Education in Brookhaven, Mississippi, to 1954," senior thesis, University of the South, 1985. For blacks as well as whites, the authority of the football coach translated easily into other administrative responsibilities. A. A. Alexander, who for decades guided black Brookhaven's schools, came to Brookhaven from Jackson's Lanier High, where he had been football coach (28). The black high

school at the time of the dismantling of the dual system was A. A. Alexander High School. In a pattern common in Mississippi towns, it is now Alexander Junior High. Alexander added the eleventh grade (1934) and the twelfth grade (1935) to the black school system. See "History of Brookhaven Public Schools," 6.

34. After being passed over for the coach/athletic position at Brookhaven High, Alexander Junior High football coach Levander German filed an EEOC complaint against the school system. See School Board Minutes, January 28, 1988, 664. The job advertisement stipulated that the successful applicant should hold a graduate degree; German did not. As of 2004, German is principal of Alexander Junior High.

35. Willie Morris, *Yazoo: Integration in a Deep-Southern Town* (New York: Harper's Magazine Press, 1971), 127–28.

36. Interview with Dr. Dorothy Logan-Alexander, June 3, 2004; interview with Carl Holloway, June 2, 2004.

37. *Daily Leader*, February 22, 1988.

38. *Daily Leader*, February 23, 1988.

39. *Daily Leader*, February 4, 1988.

40. *Daily Leader*, February 29, 1988.

41. *Daily Leader*, February 24, 1988.

42. City of Brookhaven, minutes of a meeting of the mayor and the board of aldermen, April 5, 1988, 363. The permit was granted for April 23, 1988. Other than the Nationalist Movement parade permit request, the City Council minutes from January to June 1988, make no mention of the Coach Rutter controversy.

43. Interview with George Brumfield, December 22, 2000.

44. School Board Minutes, April 21, 1988, 685. The school board voted four to one to accept Brumfield's recommendation; George H. Edmonson voted against the proposal. *Daily Leader,* April 22, 1988.

45. "Supporters Carried Flags and Signs During Saturday's march." Article available at www.nationalist.org/news/archives/1988/brookhaven.html.

46. Mississippi State Tax Commission figures show the following gross sales tax receipts for Lincoln County for the years 1986 to 1990: $227,059,141; $217,173,314; $246,303,795; $208,135,120; and $218,374,728. The counties surrounding Lincoln are Pike, Lawrence, and Copiah. For Pike County, gross receipts for the year 1988 were lower than 1987 and the lowest of the five-year period; for Lawrence, less than one million dollars higher than 1987; for Copiah, higher than 1987 (Jarvis Yancy to Trent Watts, February 24, 2004).

47. *Daily Leader*, March 7, 1988.

48. *Daily Leader*, February 12, 1988.

49. *Daily Leader*, March 8, 1988.

50. *Daily Leader*, April 22, 1988; *Clarion-Ledger*, April 23, 1988.

51. *Daily Leader,* May 3, 1988.

52. Interview with Donald Paterson, December 20, 2000.

53. Interview with Carl Holloway, June 2, 2004.

54. Michael D. Koehler, *Football Coach's Survival Guide: Practical Techniques and Materials for Building and Effective Program and a Winning Team* (West Nyack, NY: Parker, 1992), 11. Koehler further emphasizes the paternal and character-building role of the coach; he is "head of a family which takes pride in the personal as well as the physical accomplishments of each of its members" (vi).

55. *Clarion-Ledger,* October 23, 2003.

56. See www.city-data.com/city/Brookhaven-Mississippi.html (accessed June 17, 2004).

57. *Clarion-Ledger,* March 24, March 27, August 27, September 14, 2001.

Neo-Confederates in the Basement

The League of the South and the Crusade against Southern Emasculation

K. MICHAEL PRINCE

It's only in the South that the past is a curse, an industry, an institution, a constant companion who's not always soft-spoken and discreet.
—HAL CROWTHER, *Cathedrals of Kudzu*

It has often been said that, though Germany and Japan lost the war, they won the peace. By the same measure, it might also be said that the South lost its war but won the peace that followed—and did so by, as Walker Percy put it, "taking over the national myth."[1] Percy was, of course, referring to what some have dubbed the "Dixiefication of America,"[2] in particular its entertainments and its politics. This phenomenon is merely an extension of the post–Civil War national romance with southern myths and the southern mystique that grew out of them.

There are others, however, who see things in quite the opposite way. Rather than a triumphant South, they see a South on the verge of surrendering to prevailing national myths. The "Americanization of Dixie" poses a threat, as they see it, not only to the South's sense of itself but to the historical, cultural, and political underpinnings supporting the South's separate and distinct identity. For them, the glass is already at least half empty and getting emptier all the time. Thus it is that those in the southern heritage movement, with the neo-Confederate movement at its core, have take up the cause once more, to fight what they see as the manly fight of their ancestors in defense of southern honor and southern identity.

If manliness—at least from the point of view of males—may be defined as the ability to set one's own course, to exercise independent control over one's destiny and, as such, to reject submissiveness to outside dictates, then emasculation could be defined as the loss of this sense of self-sovereignty, accompanied by resentment over the imposition from outside of norms and rules that do not adhere to or, indeed, discredit and undermine what one considers a good and proper way of living. The southern heritage movement is largely an expression of wounded pride and injured machismo, an attempt to reestablish control over regional self-defini-tion and to reassert a Burkean view of the way things ought to be. The southern traditionalists and neo-Confederates of the southern heritage movement set them-selves against the tide of social and political dislocation that they see undermining "normality" and traditional order. For them, the struggle is embodied in the battle to define the southern past and through it southern identity. It is there that they have chosen to take their stand.

The South has been chasing after a durable identity for the past century and a half or more—at least since the "late, great unpleasantness." Every time the South thinks it has a tight hold on its identity, along comes another "New South" to knock it off balance and set it grappling for a tighter grip on something more stable and everlasting. The most recent New South came in the guise of the social and political shifts of the 1960s—and their echoes in the "multiculturalism" of the 1970s and 80s. The social-cultural change that swept the nation during the 1960s—civil rights, the sexual revolution, the women's movement, etc.—posed a direct challenge to the fundamentally conservative and masculine mores of the traditionalist South. In its wake came the politics of social reform carried out by an "activist" government and urged on by national media. These agents of change not only encouraged these developments (by encoding them in law, for example), they also further undermined the local community's sense of autonomy—of its ability to deal with change as *it* saw fit. Together, they posed an elemental threat to the southern way of life, as defined by regional traditionalists.

But it was the multiculturalist "assault" on the South—on its historical mem-ory and, in particular, on its symbols and heroes—that finally led southern tradi-tionalists to feel compelled to mount a countercharge. Acceding to or tolerating social and cultural change was bad enough, they felt, but acquiescing to "libel" on the southern past, to a concerted campaign to discredit Confederate-era gallants and to remove or eliminate the South's premier symbol, the Confederate "battle flag"—that was too much. It was an affront. It smacked of the kind of revisionism, of retreat and even surrender that many tradition-minded southerners were not prepared to accept. Submission to the dictates of effete cultural elites amounted to nothing less than the emasculation of southern heritage.

The Southern Heritage Crusade

It has become a truism, nearly a banality, to describe the South as a "past-haunted" landscape. Writer Hal Crowther recalls an occasion when he was "reproached . . . sorrowfully" by a southern gent upset with him for his self-proclaimed fatigue with everything having to do with the Civil War. "With tears in his eyes," Crowther recounts, the elderly man reprimanded him for his callous indifference, saying, "My family lived on rats during the siege of Vicksburg . . . and we've never gotten over it."[3] It is this sort of visceral clinging to the past, this "retro-fixation," as Crowther puts it, that makes of southern history a kind of sacred script, its symbols holy relics. Attacks on them are taken as almost a form of sacrilege, eliciting a gut reaction from those who hold them dear, prompting a call to arms against the forces of negation and disorder.

Thus, the southern heritage movement was born, its purpose being the defense of those southern (primarily Confederate) symbols, monuments, memorials, and historical figures under attack by the forces of multiculturalism, historical revisionism, and "political correctness." Though they tend to be politically conservative, most of those involved in the movement are nonpolitical, or at least do not couple their defense of Confederate heritage with a broader, integrated political philosophy. The vast majority—some of them members of older heritage organizations, like the Sons of Confederate Veterans (SCV)—are motivated primarily by a desire to celebrate and nurture the memory of their antebellum ancestors and see to it that all forms of commemoration of the Confederate past be kept intact and inviolable.

Battles over battle flags (most prominently in South Carolina), over monuments and memorials (along Monument Avenue in Richmond, Virginia, and at the Nathan Bedford Forrest monument and park in Selma, Alabama), over state flags (in Mississippi and Georgia), over the names of Confederate luminaries adorning streets, schools, or other public buildings and sites, or over Confederate insignia (Daughters of the Confederacy) and symbols (such as the "T-shirt wars" that have broken out in countless public schools across the South)—struggles like these have energized the southern heritage movement by contributing to the perception that they are part of a campaign of discrimination aimed at the South's peculiar past.

The Neo-Confederates

Although the bulk of those involved in the movement—the pulp of the peach, if you will—are the foot soldiers of the southern heritage defense campaigns, the hard core of the movement—the pit at the center of the peach, as it were—is made up of the so-called neo-Confederates (also known as southern nationalists or paleoconservatives). While the former dress up in Confederate gray, march in support of the rebel flag, or raise their voices to preserve the "good name" of their ancestors, neo-Confederates take matters one step further—and a lot more seriously. Most heritage defenders take little or no interest in political philosophy, constitutional theory, theology, or deep historical explication—and certainly have no time to contemplate secession, the rebirth of the Confederacy, or similar castles in the air. These are all, however, matters near and dear to the hearts of all neo-Confederates.

Neo-Confederatism is a form of political religion based on a faith in a certain fixed reading of history, of the kind described by Charles Reagan Wilson.[4] It is, in effect, an alternate civil religion, a counter to the prevailing American civil religion. Its adherents see in contemporary American government and culture a threat to the social order they believe is best: that of the traditional South. In essence, it is an expression of the general southern "weakness for religion," a "secular faith that [goes] beyond ancestor worship and [offers] its own reactionary theology—the past (agrarian, antebellum) as heaven and the future (urban, industrial) as hell."[5] The aim of neo-Confederates is to bring all of America into line with their particular beliefs about government, economics, and society—to rescue the nation from its erring ways. Failing that (a likely outcome, in their view), they seek to separate themselves from America, in order to protect and preserve what they see as the only viable alternative to an increasingly degenerate and dictatorial order. In the words of the League of the South, the premier neo-Confederate organization, the movement aims to "fight a tyrannous central government that refuses to be restrained by the Constitution" and to secede "from the mindless materialism and vulgarity of contemporary American society."[6]

The neo-Confederate movement traces its lineage (a matter of great importance to its members) back to the founding of the republic. It is only the early American republic—in particular in the period of the Articles of Confederation—that neo-Confederates find a political and social order that accords with their views about the proper role of government and the proper ordering of society. The American Revolution, according to this view, constituted merely the *first* effort to break free from the chains of centralized government. The southern struggle against the North during the Civil War, sometimes referred to as the "Second War for Independence," or the "War for Southern Independence," was its legitimate (though failed) successor, aimed at righting the imbalances and abuses that had grown up over time. The movement traces its intellectual genealogy from the anti-Federalist critique and Jefferson's agrarian vision for America, on through antebellum leaders and opinion makers like John C. Calhoun, John and Edward Randolph, William Loundes Yancey, Robert Lewis Dabney, James Henley Thornwell, John Taylor of Caroline, and George Fitzhugh of Virginia. The pedigree flows almost seamlessly into the post–Civil War era with the Confederate apologists Jefferson Davis and Alexander Stephens, Edward Pollard and Albert Taylor Bledsoe, all of whom helped "birth" the Lost Cause interpretation of southern history.

Carried along into the twentieth century by the work of the United Confederate Veterans (UCV), the United Daughters of the Confederacy (UDC), and the Southern Historical Society, as well as through occasional cultural events, such as the film *Birth of a Nation*, the movement got its next big boost from the so-called Southern Agrarians and their book, *I'll Take My Stand* (together with its sequel, *Who Owns America?*). Neo-Confederates are particularly fond of those among the Twelve who, like Andrew Nelson Lytle, John Crowe Ransom, and Donald Davidson, remained true to the cause. Davidson, whom Walker Percy once dubbed "the unreconstructed Southerner," was especially important in this regard and inspired many southern traditionalists in their battle against cultural modernism and what they termed "Leviathan" centralism.[7] Those with even more direct influence on the rise of neo-Confederatism included M. E. Bradford, Russell Kirk, and Richard Weaver—along with nonsouthern economic theorists like Ludwig von Mises and his disciples at the Ludwig von Mises Institute (www.mises.org). Each in his own way contributed to the ideological mix—one might even call it a Weltanschauung—composed of economic individualism and organic social cohesion, historical resentment, assertive regional identity, cultural traditionalism, religious orthodoxy, aristocratic hierarchy, and *voelkisch* exclusivity that serve as the foundation of southern traditionalism and the neo-Confederate movement.

Contemporary leading figures in the movement include Grady McWhiney (whose controversial book *Cracker Culture* forms the foundation of the Anglo-Celtic interpretation of southern identity); his student and disciple, Michael Hill; Thomas Fleming, editor of *Chronicles*, a publication of the conservative, Illinois-based think tank the Rockford Institute; as well as professors Donald Livingston (Emory University), Clyde Wilson (University of South Carolina), and James Kibler (University of Georgia). Some observers of the movement have suggested that "these individuals comprise a nascent [southern] nationalist intelligensia" similar to those that stood at the core of many nationalist movements during the heyday of European (especially Eastern European) nationalism in the nineteenth century.[8] Doubtless League of the South members like to see themselves as an intellectual vanguard, but regardless of their relative political influence, these figures have been of central importance to the development of the neo-Confederate movement.

The League of the South

There are numerous organizations and groups actively engaged on behalf of the neo-Confederate cause (though some of them exist only in a virtual sense, with no structure or membership beyond an Internet presence and the person who maintains the website). Internet-based "organizations" like Free South and Free Mississippi, the Confederate Alliance Group, southerncaucus.org, shucks.net, or ronholland.com, along with publications (many only available online) like *Southern Partisan*, Dixie Daily News, the *Southern Patriot*, and *Southern Events*, and southern-oriented law firms like the Southern Legal Resource Center, as well as purveyors of southern traditionalist literature and audiovisual materials like Apologia Books, constitute just a few of the multitudes of neo-Confederate, southern traditionalist, states' rights and Confederate heritage groups associated with the southern movement in general and the neo-Confederate movement in particular. Many of these have banded together (albeit loosely and, again, virtually) into web rings with names like Confederate Web Ring or Dixieland Ring to form what amounts to an electronic Confederate community.

Far and away the most important of these southern nationalist organizations, however, is the League of the South, which, together with its own Institute for the Study of Southern Culture and History and the various state-based branches of the Southern Party (to which the League of the South also gave birth), forms the hub of neo-Confederate thinking and organizational activity. Founded in Alabama in 1994, the League of the South is not only the centerpiece of the movement, it virtually *is* the movement. No other organization or group exercises as much influence over the direction of the neo-Confederate movement, and few others (with the possible exception of the SCV and UDC) rival it in activism in defense of southern heritage.

It is no surprise, then, that all the leading figures in the neo-Confederate movement have come together under the auspices of the League of the South. Indeed, most of them helped to found it. Michael Hill serves as league president and lead spokesman. Clyde Wilson is director of the Institute for the Study of Southern Culture and History, a post formerly held by Grady McWhiney. Both Wilson and Thomas Fleming served as past League of the South directors. James Kibler heads up the organization's home-schooling and secondary education program. Donald Livingston of the Ludwig von Mises Institute has chaired the league's education committee. All have written extensively for League of the South publications, spoken and lectured at league-sponsored events, and otherwise helped the organization become the central organ of the neo-Confederate movement.

The surge in neo-Confederate cultural separatism in the early 1990s was linked to and partly inspired by the post–cold war breakup of the Soviet Union and its imperial order in Eastern Europe, along with the accompanying reinvigoration of national identities there and in other parts of the globe. Separatist movements in Quebec, Basque Spain, and, especially, Northern Italy, served as models for the then-coalescing neo-Confederates. The League of the South (which originally called itself the Southern League) took its name from the northern Italian separatist party, Lega Nord, and from the antebellum states' rights, proslavery association, the League of United Southerners, brought into being by southern secessionists William Loundes Yancey and Edmund Ruffin.

Those interested in matters relating to states' rights versus federal power, religious faith and freedom, southern history and culture, foreign intervention, political philosophy, and cultural decline—along with all those concerned with the three Gs: God, guns, and government—were exchanging their ideas and criticisms of contemporary affairs long before the creation of the League of the South, through articles published in right-wing newsletters like *Chronicles* and southern heritage / states' rights magazines like *Southern Partisan*.[9] Many are self-described "paleoconservatives," constitutional strict constructionists, cultural traditionalists, and adherents of Christian orthodoxy. Many hearken back to an ideal political and social order they perceive as having existed during the early American republic—*before* the triumph of centralism, mammonism, and secular humanism that followed southern defeat in 1865.

Their writings are a mix of hard-bitten intellectualism and pep-rally inspirationalism. The tone and quality of much of the writing that goes on in southern nationalist circles often falls to the level of Spanky and Our Gang at a meeting of the He-Man Women-Haters' Club, banging on soapbox lecterns and yelling about how "we gotta do something!"[10] The writings of the League of the South, by contrast, are generally erudite, coherent, and well argued—though tendentious, strident, self-righteous, and often pedantic, condescending, and pompously old-fashioned. Since most of its members tend to be "educated and affluent, middle-aged men who work professional jobs and live in the suburbs"—some of whom are professional historians or other academics—"Leaguers" generally consider themselves a cut above, a kind of cultural vanguard whose mission is promoting an awareness of southern distinctiveness and rejecting all that runs counter to it.[11]

The Neo-Confederate Creed

While many of their political positions coincide with mainstream conservatism, it would be a mistake to lump neo-Confederates (the true believers especially, the hard core of the hard core) together with right-wing Republicans, libertarians, Buckleyites, or even the Christian right. All are conservative, but, for the most part, they feel the Republican Party is as much a part of the problem as the Democrats—especially the neoconservative element within Republicanism, with its tendency to promote an ever-increasing centralization of government power at home while pursuing an imperialistic, interventionist policy abroad. As the Southern Party puts it, "While Democrats plunder the national treasury in order to appease accredited victim groups—feminists, ethnic minorities, and homo-sexual lobbies, for example—Republicans, in the interests of plutocracy and global capitalism, sponsor policies that seriously dilute state sovereignty and local control."[12] They also reject libertarianism's emphasis on man as a purely economic entity. Though they do believe in a very muscular and dynamic form of individualism (especially individual responsibility) and free-market economics, they wish to see it bounded within a specific communal context.

As with all loosely organized groups, there is a range of opinion represented among those active in the League of the South. Some Leaguers are motivated primarily by political and social concerns—specifically, by a strict constructionist (or "originalist") interpretation of the Constitution. Others see the conflict in more religious terms: America as a "Christian" country where religious belief and practices are under attack by Washington, Hollywood, big business, and the broader forces of modernism and secularism. While most see religious belief as central to society, many members remain focused primarily on questions relating to political structures and processes, leaving religious matters to work themselves out on their own. Still another subelement of the movement takes an ethnic track, seeing southerners as possessing their own separate ethnicity or culture with Anglo-Celtic roots.

The issue of secession is also a source of some disagreement within the movement. While some prefer to promote and defend southern ways while remaining part of the United States, others see the South's only viable future as lying outside of the Union. For those in the latter camp, including League chieftain Michael Hill, all attempts at compromise or understanding with the nation as a whole are bound to failure. The power-hungry, "imperial" regime in Washington, they believe, will tolerate no variation, no divergence from the political course it chooses for the country, and no independent action or separate identity. It seeks to enforce a rigid uniformity (*consolidationism*, to use an old favorite term of southern nationalists) subversive of traditional southern belief and practice. Hill writes, "The voluntary Union of sovereign states given to us by the Founders is now a dead thing of the past. The Revolution [i.e., the Civil War] that destroyed the Constitution and our old republic has come and gone and most folks do not even realize it. What many 'conservatives' today seek to conserve is only a pale imitation of long departed principles and the way of life they once informed. In short, the current polity is well past meaningful reformation."[13] Hard-core southern traditionalists find no air to breathe in an increasingly degenerate and yet simultaneously intolerant United States. All efforts at adjustment or accommodation, as they see it, can only lead to southern self-denial and, eventually, self-destruction. American national culture will never be satisfied, they say; it will always demand more concessions from the South. All attempts at settlement will only lead to conformity, to a watering down of southern qualities until they are emptied of all meaning. Hill claims, "When we [southerners] and our symbols cease to be threatening, divisive and offensive to our enemies, then it can only mean one thing: We have lost."[14]

The "loss" Hill refers to is that of southern distinctiveness, of everything that makes the South what it is. Such a loss would mean the final, ignominious defeat of the cause the old Confederacy struggled to defend and post–Civil War southern patriots sought to uphold over generations. It would neuter the South by making it subject to the demands of an effete and degenerate elite. "The real lost cause," Hill contends, "is the American Empire and any attempts to reform it."[15] Better, then, to secede now and save what can still be salvaged of the traditional South before it is vitiated of all that makes it southern.

The neo-Confederate movement, as part of the larger heritage movement, derives much of its appeal from the sense of an increasing sameness in American life, of a cultural homogenization driven by the standardization of mass society, government policies, and the influence of big business and, especially, big media— and a submissiveness to the whims of fashion and acceptability. Southern heritage sympathizers mourn the loss of specific identity, the rootlessness, and, to a degree, the commercialization of modern America, and they yearn for the bonds of place and tradition. While the South certainly shares a pool of memory and folkways that constitute a coherent and distinct cultural and historical identity, the neo-Confederate interpretation of what exactly constitutes "southernness" is severely cramped and disturbingly exclusivist. Their tendency to limit the definition of who is southern to those who believe as they do is, ironically, itself typical of the kind of rigid uniformity to which they object in the national American myth.

The same exclusivist urge expresses itself in the neo-Confederate opposition to immigration and in their anti-interventionist, isolationist stance in foreign affairs. In the southern nationalist view, a true culture is like a family. It is based on bonds of "kinship, language, faith, and myth"; it has a common history "with shared civilizational and religious roots," and as such is the opposite of the "abstract proposition" represented by and embodied in the United States.[16] Their aversion to immigration is more than mere nativism, however; it stems from their view that the South constitutes an "organic" culture, which any influx from outside (even from other parts of the United States itself) threatens to erode and eventually destroy. There is in this an unmistakable echo of "mongrelization," that fundamental critique of racial and ethnic mixing espoused by southern racial segregationists of an earlier day. But, unlike that generation of white supremacists, neo-Confederates base their critique of mixing less on race than on culture and the destructive power of social engineering as practiced by government and academic elites.

There is an undeniable racist element (along with a lot of unenlightened thinking about race) in neo-Confederate circles. They are indifferent and even hostile to all the means and measures taken to eliminate the effects of historic racism and to alter racist behavior and practices. This is bound up together with their beliefs about the proper role of government in dealing with social problems. In the view of paleoconservatives (as distinguished from contemporary conservatives), society should be largely self-regulating. Government has no business promoting, let alone enforcing by law, social change or "self-actualization." A citizen has a duty to his fellow citizens, but he should fulfill that duty of his own volition. He should not be forced to do so by government decree. If he fails to perform his social obligations, his fellow citizens should appeal to his sense of morality and personal responsibility, mainly through religious institutions and the religious impulse. The only reason this chain of moral accountability no longer functions properly, say paleoconservatives, is because the antireligious character of modern society prevents religion from performing the enforcement role it traditionally served.

In practical terms, however, the distinction between race and culture quickly breaks down, for, according to their view, any society that chooses to practice racial discrimination may do so, if it is a cultural convention traditional to that society or meant as a means of preserving cultural cohesion: "Segregation is not evil or wrong. It is simply the policy to promote the integrity of a group."[17] Moreover, at least some in the movement take for granted the existence of racial distinctions (beyond mere outward appearance), just as they take for granted essentialist differences between world cultures. It is no stretch of the imagination, then, to conclude that those who reject the mixing of cultures (through immigration) might just as easily reject the mixing of races, since race is one of the "carriers" of culture. As Samuel Francis, editor of *Chronicles*, wrote, in a piece reproduced on the website of the South Carolina League of the South:

> Disparities between races—rebaptized as "prejudice," "discrimination," "white supremacy," and "hate," to which state and local governments are indifferent or in which they are allegedly complicit—provide constant targets of convenience for managerial attacks on local, private and social relationships. Seen in this perspective, as a means of subverting traditional society and enhancing the dominance of a new elite and its own social forms, the crusade for racial "liberation" is not distinctly different from other phases of the same conflict that involve attacks on the family, community, class, and religion.[18]

Accordingly, the League of the South supports what it calls the "right of free association," which of course includes the right *not* to associate, as well as the freedom from being *forced* to associate (through government intervention, in the form of desegregation, antidiscrimination laws, and affirmative action). As the league puts it, "People of different cultures should pursue their own interests without interference from bureaucrats and social engineers who push such enormities as global democracy and multiculturalism."[19] Ironic, then, that neo-Confederates have adopted the rhetoric of multiculturalism, claiming for themselves a separate southern ethnicity that, they say, merely seeks the same measure of respect and equal treatment as that afforded to other racial and ethnic groups.

The neo-Confederate worldview is all of a piece: The "foreign," nonsouthern (nonwhite) elements whose mere presence undermines the cultural cohesion of the South also tend to encourage liberal government programs—a government of handouts and set-asides—and so foster the growth of ever bigger and ever more centralized government. They are, in effect, in league with the powers of "tyranny" arrayed against the South. While (white) southerners seek to preserve freedom, tradition, and cultural identity, these "alien" peoples help to encourage the sort of regime that further destroys southern freedom, undermines southern tradition, and advances the obliteration of southern identity.

It is no surprise that neo-Confederates also reject most every form of foreign involvement, opting instead for "armed neutrality in the tradition of Switzerland," an immediate end to foreign aid, as well as immediate U.S. withdrawal from the United Nations, the North Atlantic Trade Organization (NATO), and other "entangling alliances" and treaty commitments.[20] Neo-Confederates need look no further than their own southern past to find reasons for opposing intervention overseas: the march of Union armies into the South to crush southern independence negates any support southerners might have for the United States as world policeman. But, say neo-Confederates, neither should we seek to ensure a right to national self-determination abroad, since this, too, binds us to endless foreign involvement and "strengthens the central state here at home."[21] Many in the movement felt confirmed in these opinions by the passage of the Patriot Act in the wake of the September 11, 2001, terrorist attacks.[22]

Moreover, according to neo-Confederates, those attacks were, in effect, directed against the New World Order, against globalism and the "American Empire"—against "the post-Christian religion that leftists see as a planetary state and 'conservatives' see as benevolent American hegemony."[23] And though sympathetic to those who lost their lives and their loved ones in those attacks, neo-Confederates were somewhat less than charitable toward the institutions targeted. "The people and institutions that were attacked on Tuesday the 11th were the same people that on Monday were working to destroy our heritage, culture and our people," wrote the head of the Texas chapter of the League of the South.[24] League president, Michael Hill, wrote on September 12, 2001, that the attacks were "the natural fruits of a regime committed to multiculturalism and diversity, hallmarks of an empire rather than a nation."[25]

The Program for Southern Self-Preservation

Given this sort of resentment, the feeling of being put upon from all sides—by the forces of globalism, modernism, multiculturalism, statism, secularism, centralism, materialism, and cultural "consolidationism"—it seems perfectly natural to southern nationalists that they do what they can now to try to preserve what they have left before it is too late. Their support for home schooling and other education programs is the result, an outgrowth of their concern for cultural and heritage preservation, and an expression of their separatist views. It is, in effect, a form of secession in miniature, and as such constitutes a means not only of defending the South against "outside" influences but also of preparing themselves and, especially, their children for cultural and, eventually, political separation from the United States. Neo-Confederate home schooling is a subset of the larger home-schooling movement and shares with it a largely traditional and conservative interpretation of Christianity, personal morality, and social norms. Both reject what they see as the secular humanist, antireligious character of the public school system and see in home schooling a means of avoiding those influences and allowing the home to fulfill "its God-given reason for being on earth."[26]

Additionally, however, southern nationalists see in home schooling a way to avoid having their children indoctrinated in antisouthern propaganda. Neo-Confederates consider public schools as weapons in the culture war against the South and southern history (what some have referred to as "cultural genocide"). They oppose the

> Northern-inspired public educational system under which generations of children have been inculcated with the flawed egalitarian social principles borrowed from the French Revolution . . . [which] have degenerated into

an insidious form of authoritarianism broadly described as "political correctness," the express purpose of which is to subvert the symbols, traditions
and institutions of Western Civilization . . . a major focus of this subversion
is the South, whose symbols, anthems and monuments are besieged by a
zealous, unrelenting campaign of cultural cleansing.[27]

"Government schools" (another favored neo-Confederate term) are a failure and
a threat, the product of a northern, Unitarian experiment based on a state-con-
trolled, centralized Prussian model.[28] Neo-Confederates find their preferred model
in the so-called "subscription schools" of the antebellum South, a form of private
school system that allowed parents total control over their children's education.[29]
As additional means of preserving southern culture, the League of the South also
encourages the establishment of so-called hedge schools, modeled on Irish institutions of that name set up to preserve Irish culture under British rule, as well as
southern culture clubs, a "Southern Scouts" program, and local restaurants spe-
cializing in traditional southern cuisine.[30]

Southern nationalists do not stop there, however. Not satisfied with anything
less than total separation from U.S. cultural life, many have taken up the cause of
what they call "verbal independence." They promote the use of "southern spellings" based on British orthography as set down in the Oxford English Dictionary
and the King James Bible. Proponents of verbal independence view Noah Webster
as probably the first Yankee imperialist. As a "consummate Yankee codifier and
the chief centralizer of the language," Webster committed an "assault on diversity
that culminated in his famous conformist dictionary."[31] Southern nationalist writing, in contrast, hearkens back to the spellings preferred by the likes of William
Gillmore Simms, Edgar Allen Poe, and William Faulkner. Some of the rules they
follow include using an *s* instead of a *z* in words like *centralisation;* using *ou* rather
than *o* in nouns like *honour;* reversing the order or *e* and *r* in words like *centre;* and
omitting the apostrophe from words like *wont* and *cant*. The campaign also champions the use of "typically southern" terms like *mash* (rather than *push*), *dinner*
(and not lunch), *raise* (not *rear*), and *tote* (not *carry*)—along with the preservation
of the southern drawl and other aspects of southern dialect.

As one would expect, the history and arts curriculum they have developed to
support home schooling aims to counteract what southern nationalists see as the
pernicious effect that "political correctness" has had on Americans' interpretation of history, especially southern history, and also to underpin the campaign for

southern cultural independence. As a consequence, many of their reading selections are from an era unsullied by contemporary historical interpretation. "American history textbooks used in Southern public high schools until the 1950s are often quite good," advises the League of the South Institute, "with solid and unbiased presentations."[32] Works by Ulrich Philips, Francis Butler Simkins, Robert L. Dabney, Charles Adams, Albert Taylor Bledsoe, William Gillmore Simms, Frank Owsley, Avery O. Craven, and E. Merton Coulter are on the list—along with books by familiar prosouthern writers, like Russell Kirk, M. E. Bradford, Richard Weaver, Thomas diLorenzo, James Kibler, Steven Wilkins, Andrew Lytle, Mark Winchell, Thomas Fleming, Grady McWhiney, Donald Davidson, and the Kennedy brothers, Ronald and Donald, whose books (*The South Was Right! Why Not Freedom?* and *Was Jeff Davis Right?*) are standards of the neo-Confederate movement. Other favored titles include *North Against South; Yankee Leviathan; So Good a Cause; The Real Lincoln: A New Look at Lincoln, His Agenda, and an Unnecessary War;* and *Why the South Will Survive* (an early collection of southern nationalist essays meant as a successor to *I'll Take My Stand*)—along with works by or about numerous southern and Confederate heroes (Robert E. Lee, Jefferson Davis, John C. Calhoun, John Randolph, Thomas Jefferson, Nathan Bedford Forrest, Thomas J. "Stonewall" Jackson, J. E. B. Stuart, Francis Marion, Daniel Boone, and Davy Crockett). Neo-Confederate reading lists also include books by more recent authors, like John Shelton Reed and Eugene Genovese, whose later works are considered sufficiently southern-friendly to be acceptable in traditionalist circles.[33]

Southern nationalists' tastes in literature run from Joel Chandler Harris, Margaret Mitchell, Caroline Gordon, Owen Wister, Flannery O'Connor, and William Faulkner to Shelby Foote, Walker Percy, Wendell Berry, and Fred Chappell. Their preferences in movies include obvious choices like *Gone With the Wind, Song of the South,* and *Birth of a Nation* (though the latter is criticized for presenting "too favorable a view of Lincoln"), as well as *Jezebel, A Trip to Bountiful, True Grit, The Alamo,* and *The Hunley.*[34] More recent films that have won southern patriots' hearts are *Ride with the Devil* (a sympathetic portrayal of southern-guerillas in the "dirty war" along the Kansas-Missouri border, in which, according to one neo-Confederate reviewer, the attack on Lawrence, Kansas, becomes "understandable and even justifiable");[35] *Pharaoh's Army* (a small-scale drama of the Civil War in Kentucky, which includes a black character with southern sympathies); and *The Patriot* (Mel Gibson's film about the South in the Revolutionary War). Interestingly, they also seem to have enjoyed *Gangs of New York,* in part, no doubt, because of the film's unflattering portrayal of anti-immigrant sentiment and the squalid, brutal life in northern slums but also because of its graphic depiction of northern racism (during the 1863 New York draft riots) and the brutality of federal intervention. By contrast, the film *Cold Mountain* got a thumbs down from neo-Confederate viewers, who were taken aback by what they felt was the film's stereotypical portrayal of degenerate and depraved southerners and its antiwar disavowal of the rightness of the southern cause.[36]

Far and away the most eagerly anticipated and lavishly praised film of recent times, however, was the prequel to *Gettysburg*, the Ted Turner–produced *Gods and Generals*. League of the South leader Clyde Wilson called it "an American cultural event of major significance" and "an arresting example of how a people's history should be told."[37] Neo-Confederates were especially pleased with the positive, even heroic portrayal of the story's main character, Stonewall Jackson, and in particular with its unapologetic depiction of his pious Christian faith.[38] Also appealing from a southern traditionalist viewpoint was that the only black characters in the film remained loyal to the South and to their southern masters. Furthermore, Union troops (in the scene recreating the attack on Fredericksburg, Virginia) are depicted as marauders, while Confederate troops are portrayed as noble warriors.

In tune with a Civil War history buff's preference, the movie was "put together with love and affection for the details of the campaigns, the gear and the setting," but it glides past any real consideration of the causes of the war and handles with kid gloves the issue of slavery, "minimiz[ing] the actual conflict and animosity between Union and Confederate."[39] The film is not so much inaccurate as it is incomplete and one-sided. It is a film told almost entirely from a Confederate perspective. It shows Confederate-era southerners the way they preferred to see themselves: pious, decorous, valiant, loyal, noble, determined, familial, and very sentimental. Therein lies the film's charm in neo-Confederate eyes.

The Emasculated South

What irks southern traditionalists most is the sense that southerners are no longer able to feel this way about themselves and, more than that, the sense that the South has lost its cultural sovereignty by not being allowed to determine for itself what aspects of its history it wishes to preserve and revere. The overturned orthodoxies and the upended memorials to what were once thought of as the glories of the southern past are to neo-Confederates signs and symbols not of a natural process of change and reexamination but of social disorder, the decline and degradation of civilization itself. The values represented by the Old South offer, to them, the best (and last) example of the kind of social order that provides for a civilized life. The South has lost much of what once made it southern and is in grave danger of abandoning or surrendering even more of its former character, say neo-Confederates. In losing or abandoning that which was once typical of the South, the region has become a mere shadow of its former self. It has, in effect, become an *emasculated* South.

Writing about George Wallace, one southern nationalist sees in this erstwhile segregationist's transformation a "chief example of a repentant Southerner asking for forgiveness for opposing the new order." For him, this change symbolizes the South as a whole: "the sad story of the emasculation of a people and their surrender to alien might and ideology."[40] Neo-Confederates (and with them many southerners generally) resent the suggestion that they should now apologize, ask pardon, or atone for the southern past. They are offended at what they see as a "heritage of shame and dishonor" resulting from historical reinterpretation and imposed on them by the dictates of political correctness. Their writings are full of angry denunciations of the "Yankee Empire" and anguished lamentations over the "relentless and senseless attacks against our heritage."[41] Especially galling to neo-Confederates is what they feel to be the general assumption that "the North is normal, the standard of all things good," while the South is "the unique repository of evil in a society that is otherwise shining and pure."[42] This is the old sore, the belief that the South has been unfairly forced to bear the burden of its (and the nation's) past sins while the rest of the country (especially the North) revels in the glories of victories won and moral causes upheld.

The primary field of battle in this grand cultural struggle involves contemporary reinterpretations of the southern past—in particular of the antebellum and Confederate eras—and the symbols and monuments of that time. As a result, the campaign waged by southern traditionalists is, by and large, backward directed, aimed at refighting old battles. It is an attempt to revert to an earlier reading of southern history and to maintain control over that history as part of an effort to rescue the region's tarnished reputation—to cleanse it and thus restore its manly honor.

For neo-Confederates, Faulkner's dictum is reality: the past is *not* past; indeed, the past is really the *present*—contemporary conflicts reflect struggles of the past or are direct continuations of them. The underlying principles are the same. Although defending the Confederate flag and similar outward symbols are essential elements in the campaign, they will not suffice, neo-Confederates insist, for they simply represent matters more fundamental in nature. Defending southern heritage involves more than protecting Confederate symbols; for them, it involves defending what the flag *symbolized*, what it stood for, and vindicating the principles of the southern cause it represents.

Contrary to general belief, say southern nationalists, it is the central (federal) government (the Union, Lincoln) that must bear the blame for four years of bloodshed. It is taken as a matter of faith in neo-Confederate circles that the Civil War was not caused by the conflict over slavery but rather by a lust for power on the part of the federal government, industrial interests, and the North in general. In their view, the Confederacy was the true heir and defender of the principles (especially states' rights) on which the early republic was founded. As Presbyterian minister and League of the South leader, Steven Wilkins, has written: "Slavery . . . far from being the cause of the war, was merely the pretext for revolution"—a revolution against the form of government envisioned and established by the Founding Fathers.[43] Thus, freeing the South of the guilt associated with slavery and secession becomes a central purpose of the neo-Confederate struggle—a struggle with which some activists so closely identify that they sometimes appear ready to take up a defense of slavery itself.[44]

The aspect of their culture war that has gained most public attention has been the battle over monuments to Confederate-era leaders and the struggle over Confederate symbols—most notably, the "Southern Cross" banner, more commonly called the "rebel flag." But to those in the southern heritage movement, the rebel flag has ceased to be merely a symbol of one period in the southern past. For many, it has become more than an emblem representing the Confederate soldier and those who gave their lives for southern independence. For them, the flag has taken on an almost personal significance, and in the process it has been loosened from the bonds that once tied it to a specific part of the past. The rebel flag has, in effect, become a symbol of southern self-respect, a mark of individual and communal sovereignty, as derived from regional historical experience and identity. Fealty to the past strengthens a feeling of regional distinctiveness and communal solidarity, helping to buttress a general sense of cultural autonomy and self-esteem. Attacks on these symbols, then, constitute more than an attack on the integrity of the past. They are assaults on the dignity and personal integrity of southerners living and dead—in southern terms, on "me and my kin." Standing up against these attacks becomes an exercise in character, the performance of manly duty in defense of communal reputation and familial honor. Allowing the rebel flag to become an embarrassment would mean surrendering to a heritage of shame.

As previously mentioned, the bulk of those involved in the Confederate heritage movement are chiefly interested in battles over banners, place names, and monuments; in other words, in the outer symbols of the Confederate era, not in the politics of secession, as neo-Confederates are. But the line between heritage defense and neo-Confederatism is fluid and indistinct at best. The motivations of participants range from those interested in Civil War reenacting to those who seriously advocate political separation. For neo-Confederates, the flag is just the proverbial tip of the iceberg, the abuse directed against it symbolic of deeper flaws in contemporary American society. For them, the flag and its defense serve as a kind of recruitment tool, a means of making southerners more aware of the larger issues they feel are at stake. The struggle over the Confederate flag is, for them, symbolic of a more profound underlying conflict and its defense an instrument in reestablishing sovereignty over the region's historical identity.

Feeling unfairly, even unjustly burdened with the judgments of history, neo-Confederates see themselves as self-appointed champions of southern integrity and incorruptibility. In this war over history, much of their energy is aimed at defending secession—as a historical and contemporary right—as well as the good names and noble character of Confederate leaders. Indeed, the two campaigns are inextricably linked, for if it cannot be established that the act of secession was both just and justified, then the cause itself is tainted and along with it the stature and reputations of those who fought on its behalf.

Neo-Confederates give significant attention to the greatness of their Confederate-era ancestors.[45] Honoring the dead and the cause for which they sacrificed is meant to do more than vindicate the past and glorify the deeds of Confederate leaders, however. It also serves a didactic function. By celebrating the lives and works of Confederate heroes, neo-Confederates hold up those figures as role models in conduct and conscience. The Confederates of old are taken as exemplars of a type ready to stand staunchly on principle against the forces of compromise and conformity—which is also how neo-Confederates see themselves. Southern nationalists admire Robert E. Lee or Stonewall Jackson not only, perhaps not even primarily, as Confederate military heroes but as models of character, representatives of chivalry and gentle manliness worthy of emulation.

As they see it, the character of Lee can act as an antidote to the degenerative effects of modern American life: "Today a generation that is entertaining itself to death to avoid facing reality needs a Lee to call it back to its senses," writes one southern traditionalist.[46] Another, reviewing Steven Wilkins's book, *Call of Duty: The Sterling Nobility of Robert E. Lee,* laments that "our wonderful country is passing through a period of decline, of mediocrity, of pusillanimity, of cultural decadence that would have stupefied our ancestors."[47] Lee serves as the antithesis of all that, an exemplar of "honor versus duplicity; magnanimity versus self-absorption; self-discipline versus self-indulgence; steadfastness versus vacillation; probity versus baseness; courage versus cowardice; realism versus credulity."[48] Lee is a man of "splendid character and courage . . . iron resolve in the face of adversity . . . uncompromising integrity, and . . . deep Christian faith."[49] Wilkins's book makes Lee the epitome of all that is virtuous: "Christianity, fatherhood, courage, duty, humility, self-control, self-denial, humor, kindness, trust in God" and, as such, representative of all those supposed qualities of the man of the Old South that neo-Confederates find so endearing and virtuous and that they wish to see revived in the South they envision.[50] It is a vision of a South redeemed, freed from past guilt and from the corrosive effects of modernity and in full control of its own destiny.

Modern America is the opposite of that good society, it is the thing to be rebelled against. Contemporary America's degenerate values have infected fundamental southern folkways, disrupting the very backbone of southern life, the family—what D. L. Dabney called the "little commonwealth"—where "alien ways have displaced our southern manners and impoverished our lives," resulting in a disorder that "set[s] children against mother and father, wife against husband, woman against man."[51] To neo-Confederates, the origin of the present state of affairs is clear: "all this is the legacy of the South's defeat."[52] And so, "the question of who was right in the old struggle is not so hard to answer after all. Look around you. Do you like what you see? If not, you have answered the question in my favour."[53]

The strong conservative Christian element in the neo-Confederate movement, while not all-encompassing, is nevertheless undeniable and ever present. Paleoconservatism has been defined as "the expression of rootedness: a sense of place and of history, a sense of the self derived from forebears, kin, and culture—and identity that is both collective and personal.[54] This is the basis for the *voelkisch* side of the movement. For the religious side, however, "culture implies far more than common food, dress, or accent."[55] It is a "spiritual community," one which in the South rests on "Protestant Christianity of the Reformation type"—a faith that held sway throughout the country "through the early nineteenth century," until the "Northern section of the country slid away to embrace the heresies of Deism, Unitarianism and Transcendentalism," discarding the "doctrines of God's sovereignty and man's depravity" for the idea of "a sovereign, perfectible man" who was "not saved by grace but by social and political reform," a view which the South rejected as a form of "semi-paganism," choosing instead to hold fast to "the old Faith."[56] This, say religious-minded neo-Confederates, is what at bottom distinguished the South from the rest of the country and was the true, underlying cause of the Civil War. Resistance against modern American heresies is the foundation of traditional southern life to which the region should return.[57]

The same things that forced separation in the nineteenth century underlie the call for separation now. The cause is the same, say neo-Confederates, because the battle is the same. The South was "the last bastion of Christendom" because it was the last to uphold a common-law system of "God-given liberties." "Secession was not driven by a desire to rebel but by a zeal to preserve the old order."[58] All the secondary attributes of masculinity—patience, perseverance, honesty, integrity, loyalty, courage, conviction, strength, along with the willingness to take responsibility for one's actions, to accept risk and to sacrifice—only become "true and proper manhood" when they serve to keep "out anything and everything that would bring corruption and destruction."[59] Thus, "true and proper manhood" lies in the submission to God's will and word—not only in abiding by and holding to them but also in moving others to do the same, and in separating oneself from those who refuse or fail to do so—to "secede" from sin. For many neo-Confederates, all else flows from this fundamental call to defend God's order—everything from their strict construction of the Constitution and their views on states' rights, governmental power, and personal responsibility, to their beliefs about social order and cultural coherence. Securing and promoting this order was, as they see it, the cause of southern secession in 1865 and serves as grounds for separation, in some form, today. Their aim is to restore the proper ordering of society and government—and in the process to redeem southern honor through the application of the "right" interpretation of history.

For neo-Confederates and southern traditionalists, submission to the dictates of contemporary norms—whether in the form of progressive historical reinterpretation or new forms of social behavior—is nothing less than a sin. It is a sin against the past and against a way of living defined by God. They do not want to see the South subsumed into a greater American whole. Only by maintaining southern distinctiveness can they cleave to the proper path and save themselves and their region from cultural destruction. Only by reasserting control over regional self-definition and reestablishing cultural sovereignty can they arrest the slide toward southern emasculation and amalgamation.

Some of their numbers are not prepared to wait any longer and have already taken the first step toward "abjuring the realm." At Lawrenceburg, Tennessee, League of the South activist Pat Baughman has set aside parcels of land for what he calls a "Confederate Colony," a place where southern nationalists and heritage devotees can revere their ancestors, preserve southern culture, educate their children (at home), practice their religion, and fly the Cross of St. Andrew as they see fit.[60]

It is hard to say whether an experiment like this will become a seedbed of southern radicalism or merely a comfortable retreat for the Confederate country-club set intent on flying their rebel banners wherever and whenever they like. Most neo-Confederates likely find sufficient sustenance in simply being part of the movement, in engaging with the like-minded in free-floating discussions about Confederate heroes and in dreaming about the glorious future of a new Confederacy. Despite the lack of any real achievements, they will continue to meet, discuss, and party together. Some will drift off disappointed and fail to join with any other group. A few, dissatisfied with the lack of concrete success and frustrated over continuing regional emasculation, may gravitate to more radical forms of individual or group action in order to reassert what they feel is the proper manly control over their collective destiny. In any event, one thing remains clear. The South may have lost the Civil War, but the struggle over southern history goes on.

NOTES

1. Walker Percy, "Red, White, and Blue-Gray," in *Signposts in a Strange Land* (New York: Farrar, Straus, and Giroux, 1991), 79.

2. See, e.g., John T. Edgerton, *The Americanization of Dixie* (New York: Harper's Magazine Press,

1974); Peter Applebome, *Dixie Rising: How the South Is Shaping American Values, Politics and Culture* (New York: Times Books, 1997); Michael Graham, *Redneck Nation: How the South Really Won the War* (New York: Warner Books, 2002).

3. Hal Crowther, "Eating Rats at Vicksburg," in *Cathedrals of Kudzu* (Baton Rouge: Louisiana State University Press, 2000), 64.

4. Charles Reagan Wilson, *Baptized in Blood: The Religion of the Lost Cause, 1865–1920* (Athens: University of Georgia Press, 1980).

5. Crowther, "Apostles," in *Cathedrals of Kudzu*, 83.

6. www.leagueofthesouth.net/static/homepage/intro_articles/ls-faq.html (accessed June 25, 2007); www.leagueofthesouth.net/static/homepage/intro_articles/ls-grand-strategy.html (accessed June 25, 2007).

7. Percy quote from Crowther, "Apostles," 81. See also "The Patron Saint of Southern Traditionalists," in *Southern Events,* available at www.southernevents.org/patron_saint_of_southern_traditi.htm (accessed January 19, 2004).

8. Euan Hague, "Texts as Flags: The League of the South and the Development of a Nationalist Intelligentsia in the United States, 1975–2001," *HAGAR—International Social Science Review* 3, no. 2 (2002): 301.

9. Ibid., 323.

10. A sampling of the shrillness of some in the movement can be found in the articles collected under the title *The Future of Dixie and the Southern Movement—Where Do We Go from Here?* previously available online at southerncaucus.org (accessed February 2, 2004), now only available in printed form; see www.lulu.com/content/43848 (accessed February 2, 2004).

11. Monte Paulsen, "Suburban Rebels Find Assemblage in 90s-Style Trenches," *State* (September 28, 1997).

12. See Southern Party of South Carolina frequently asked questions at www.southernpartysc.com/faq.htm (accessed February 2, 2004).

13. Michael Hill, "Should We Stay or Should We Go?" in *Southern Events,* www.4noel.com/bruce/secesh.html (accessed June 25, 2007).

14. Ibid.

15. Ibid.

16. Srdja Trifkovic, "Let the Counterrevolution Begin," in "What Is Paleoconservatism?" *Chronicles* (January 2001), available at antiwar.com/rep/trifkovic3.html (accessed June 25, 2007).

17. William L. Cawthon, "George Wallace and the South," at www.dixienet.org/spatriot/vol15no6/wallace1.htm (accessed February 2, 2004).

18. Samuel Francis, "Paleoconservatism and Race," in "What Is Paleoconservatism?" *Chronicles* (January 2001).

19. "League of the South Position Papers—Our General Worldview" at www.dixienet.org (accessed January 24, 2004).

20. See the Southern Party's "Our View of Independence" at www.southernpartysc.com (accessed February 15, 2004).

21. Scott P. Richert, "Mr. Wilson's Wars: Devolution or Evolution?" in "What Is Paleoconservatism?" *Chronicles* (January 2001).

22. See, for example, Steven Yates, "The New (Pseudo) Patriotism," *South Carolina Patriot* (Winter 2002), available at www.lewrockwell.com/yates/yates43.html (accessed June 25, 2007); or Kelly Patricia O'Meara, "Police State," *South Carolina Patriot* (Winter 2002), available at www.ratical.org/ratville/CAH/policeState.html (accessed June 25, 2007).

23. Thomas Fleming, "The Pornography of Compassion and the Cost of Empire," *Chronicles* extra (September 18, 2001), available at listserv.acsu.buffalo.edu/cgi-bin/wa?A2=ind0109&L=twatch -l&D=1&O=D&P=71069&F=P (accessed June 25, 2007).

24. Jeff Adams, "American Spirit," *South Carolina Patriot* (Winter 2002).

25. Hill quoted in Joseph Stroud, "Fighting a Losing Battle," *State*, May 18, 2003, reproduced by the South Carolina League of the South at www.palmetto.org (accessed January 25, 2004).

26. Robert W. Watson, "Resisting the Devil, or How to Vex the American Empire," in *The Future of Dixie and the Southern Movement*.

27. "The Asheville Declaration: A Second Declaration of Independence" (by the Southern Party of North Carolina), available at www.spnc.org/declaration.htm (accessed February 12, 2004).

28. See T. C. Pinckney, "We Are Losing Our Children," *South Carolina Patriot* (Winter 2002), available at http://www.exodusmandate.org/art_we_are_loosing_our_children.htm (accessed June 25, 2007).

29. Clint E. Lacy, "Public Education: The #1 Problem in the Southern Movement," in *The Future of Dixie and the Southern Movement*.

30. K. Michael Prince, *Rally 'Round the Flag, Boys! South Carolina and the Confederate Flag* (Columbia: University of South Carolina Press, 2004), 59–60.

31. James E. Kibler, "Verbal Independence," at leagueofthesouth.net/static/homepage/intro_articles/verbal/verbal_independenc.htm (accessed February 22, 2004).

32. LSI Homeschooling Section at lsinstitute.org/Homeschool.htm (accessed February 24, 2004).

33. Clyde Wilson, "The South and Southern History" at www.lewrockwell.com/orig/wilson5.html (accessed February 15, 2004).

34. Ibid., and LSI Homeschooling Section.

35. H. Arthur Scott Trask, "A Southern Braveheart," at www.dixienet.org/spatriot/vol7no2/special .htm (accessed February 23, 2004).

36. See Ilana Mercer, "Hollywood's Hateful Hooey about the South," at www.wnd.com/news/article.asp?ARTICLE_ID=36413 (accessed February 15, 2004).

37. Clyde Wilson, "Reclaiming the American Story," *Chronicles* (March 2003), available at www .chroniclesmagazine.org/Chronicles/February2003/0203Wilson.html (accessed June 25, 2007). See also George Ewert, "White Washing the Confederacy," at www.splcenter.org/intel/intelreport/article .jsp?sid=47 (accessed February 10, 2004).

38. See "Movies and Myths: A Conversation with the Maker of Gods and Generals," *Southern Partisan* 22, no. 6 (2003): 16–21.

39. See Patrick Rael, "Gods and Generals Is Good Hollywood—Don't Go See It," at History News Network, hnn.us/articles/1280.html (accessed February 26, 2004).

40. Cawthon, "George Wallace and the South."

41. Doug Hagin, "When Will Southerners Be Left Alone?" RenewAmerica Web site (January 19, 2004), www.renewamerica.us/columns/hagin/040119 (accessed June 25, 2007).

42. Clyde Wilson, "The Yankee Problem in America," at www.lewrockwell.com/wilson/wilson12.html (accessed January 21, 2004); and Clyde Wilson, "Dispelling Southern Myths," at www.dixienet.org/spatriot/vol1no2/thesouth.html (accessed February 23, 2004).

43. Rev. J. Steven Wilkins, *The Great Civil War Debate* (DVD), American Vision (released July 2005).

44. See for example Christian T. McCall, review of *The Great Civil War Debate*, at www.freerepublic.com/forum/a392b552b5148.htm (accessed June 25, 2007).

45. The League of the South organized a four-day "summer school" program in July of 2003 focusing on the "honorable deeds and personalities of the [Confederate] struggle" through a series of lectures presented by league scholars, with titles like "The Achievements of General Bedford Forrest"; "Wade Hampton: South Carolina's Hero"; "Jefferson Davis: The South's Complete Hero in Toto et in Extenso"; and "Why the Confederate Soldiers are Admired by the Civilized World." See "'Unsurpassed Courage and Fortitude': Heroes of the War for Southern Independence, Eighth Annual Summer School of the League of the South Institute for the Study of Southern Culture and History," at www.lsinstitute.org/Eighth.htm (accessed February 15, 2004).

46. David Alan Black, "Why I Celebrate Robert E. Lee's Birthday" (January 13, 2004), www.daveblackonline.com/why_i_celebrate_robert_e.htm (accessed June 25, 2007).

47. James Thornton, "Lessons in Nobility," *New American Magazine* (May 29, 1995), available at www.westberry-moses.com/main/honor/csa.htm (accessed June 25, 2007).

48. Ibid.

49. Ibid.

50. Ibid.

51. Franklin Sanders, "The Southern Household," and "Who Are We and What Do We Want?" www.southernevents.org/who_are_we_and_what_do_we_want.htm (accessed June 25, 2007).

52. Wilkins, *The Great Civil War Debate*.

53. Ibid.

54. Chilton Williamson Jr., "What is Paleoconservatism? Man, Know Thyself!" in "What is Paleoconservatism?" *Chronicles* (January 2001).

55. Steven Wilkins, "Christianity, the South, and the Culture War," *Patriotist*, available at www.geocities.com/mosouthron/culture.html (accessed June 25, 2007).

56. Ibid.

57. See Euan Hague and Edward H. Sebesta, "The US Civil War as a Theological War: Confederate Christian Nationalism and the League of the South," *Canadian Review of American Studies* 32, no. 3 (2002). For the neo-Confederate view of a postsecession South, see Clyde Wilson, "After Independence," *Southern Patriot* 4 (1996).

58. Wilkins, "Christianity."

59. Steven Wilkins, "Biblical Masculinity," at www.auburnavenue.org/SermonSeries/Biblical Masculinity/MasculinitySermon.Index.htm (accessed February 15, 2004), and on *Biblical Masculinity*, 21-CD set, Covenant Media Foundation.

60. See www.slrc-csa.org/site/updates/2005/03-11-2005-udt.php (accessed June 25, 2007).

"The Most Man in the World"

Nathan Bedford Forrest and the Cult of Southern Masculinity

COURT CARNEY

In 1998, Nathan Bedford Forrest, brandishing a pistol and a sword, emerged from the Tennessee woods atop his horse, two stories tall and surrounded by Confederate flags and barbed wire. Located in a small private park outside of Nashville and sculpted by Jack Kershaw, an avowed segregationist and one-time attorney to Martin Luther King Jr.'s assassin, the Forrest statue ostensibly represented the New South in an amalgam of fiberglass and silver and gold paint. Local black legislators protested the statue as racist and decried in particular the Tennessee Department of Transportation's decision to increase visibility of the private land by ordering state convicts to remove the brush from the nearby highway. Despite the protests, several hundred people gathered in the park to witness the unveiling, an event undeniably connected to issues of race. One attendee, for example, noted that he had "lived in an integrated neighborhood for 17 years, and that's where I've learned that the mixing of the races doesn't work." The South Carolinian also blamed crime generally on African Americans, "who are primarily criminal as a group." With destination unknown, Forrest once again led white southerners into battle. "He's crying 'Follow me!'" Kershaw said of the Confederate general. Still, the ranks were not without some rancor, as one Tennessean proclaimed the statue simply as "the ugliest piece of overblown yard art imaginable."[1]

Racial controversy resonated from the Kershaw statue, but this fiberglass effigy also suggested a more contemporary identity: Forrest as a new archetype of violent, white southern masculinity. The racial context of Confederate flags gives way to the exaggerated—and near comic—virility of the general himself with his raised sidearm, aggressive horse, and phallic saber. Since the Civil War, admirers of Forrest have generally accentuated the general's virile heroism. In the late 1860s, for example, a Tennessean asserted that "no man more unflinchingly true and gallant is to be found than General N. B. Forrest." At his death in 1877, one eulogist remarked that Forrest was "the greatest man eviscerated" by the Civil War. In 1905, another speaker placed Forrest in a global context and declared him "the most masterful and marvelous man that ever figured in the world's great history." The next year an orator proclaimed Forrest a "manly man, fearless and true." Following World War II, Forrest's connection to issues of masculinity grew more pronounced as the general came to serve as a particular illustration of southern honor through virility and violence. More than any other admirer of the general, the writer Shelby Foote faithfully promoted Forrest as a paradigm of southern manliness.[2] By the late 1990s, due in large measure to Foote's work, the Forrest image had developed into a complicated symbol of southern honor and manhood as well as racial prejudice and intolerance. The general's military service obviously played a large role in this image, as did his recalcitrant attitude of forgoing submission. A southern hero to be sure—especially when his image was emblazoned with Confederate iconography—but Forrest also stood for a more primeval tradition of manliness and courage. Women (and women's organizations) certainly played a role in honoring Forrest, but unlike Robert E. Lee or Stonewall Jackson, Forrest noticeably appealed more to men. By the late twentieth century, groups like the Sons of Confederate Veterans (SCV) eclipsed the United Daughters of the Confederacy (UDC) as gatekeepers of Confederate legitimacy, and Forrest (more than any other Civil War personality) personified violent masculinity. Forrest became quite clearly, in the words of Foote, "the most man in the world."

Almost single-handedly, Shelby Foote contorted Forrest into a symbol of martial virility. By downplaying the racially charged aspects of the general's life—he was an antebellum slave trader, a commanding officer during a racially motivated massacre, and an early leader of the Ku Klux Klan—Foote ably constructed a useful symbol of southern honor and masculinity. A native of Greenville, Mississippi, who moved to Memphis as an adult, Foote first became interested in the Civil War and Forrest as a young man living among the folk history, memorials, and other shadowed remembrances of the general. Throughout the 1950s, as he established a career in writing, Foote implicitly and explicitly began to create and define a usable image of Forrest. Elements of the general's biography infiltrated Foote's characters, and in 1952 Foote published his fourth novel, *Shiloh*, a book based on one of the only major battles in which Forrest fought.[3] Unlike in the actual 1862 battle in Tennessee, Forrest plays a rather large role in the novel, and one character stands in awe of the general who engages a much larger force of Union soldiers. On the battlefield Forrest sits atop his horse, "hacking and slashing, riding them down. His saber looked ten feet long; it flashed and glinted." Overall, Foote's *Shiloh* presents Forrest as a warrior-god, a man possessing both superhuman strength (at one point a wounded Forrest hoists a Union soldier onto his saddle to serve as a shield) as well as unwavering courage and bravado.[4] For Foote, Forrest represented a particular type of southern manliness and honor, and as early as 1952, Foote had created the template to which he would continue to return over the next fifty years. Despite any reservations Foote may have had concerning Forrest's actions involving African Americans—and in many ways Foote held somewhat progressive views for a southerner in the 1950s—the writer's comments about the general consistently underscore his unflagging admiration of Forrest.[5]

Foote's image of Forrest would become the definitive one from the 1950s onward, and although the writer's admirers tend to connect him to William Faulkner, Foote's Civil War–themed work fits more comfortably within the style and tradition of Andrew Lytle. One of the Southern Agrarians, Lytle used Forrest as a social symbol of southern honor and virtue, as well as a political symbol of perseverance against northern industrialism. In 1931, Lytle published *Bedford Forrest and His Critter Company,* a book that served both as a nominal biography of the general and as a strongly argued critique of northern society and culture. In it, Lytle posits several themes that would prove long lasting within the emerging cult of Forrest. At the heart of Lytle's book stood a strong commitment to the southwest—the area near the Mississippi River routinely given short shrift (in Lytle's opinion) by Civil War scholars—and a class-based focus on southern yeoman. Forrest served less as a biographical subject for Lytle than a political symbol used to explore the social context of the 1930s. The power of Lytle's book concerned its political timeliness, not its biographical accuracy. To Lytle, Forrest exemplified the logistic and cultural significance of the area, and the general also represented the honor-bound planter and slaveholder who paternalistically looked after what Lytle referred to as the "plain people" of the South.

Throughout *Bedford Forrest,* Lytle draws a consistent distinction between the college-trained generals in the East—such as Lee and Jackson—and the untrained, natural genius of Forrest. Forrest's performance during the Civil War reinforced Lytle's contention that the Confederacy lost the war in the West because Jefferson Davis and his Richmond advisors never understood Forrest's genius. Forrest became for Lytle the selfless hero who won important victories only to be betrayed by military politics. Furthermore, since he represented the patriarchal clan leader of the white rural South, Confederate leaders' neglect of Forrest showed a disregard for the nonplantation South. "Davis and his advisors made one great mistake that overshadowed all other errors of policy: they chose to rest the foundations of the Confederacy on cotton and not the plain people." Lytle's concern for the plight of the "plain people" reflected his Agrarian stance in remonstration of the "modern juggernaut" of progress and northern industry.[6] Race also played a role, and as grand wizard of the Klan, Forrest represented for Lytle "the last ruler of the South" who helped shatter Reconstruction. "At the most tragic moment of Southern history," Lytle asserts, "when all seemed lost beyond redemption, he appeared, unexpectedly, mysteriously, almost supernaturally and snatched the enjoyment of victory from the enemy's hands, from those Black Republicans who had set out to destroy the South and the Old Political Union." A paternal clan leader of the plain people of the South and a Klansman who served as the final protector of the Old South, Lytle's Forrest "had shown himself to be the hero who could save absolutely."[7]

Along with these political issues, one of the more influential elements of Lytle's book is his emphasis on the vigorous Forrest. Lytle presents a dashing and reckless general capable of incredible military success and possessing almost supernatural strength.[8] Before the 1930s, the general's biographers and admirers noted his bravery, but writers rarely spoke in graphic terms concerning his fighting and killing. After Lytle, however, the theme of Forrest as a manly hero fighting to defeat Yankee industrialism proved powerful in Memphis throughout the Great Depression. The United Daughters of the Confederacy—a chief sponsor of public commemorations of Forrest's birthday—began to promote a variety of Forrest-themed academic lectures, public talks, and radio addresses. No longer a stately image, the portrayal of Forrest in the late 1930s resembled Lytle's vigorous hero. A newspaper article in 1937, for example, related the story of Forrest using his hand to plug a wound in his horse's neck to delay the animal's death long enough for the general to finish fighting. The image of a quick-thinking and bloodied—yet miraculously uninjured—warrior replaced the earlier, more composed perception of Forrest popular during the late nineteenth century. The general's sword even attracted enthusiastic attention when Mary Forrest Bradley (the general's granddaughter) allowed a reporter to photograph the weapon for the first time. The Memphis *Commercial Appeal* published the picture and observed that "the bloodstains thereon are plainly visible."[9] Lytle had effectively removed Forrest from irrelevance by refashioning him not simply as a naturally intelligent, if doomed, warrior, but as a protean political symbol of southern honor, aggression, and manliness. Although the UDC helped craft Forrest into a socially acceptable icon, the organization would soon shy away from connecting Forrest explicitly to the theme of bloodlust. Forrest emerged from World War II as a bloodier and, with one notable exception, more gender-specific hero.

In 1952, the same year that Foote published *Shiloh*, Aileen Wells Parks published *Bedford Forrest: Boy on Horseback*. Parks—who had previously written a book on Davy Crockett—transformed Forrest into a template for masculinity. Focused on Forrest's childhood, Parks's book emphasizes his civic (rather than martial) virtues. Patriotic and honorable, Forrest respects his parents and authority figures (he listens attentively to a speech by the governor of Tennessee) and obediently goes to school.[10] To Parks, Forrest easily connected with basic American heroes: a self-taught, self-reliant individual fighting for his beliefs. Still, Parks emphasizes the mythic, and one soldier describes Forrest as a larger-than-life warrior who "when he raised his sword in that left hand of his and yelled 'Charge!' he looked ten feet tall." Echoing Lytle, the veteran emphasizes the general's lack of military education and notes that "he went to school less than most boys did." Parks's only battle scene focuses on Forrest's protection of a Confederate retreat, but even then Forrest exhibits more courage and heroism than other men. Ignoring slavery and the Ku Klux Klan, Parks ends her book with a reiteration of her theme of patriotism: Forrest signifies the brave soldier who fought loyally for his country. "The general," Parks tells her readers, "would expect you to be a good citizen too." There is not much bloodshed, as children were the intended readers, but Parks subtly incorporated Lytle's imagery with a more traditionally American setting.[11]

In many ways Parks's book remains an aberration because she tends to invert many of the basic myths surrounding Forrest: the uneducated general enjoys school, the aggressive warrior respects the feelings of others, the secessionist is praised as a patriot. But Parks's interests lie more in establishing Forrest as a social role model than in recreating an accurate description of a Civil War battle. The appearance of the book (along with Foote's *Shiloh*) underscores the general's renewed visibility. In 1958 hundreds of Memphians gathered throughout the city to commemorate the general's birthday, and in one of several speeches delivered that day, one lecturer echoed Parks almost directly by asserting that "as New England points to Paul Revere and Virginia points to George Washington, so does the South point with pride to Forrest." The speaker deemed it necessary to place Forrest in a larger context than the Civil War; Forrest was as great a patriot as George Washington.[12] One reason for the tremendous interest in Forrest in 1958—apart from the recent publications—relates to the volatile state of southern race relations in the late 1950s. Mary Forrest Bradley commented that the Supreme Court's decision to desegregate public schools in *Brown v. Board of Education* helped explain the larger number of celebrants on her grandfather's birthday. Although admirers of Forrest rarely made such explicit references to the role of race in the homage offered their hero, Bradley's comments suggest that Forrest remained a powerful symbol of white supremacy. As the South's racial hierarchy fell under attack, commemorating the first leader of the Klan became even more important to white Memphians. Along with the larger crowds it drew, the 1958 birthday celebration of Forrest involved the conspicuous use of the Confederate flag. Absent since the early twentieth century, Confederate flags made a dramatic reappearance in the midst of the segregation crisis. The Confederacy, and Forrest in particular, served as useful symbols of white defiance of desegregation.[13]

By this period Shelby Foote clearly stood as the foremost promoter of Forrest, and though the general continued to appeal to antisegregationists, Foote emphasized broader facets of the general's meaning. To Foote, Forrest signified an element of southern history larger than racism, and the writer hardly condoned the use of Forrest in the fight to maintain segregation.[14] The increased visibility of African Americans within Memphis politics coincided with the near abatement of Forrest-related festivities within the city. Demographics and local politics played large roles in the near invisibility of Forrest in the 1960s, but Foote's constant presence may have helped temper some the more overtly racist sentiments. In a 1969 speech, Foote announced that as a slave trader Forrest "served as an example of much that was wrong about the South." As the civil rights movement began to make race a defining feature of the Forrest image, Foote countered by reclaiming the general as a suitable model for manhood. Noting the lack of black Memphians at the celebration, Foote stated that "I am sorry there are no Negro citizens here today because Forrest is a man they could admire." On one level, these comments are consistent with Foote's views throughout his life. On another level, however, the context of this speech proved Foote's inability to understand any conception of Forrest that was different from his own. In the midst of a troubling period of social and economic turmoil for the city—the previous year Martin Luther King had traveled to the eventual site of his murder to address a Memphis sanitation workers strike—Foote turned a blind eye to his surroundings. "This is a truly great man," Foote argued, "deserving of the love and respect of the whole country."[15] If only, Foote seemed to say, people could focus on the general's heroism and manliness rather than the more troubling aspects of his life, Forrest could reclaim his place simply as a southern hero.

Forrest emerged from the 1960s an embattled icon as white admirers countered race-related attacks on their hero with appeals to southern manhood and honor. Foote, as usual, served as the arbitrator for the discussion, and a few years after publishing *Shiloh* he began work on a three-volume history entitled *The Civil War, A Narrative*. The first volume, *Fort Sumter to Perryville*, appeared in 1958. Five years later Foote published the second volume, *Fredricksburg to Meridian*. In his history Foote argued in concert with Lytle that the Confederacy lost the war in the West. Soldiers such as Forrest and John Hunt Morgan symbolized the rough heroism of the western theater, and Foote emphasized their exploits more than most previous writers. Published in 1974, the final volume of the trilogy, *Red River to Appomattox*, displayed even more Foote's admiration of Forrest. Fort Pillow and Brice's Crossroads, two relatively minor battles routinely disregarded in most accounts of the war, received extensive commentary by Foote. In the narrative's last installment, Forrest clearly emerges as the lost hope of the Confederacy—a victor among the defeated. In these volumes Foote presents no new information regarding Forrest's life, nor does he substantially add to his own views of the general. Instead, this high-profile series helped codify Forrest as a significant hero deserving academic and critical respect for his wartime activities.[16]

Foote's emphasis on Forrest as manly warrior appealed to the Memphis chapter of the Sons of Confederate Veterans (SCV), an organization that regularly asked Foote to speak at memorial events for the general throughout the 1980s. Unlike the UDC in the 1930s—which despite emphasizing a more energetic image of the general also struggled to make Forrest acceptable—the SCV focused squarely on the idea of Forrest as a masculine and violent hero. Foote's perspective, of course, dovetailed directly with this theme, but the SCV also tended not to shy away from the politics of race. Thus, despite whatever reservations Foote may have had about connecting the general to racial issues, by the 1980s, Forrest, pro-Confederate groups, and, by extension, Shelby Foote stood at the center of a brewing controversy over the meaning of Civil War symbols and the role African Americans should have in the commemoration of these events. In 1985, the Memphis *Commercial Appeal* published an interview with Foote in which he again quickly glossed over Forrest's connection to slavery and the Ku Klux Klan. Foote claimed weakly that Forrest, as a slave trader, "avoided splitting up families or selling to cruel plantation owners." Foote also attempted to distance his hero from the terrorist tactics of the KKK by noting that Forrest "was not a Klu Kluxer in the way we know them today."[17] These feeble pronouncements did little to end the controversy and, in many ways, offered black commentators an opportunity to respond publicly to such claims about Forrest. This debate surrounded the existence of a Forrest statue in Memphis as civil rights activists protested the honoring of a slave trader. Maxine Smith, executive secretary of the Memphis chapter of the National Association for the Advancement of Colored People (NAACP), asserted that "the presence of this park is a daily slap in the face to blacks throughout the city, and we intend to see that it's removed." Smith also demanded the removal of the statue, the reinterment of Forrest, and the renaming of the park. "Let the historians and all those who are so fond of the general," Smith charged, "take him and do what they want with him."[18]

In response, Foote claimed that "while I can understand why blacks might see the statue as a symbol of racism, I think they've overlooked the facts about Bedford Forrest." "He was certainly not," Foote contended, "the villain they perceive him to be." "You have to take the past as it is," Foote explained. "Bedford Forrest and Abraham Lincoln were, in my opinion, the two absolute geniuses to emerge during the Civil War. To try and remove a monument to either one of these men is just crazy." "The day that black people admire Forrest as much as I do," Foote concluded, "is the day when they will be free and equal, for they will have gotten prejudice out of their minds as we whites are trying to get it out of ours."[19] Black Memphians reacted immediately to Foote's insensitive comments. In an article entitled, "Foote, You Put It In Your Mouth," a writer for the *Tri-State Defender* called the appeal for African Americans to admire Forrest, "outrageous, insulting, bigoted and racist!" "Black people are already free and equal," the writer asserted, and "they did not get that way . . . by admiring Nathan Bedford Forrest." "Forrest is your hero," the writer alerted Foote, and "why you are so enamored with him, only you can answer for sure, but it is not hard to guess. You are a relative, if not by blood at least in spirit and outlook." Inverting Foote's own words, the writer concluded that "the day you become as sensitive to the feelings of Black people as you are to those of Whites who admire Nathan Bedford Forrest you will be free, for you will have gotten the racist prejudice out of your mind that you want to force your hero on the descendants of his victims."[20] Foote had steadfastly portrayed Forrest as a hero for everyone, and black southerners took particular offense at the public idolatry of a slave trader, leader of the massacre at Fort Pillow, and grand wizard of the Ku Klux Klan.

The attack on Forrest riled a number of white southerners already angry at the national focus on black equality. This white southern malice also stemmed from the perceived slights slung at their hero; an attack not simply on Forrest but on southern honor and masculinity. In an editorial for the conservative and militantly prosouthern magazine, *Southern Partisan,* Matthew Sandel argued that the fight over Memphis's Forrest Park was "a petulant nastiness," and served as "a sure sign that the civil rights movement is over." The conservative backlash against any progress made in the 1960s filtered through much of this rhetoric. The NAACP—defined by Sandel as the "National Association for the Advancement of Comfortable People"—had "no more real worlds to conquer," he explained, "only the inner world of a growing black paranoia." Sandel singled out Benjamin Hooks, the national director of the NAACP, for specific scorn. If Hooks and his associates "push [Forrest] too far," Sandel writes, "he may just come roaring out of the grave one day, eyes flashing, teeth-clenched—and then you will see some well-fed, middle aged black men run like they haven't run in years, on their way to catch the train to Yonkers, to confront the challenge they have so cravenly avoided for so long." At once antiblack (with its attack on the NAACP), antinorthern (with its glib comment about Yonkers), anticoward (with its image of ghostly fright), and anti-unmanliness (its condescension towards the unfit man past his prime), Sandel's comment succinctly combined every element involved in Forrest's image in the late twentieth century. Forrest provided racial conservatives dismayed at the change in demographics and politics since the 1960s an archetype of masculine virtue. Foote (and to some extent Lytle) may have carefully ignored the more unabashedly racist elements of Forrest's life, but by the 1980s these elements only buttressed the newly unfettered thematic of manhood.[21]

In 1990, two years after the racially charged campaign to remove the Forrest statue, PBS aired *The Civil War*, a multipart documentary directed by Ken Burns. Burns borrowed heavily from Shelby Foote for the film's presentation of Forrest. Through Foote, one of the most prominent voices in the entire production, Burns depicts on film the Forrest that Foote had described in print. In terms of the larger scope of the documentary, however, Burns's interests lay more in eastern Virginia than in West Tennessee. Without placing Tennessee into a larger context, Burns tends to exaggerate Forrest's role in the war. Thus, Forrest becomes omnipresent within the war and to a large extent in the documentary itself, as he appears in six of the nine episodes. Like Foote, Burns tended not to dwell on the unsavory aspects of Forrest's life and presents him simply as a courageous warrior who charismatically led his troops to victory.[22] With its overwhelming focus on the ingratiating Foote, the documentary helped to legitimize the writer's views on Forrest and the war. In one episode, for example, Foote describes his thrill in meeting Forrest's granddaughter who allowed him the chance to wave the general's sword over his head. Throughout the film, Foote reiterates a number of comments he had been making for thirty years, including his claim that Lincoln and Forrest represented the two geniuses of the war. In the end, Forrest's charismatic life overshadowed Fort Pillow and the Klan, and the film leaves viewers with Foote's contention of Forrest as "the most man in the world." Seen by millions of people in homes and classrooms throughout the country—one historian estimates that about forty million viewers watched at least one episode of the series—*The Civil War* had a profound impact on public interest in the Civil War in general and Forrest in particular. Many people who had never even heard of Forrest could, after watching Burns's documentary, consider him a military genius who summed up years of military training in one homespun phrase, "Get there first with the most men."[23]

After the Burns film, the image of Forrest underwent a revival of sorts, and this increased interest connected to a renewed controversy over the Confederate flag. With explicit and pointed rhetoric, admirers of the general spoke in defensive terms as their symbols and heroes fell under attack. Some white southerners responded by accusing African Americans of racially motivated hatred. In 1993, for example, one member of the SCV asserted that "when a civil rights group turns into a hate group, you can't hide it." "We in the South today," he continued, "didn't enter the latter part of the 20th century as secessionists. We entered as Americans. But now that we're here, I'm not so sure." An attack on Forrest signified an attack on a specific way of life held dear by neo-Confederates. To members of the SCV and likeminded white southerners, Forrest symbolized their past and their South. In 1996, four hundred people stood in Forrest Park to hear Shelby Foote, wearing a T-shirt with the words "Honor the Old Warrior," reiterate his comments on the general. By the late 1990s, the SCV and Civil War reenactors were the diligent preservers of Forrest's memory and helped spread awareness of Forrest's courage and military greatness.[24]

Like the Confederate flag, Forrest signifies a remarkable degree of cultural ambivalence, as white southern pride merges uneasily (and not so uneasily) with racial animosity. Unlike the Confederate flag, though, Forrest represents a clear image of masculinity. Masculinity has long been a part of Forrest's appeal, but it once was a manliness that spoke to a broad audience. In 1906, for example, the United Daughters of the Confederacy could declare Forrest "a manly man, fearless and true."[25] Even for a women's group, Forrest easily stood for honor and strength. By the end of the twentieth century, this vague conception of masculinity gave way to a much more specific vision of manliness connected explicitly to violence and unapologetic aggression. Bloodlust replaced chivalry, malicious violence eclipsed moral courage, and Forrest no longer represented the honor-bound masculinity of the Old South. Part of this shift relates to a larger cultural acceptance of violence, but few other Civil War personalities became so closely defined by a bloody image.[26] Furthermore, by the end of the twentieth century, many Americans openly renounced Forrest as an appropriate template of race or manliness. White southerners sympathetic to Confederate ideals no longer held a monopoly on the cultural value of their heroes and symbols, and they lashed out at their critics. The civil rights movement of the 1950s and 1960s provided African Americans with a public voice, and by the 1980s, many of the heretofore unquestioned status symbols of the South became targets of derision. At the dawn of a new century the general remained "the most man in the world," but more than ever before critics and admirers alike contested the meaning of what this image represented.

In 1905, fifty years before Shelby Foote's *Shiloh* was published, one hundred years before Jack Kershaw's statue appeared, the city of Memphis erected a tribute to their hometown hero. That year, on a windy spring day, Confederate veterans, loyal white southerners, and curious onlookers gathered in a downtown park to witness the unveiling of Charles H. Niehaus's bronze statue of Forrest sitting atop his horse. Calm and relaxed, the Forrest of Niehaus resembles little the Forrest of Kershaw. Standing at one-and-a-half life size, the 1905 statue embodies a reposed stateliness, with Forrest signifying the resolute warrior. In the early twentieth century, Forrest represented an almost genteel code of masculinity as admirers of the general emphasized his moral courage as much as his physical strength. In many ways, the unveiling of the Forrest statue imbued the general's admirers with a strong sense of civic pride and urban boosterism. After decades of disease, financial woes, and demographic change, Memphis needed a symbol of strength and perseverance. In 1998, Jack Kershaw crafted in fiberglass the post-Foote Forrest, with its exaggerated recklessness and caricatured masculinity. Separated by one hundred years, 600 miles, and generations of meaning, two versions of Forrest serve as an explicit reminder to the volatile nature of memory, the changing perceptions of race relations, and the enduring questions of manhood. The symbolic transformation of Forrest from a placid representation of urban pride to a bloodthirsty proponent of violence mirrored a concurrent shift in cultural conceptions of masculinity.[27] More than at any other point since the Civil War, Forrest, astride his rearing horse with a gun and a saber, signified an unashamedly violent strain of southern manliness. No longer simply a racially contentious figure, by the end of the twentieth century, the image of Nathan Bedford Forrest illustrated the incontrovertible and complicated nexus of masculinity, violence, race, and honor in the South.

NOTES

1. *Nashville Banner*, September 2, 1997; Jay Hamburg, "Carving a Controversy," *Tennessean*, August 30, 1997, July 12, 1998; "Forrest Statue is Simply Hideous," *Tennessean*, July 14, 1998; Paul Ashdown and Edward Caudill, *The Myth of Nathan Bedford Forrest* (Lanham: Rowman and Littlefield, 2005), 180–81.

2. Jack Hurst, *Nathan Bedford Forrest: A Biography* (New York: Vintage, 1993), 298–99; Forrest Monument Association, *The Forrest Monument: Its History and Dedication; A Memorial in Art, Oratory and Literature* (Memphis: n.p., 1905), 55 ("masterful and marvelous" quotation); *Memphis Commercial Appeal*, July 14, 1906, 7 ("manly man" quote). Foote regularly made variations of this comment throughout his life. For one example, see Geoffrey Ward, Ric Burns, and Ken Burns, *The Civil War: An Illustrated History* (New York, 1990), 270.

3. Foote's great-grandfather also fought at Shiloh. Ashdown and Caudill, *The Myth of Nathan Bedford Forrest*, 141–44.

4. Shelby Foote, *Shiloh: A Novel* (New York: Dial, 1952), 210, 212–14.

5. For a brief commentary on Foote's views on race, see C. Stuart Chapman, *Shelby Foote: A Writer's Life* (Jackson: University Press of Mississippi, 2003), xiii–xxi.

6. Andrew Nelson Lytle, *Bedford Forrest and His Critter Company* (New York: G. Putnam's Sons, 1931; reprint, Nashville: J. S. Sanders and Company, 1984), xxvi, 36; Mark Lucas, *The Southern Vision of Andrew Lytle* (Baton Rouge: Louisiana State University Press, 1986), 1–15; Alphonse Vinh, "Southern Agrarian Warrior Hero," *Southern Partisan* 14 (Fourth Quarter 1994): 42–45. For Lytle's use of Forrest as "patriarchal clan leader," see Benjamin B. Alexander, "Nathan Bedford Forrest and Southern Folkways," *Southern Partisan* 3 (Summer 1987): 27–32.

7. Lytle, *Bedford Forrest and His Critter Company*, xxvi–xxvii, 388.

8. Ibid., 84.

9. *Memphis Press-Scimitar*, July 13, 1937, July 13, 1935; *Commercial Appeal*, July 13, 1936; July 13, 1937, Forrest Clipping File, History Department of the Memphis and Shelby County Public Library, Memphis (hereafter cited as Forrest File);

10. Aileen Wells Parks, *Bedford Forrest: Boy on Horseback* (New York: Bobbs-Merrill, 1952), 23, 25, 93, 181.

11. Parks, *Bedford Forrest*, 182–92.

12. *Commercial Appeal*, July 14, 1958.

13. A number of participants in the various activities carried small rebel flags, a prominently displayed flag flew over the wreath-laying ceremonies, Forrest's great-great-grandson presented a large rebel flag to a UDC banquet, and after lunch a large cake was cut revealing a Confederate flag baked inside. *Press-Scimitar*, July 14, 1958, Forrest File; *Commercial Appeal*, July 14, 1958; C. Vann Woodward *The Strange Career of Jim Crow*, 3d rev. ed. (Oxford: Oxford University Press, 1974), 165–68.

14. In fact, Foote's perspective may have had some appeal as the civil rights struggles in Memphis in the late 1950s and early 1960s coincided with the complete abatement of public interest in the general. Reference to Forrest's involvement with the Ku Klux Klan disappeared, and the Confederate flag failed to appear as conspicuously as it had in 1958. For Memphis in the 1960s, see Robert Sigafoos, *Cotton Row to Beale Street: A Business History of Memphis* (Memphis: Memphis State University Press, 1979), 332–35; Lester C. Lamon, *Blacks in Tennessee, 1791–1970* (Knoxville: University of Tennessee Press, 1981), 104; Marcus D. Pohlmann and Michael P. Kirby, *Racial Politics at the Crossroads: Memphis Elects Dr. W. W. Herenton* (Knoxville: University of Tennessee Press, 1996), 56–57; David M. Tucker, *Memphis Since Crump: Bossism, Blacks, and Civic Reformers, 1948–1968* (Knoxville: University of Tennessee Press, 1980), 101–2; *Commercial Appeal*, July 13, 1959; July 13, 1963; July 15, 1963; July 12, 1965; July 4, 1966; July 13, 1966, Forrest File.

15. *Commercial Appeal*, July 14, 1969.

16. Shelby Foote, *The Civil War: A Narrative*, vol. 1, *Fort Sumter to Perryville* (New York: Vintage, 1958), 172, 349–50; ibid., vol. 2, *Fredericksburg to Meridian* (New York: Vintage, 1963), 68; ibid., vol. 3, *Red River to Appomattox* (New York: Vintage, 1974), 362–73.

17. *Commercial Appeal*, July 13, 1985, Forrest File; Ward, *The Civil War*, 270.

18. David Dawson, "Another Skirmish for N. B. Forrest," *Southern Magazine* (August 1988): 16; *Commercial Appeal*, May 7, 1988; May 12, 1988.

19. John Stainchak, "Behind the Lines," *Civil War Times Illustrated* 32 (January/February 1994): 18; Dawson, "Another Skirmish for N. B. Forrest," 16; *Commercial Appeal*, May 7, 1988; May 12, 1988.

20. Harry E. Moore, "Foote, You Put it in Your Mouth," *Tri-State Defender*, May 28, 1988.

21. Tom Landess, "Tilting at Statues," *Southern Partisan* 8 (Summer 1988): 6.

22. Burns, however, cannot completely exonerate Forrest for his actions at Fort Pillow. A massacre occurred at the fort, Burns asserts, whether Forrest ordered the killing or not. In a subtle narrative, the filmmaker connects Fort Pillow to Grant's decision to discontinue prisoner transfers, which in turn led to overcrowding in military prisons. Thus Forrest, Burns insinuates, was partially to blame for the horrors of Andersonville. The connection was at best indirect, and the director fails in his half-hearted attempt to balance Foote's hagiographic view with historian Barbara Fields's more critical assessment.

23. Ken Burns and Ric Burns, producers, *The Civil War* (Florentine Films, 1990), videocassette; Robert Toplin, ed., *Ken Burns's The Civil War: Historians Respond* (New York: Oxford University Press, 1996), 48–51. Foote reiterated his comparison of Forrest and Lincoln in William C. Carter, ed., *Conversations with Shelby Foote* (Jackson: University of Mississippi Press, 1989), 173.

24. *Commercial Appeal*, July 11, 1993; July 10, 1994, Forrest File; July 17, 1995; July 15, 1996; July 17, 1997; July 13, 1998. For attacks on Forrest related sites, see Ashdown and Caudill, *The Myth of Nathan Bedford Forrest*, 180–82.

25. *Commercial Appeal*, July 14, 1906.

26. Shelby Foote makes this point in a conversation comparing the roughshod Forrest to the more saintly Robert E. Lee. "In my day," he avers, "and I think still to a considerable degree, Lee was a Christ figure, without sin." Quoted in Tony Horwitz, *Confederates in the Attic: Dispatches from the Unfinished Civil War* (New York: Pantheon, 1998), 156. In his excellent cultural biography of Turner Ashby, Paul Anderson makes a similar argument regarding the Virginian cavalryman. But Ashby was more of a regional personality and never maintained a long-lasting place in the national consciousness. Paul Christopher Anderson, *Blood Image: Turner Ashby in the Civil War and the Southern Mind* (Baton Rouge: Louisiana State University Press, 2002).

27. Race certainly a played a role in the construction of the monument—and the occasion witnessed the first explicit use of Confederate iconography in years—as the city experienced increased rates of rural black migration in the late nineteenth century. Also, part of the park's tranquility relates to its secondary function: a grave site for Forrest and his wife. For coverage of the 1905 monument see *Commercial Appeal*, May 11, 1905; May 14, 1905; May 16, 1905; *Memphis News-Scimitar*, May 14, 1905; May 16, 1905. See also Forrest Monument Association, *The Forrest Monument: Its History and Dedication; A Memorial in Art, Oratory and Literature* (Memphis: n.p., 1905). See also Court Carney, "The Contested Image of Nathan Bedford Forrest," *Journal of Southern History* 67, no. 3 (August 2001): 601–30.

White Southern Masculinity and *Southern Comfort*

An Interview with Kate Davis

LARRY VONALT

Kate Davis's film *Southern Comfort* focuses on the last year of Robert Eads, a fifty-two-year-old female-to-male transsexual, who is dying of ovarian cancer. Although the film, winner of the Sundance 2001 Grand Jury Prize for Feature Documentary, describes the difficulties Robert had in getting treatment for his cancer because of his sexual nature—he had not had surgery on his genitals—the film paints a larger canvas of the lives of the transgendered in the South. Indeed, it depicts a sense of white southern masculinity that is both strongly old-fashioned and wonderfully skewed.

What can a documentary about the transgendered tell us about white manhood and masculinity in the recent South? The film demonstrates that Eads and his friends are shaped by many southern notions of manhood and womanhood even as they consciously reject some parts of what their culture tells them about what men ought to do and to be. Eads behaves graciously, even chivalrously toward his lover, Lola. He embraces his role as mentor and corrector of the younger men in his circle. He drives a truck, smokes a pipe, respects women, and prizes his family—almost stereotypical southern male traits and practices. On the other hand, Eads and his friends are painfully aware that nothing about gender is as obvious as it seems. They are conscious of the disdain or outright hostility that many of their neighbors feel toward them and provide support for each other because in many cases their own biological families do not. The film demonstrates a central thesis of this collection of essays: in the South men are made and are not just born that way.

Robert Eads lives in a mobile home in rural northern Georgia and, like his neighbors, has a strong interest in fishing and hunting. His attire—a black Stetson, black shirt and pants—echoes that of Richard Petty or Johnny Cash and reflects his social environment. In the film he tells how a member of the KKK he met at the local Wal-Mart thought he would "fit right in with the boys." But the "boys" Robert really fits in with are Cass and Maxwell, both of whom are also white southern female-to-male transsexuals. Robert refers to them as "brothers" and members of "his chosen family."

Although younger than Robert, both Cass and Maxwell, like those raised in the South who have been taught to respect their elders, treat him as if he were an older brother or even their surrogate father. Cass says that Robert's friends call "him Daddy Robert because he takes care of everybody." Being a parent plays an important role in Robert's life. Of the trans-males in the film, he is the only parent. He says of his parenthood, "I knew that God intended me to be a parent so I found a man I could deal with and married him and had two wonderful sons." His older son visits him during the making of the film and relates Robert's philosophy of life: "Being true to myself is everything that Mom has taught me. Had I gotten married I'd have chosen Mom to be my best man."

Being true to oneself is difficult but even more so for a man like Robert who found himself in a woman's body. Being pregnant and a man became for him "the worst and the best of times." Robert believes that the only time he wasn't "true to himself" as a man was when he was married to his children's father and "felt like a homosexual." Although he lived for a number of years in what appeared to be a lesbian relationship, Robert never felt like a lesbian. Like any good old southern boy, Robert says, "I was just a man that loved women. I like women; I always have."

To change their bodies to represent their true selves, transmen and transwomen undergo considerable surgery. Robert, Maxwell, and Cass all had a form of mastectomy to reduce their breasts and took testosterone to increase their masculine attributes, especially facial hair—all three have beards. Robert, however, did not have genital surgery or a hysterectomy and is dying, as he says, because he has cancer in "the only part of me that is still female."

Robert's certainty about his manhood creates difficulties for himself with his own parents. When Robert is in his parent's home, his father introduces him as his nephew and tells people that he and his daughter Barbara have had a difference of opinion. When his parents visit in the film, Robert's father tells Kate Davis, "I had dreams that my daughter would grow up and marry the President. I am very proud because I know today that in him beats the heart of my daughter Barbara." The only thing Robert's mother told him after he had had his mastectomy was to ask him why he couldn't have remained gay. Like Robert, Maxwell has difficulties with his parents. His mother refuses to acknowledge his new identity and persists in calling him by his birth name, Peggy Sue. In the film, though, she telephones him and calls him Maxwell, which becomes for him a moment to treasure.

What haunts Robert and Maxwell and other transsexuals is their former self, their "female" other. Their families know both of their selves and try to deny the new self. For someone like Robert who believes, like a good white southern male, that "family is the core, the stone that holds everything together," the family's denial becomes a "no-win" situation. "It comes down to a choice," he says, "where either you're going to spend your life being miserable to make somebody else happy or you're going to spend your life somewhat happy but having to live with the knowledge that you've made people you love miserable." Of his biological family, only Robert's three-year-old grandson knows him only as a man. "To him," Robert says, "I'm not one thing that I used to be and one thing that I am now. I am and always will be his paw paw, pure and simple. I just am."

Because of these difficulties with his biological family, Robert finds community, brotherhood, friendship, and love with other transsexuals, especially those who are members of Southern Comfort, the organization of transsexuals that meets annually in Atlanta for fellowship, partying, education, and community. Cass, Maxwell, and Robert have been coming to the Southern Comfort conventions for a number of years. The friendships developed at So-Co, as the members call it, empower them. Cass indicates how meaningful the organization is to them when he says, "Our life seems to revolve around So-Co." This year's meeting is especially important to Robert, for he will give a speech on "Trans to Trans Intimacy." So-Co has been also important to Robert's life beyond the friendships and "chosen family," for it is there that he found his perfect woman.

Lola is a male-to-female transsexual slowly accepting her new identity—she still works as a man named John. She is, according to Robert, "all the guys' wet dream," and, more importantly, a woman who loves Robert as he is. As the year captured in the film progresses through the seasons from spring to winter, we see the relationship between Robert and Lola deepen from courtship, to falling in love, to a committed love. Early in the film, Robert makes a comment about what a lovely piece of meat Lola is, but as the film nears its fatal conclusion, Robert, facing his death, says that he would like to live long enough to make Lola his wife. One trait they share that brings them together is their sense of playfulness. Although Lola teases Robert about his always playing the "Southern gentleman," lighting her cigarette and opening the car door for her, even when, because of the effects of his cancer, he can barely walk, she takes pleasure in Robert's "manly" gestures. If Lola teases Robert, Robert enjoys praising Lola's beauty and making her blush. As playful as they are, both also provide solid support to each other's life. Robert encourages and strengthens Lola's resolve to be what she wants to be, and, when Robert's illness worsens and he can no longer live by himself in his trailer, Lola brings him into her house and cares for him by creating an atmosphere of normalcy for him.

Of course, Robert is not the only transman who has a relationship with a woman. Maxwell and his girlfriend, Cori, a male-to-female transsexual, are younger than Robert and Lola. Robert sees the difference between Maxwell's relationship with Cori and his with Lola as one that is predominately sexual. To indicate the intensity of the sexuality of the younger couple's relationship, Robert talks of the time Maxwell and Cori had sex in the back of a pickup in a parking lot. Maxwell, however, believes that his relationship with Cori goes beyond the physical, that "It's definitely a mind thing." We never see Cass and his wife, a biological woman, as intimately as we do Robert and Maxwell. What we do see of their relationship is their concern about each other's well- being. Cass talks of his wife's fear that the film may bring them harm or, as she says, "may destroy everything they have" built together. Just as Robert, Maxwell, and Cass are three different individual southern men, so also do their relationships with women differ.

The climax of the film comes at the So-Co meeting where Robert presents his speech on transsexual intimacy. Robert's idea of intimacy, important to him and to the film's presentation of southern masculinity, probably evolved from his role as a parent, from what he has undergone because of his physical transformation, from his realization of his impending death, and from what he has experienced in his relationship with Lola, a relationship built not only on sex but also on trust, care, openness, and love. Robert and Lola make the experience of So-Co into a time of romance. Robert buys Lola a corsage "for the prom that never happened." For

Lola, it is the first time they "got back to that space that they shared when there was no cancer . . . it was like a gift." But that gift is not as strong as Robert's gift of love or what he calls intimacy. Despite all the transmen's emphasis on the physical metamorphosis that makes them appear to be men, they are men, as Robert says, because in their minds and hearts they believe they are men. The model of masculinity that they represent is what Robert calls intimacy, a virtue that may seem very different from what some consider the traditional view of white southern masculinity.

Since studying at Harvard, where she worked with Ross McElwee on his *Sherman's March: A Meditation on the Possibility of Romantic Love In the South During an Era of Nuclear Weapons Proliferation* (1986), a film that explores some of the difficulties of being a white male in the South, Kate Davis has been exploring the lives of those outside the mainstream society of the United States. Among films she has directed or produced are *Girltalk, A World Alive, Anti-Gay Hate Crimes, Transgender Revolution,* and *Jockey).* Kate Davis directed, edited, photographed, and coproduced *Southern Comfort.* This interview with her was conducted via e-mail.

LV: You've made at least two films dealing with transgendered people—*Transgender Revolution* (1998) and *Southern Comfort* (2001). What attracted you to the issues of the transgendered?

KD: To speak broadly, I tend to like to make documentaries which give voice to minority groups, or people who are generally misunderstood by society. For example, I have done this with troubled teenage girls in my first feature documentary, entitled *Girltalk.* Transgendered folks strike me as being particularly misperceived, as they are generally innocent (i.e., they are not violent, etc.) and yet they are considered by many to be perverted and terribly threatening to "our" healthy way of life.

On a more personal level, I can look back on my childhood and recall that I was a tomboy (by now an out-of-date term) and had real trouble with the pressure to play with dolls and other girls. I much preferred to dig worms and wondered what was wrong with that. Later, in high school, I fought more actively for gender neutrality and even took my female friend to the prom as my date. I think that from early on, though I never felt like a transsexual, I did feel that the social rules regarding gender-based behavior were arbitrary and oppressive. Robert Eads and his friends helped depict this point of view; gender in the film becomes a question of self-perception.

LV: Are you planning any more films about gender issues? Would you, for example, want to return to a film about Robert Eads's "chosen family"—Lola Cola, Maxwell, and Cass?

KD: I have considered filming again, and their stories have evolved. However, I think Robert's story stands alone, in a sense, and I'd rather leave it alone as its own film.

LV: In *Transgender Revolution* a number of the subjects in the film are southerners—Tonye Barreto-Neto and "Terry and Dina." In *Southern Comfort* the main people are southerners in that they live in the South. In your making of these two films have you observed any regional differences in attitudes toward the transgendered?

KD: I think the discrimination facing the transgendered at a systemic level—with employers, landlords, or doctors, let's say—is harsher in the South. Frankly, I doubt Robert would have met with such hostility by the medical profession if he had lived in San Francisco. Still, the basic rules of how "men" and "women" should behave are strict all over. I felt just as much discomfort with the subject of transsexuality when speaking with my liberal Upper West Side friends in New York as with straight people I met in the South.

I have left the experience of making these films feeling like prejudice is, at its root, a personality issue which is largely inborn. Just as the trait of being transgendered had little to do with class, background, or geographic location. Of course, attitudes are shaped through experience, and so intolerance can be fostered or repKD:ressed. However, so few people have any real experience with transgendered [people], so unconscious levels of intolerance are expressed in quite an unfiltered way.

LV: What about differences in attitudes between the rural and urban? When you were filming Robert at Toccoa, his home in rural, northern Georgia, did you ever film in public? Was the sequence in the grocery store, for example, shot in Toccoa?

KD: The grocery store was shot in Toccoa, and since no one knew Robert as anything other than a male neighbor, we never encountered any hostility. If anyone asked what we were doing, we told the truth; making a film about this wonderful friend. At the conference in Atlanta, however, a group of nuns came and picketed. The Southern Comfort Conference was more public than our quiet filming.

LV: The opening of *Southern Comfort* is beautifully done with Robert watching the Easter sunrise and the cocks crowing. It establishes the rural scene, shows an image of what the audience might assume is a "good old boy," and alludes to the resurrection of Jesus with the implication of life after death. Interestingly, your film has given Robert a kind of life after death. What do you see as the strongest benefits of Robert's "afterlife" for the transgender community?

KD: What has meant the most to me, over the film's awards or quotable reviews, is the acceptance of the movie by the TG community. Lola, Maxwell, and the others have received hundreds of e-mails and letters, and many speak to the idea that it was about time a film presented a transgendered person as a human being first. I was first drawn to Robert because he broke the stereotype of a TG person as a theatrical cross-dresser. (This image is naturally emphasized by the media.) And so I would hope that Robert's story may live on to offer transsexuals and others a positive image of a TG person living his life with dignity and the courage to believe in himself in the face of adversity.

LV: Have there been any unhappy situations as a result of the film's release? In the film, for example, Cass speaks of his wife's fear that something bad might happen to their marriage because of the film's release.

KD: Stephanie was, and continues to be, fearful of the film's impact. As far as I know, there have been some strains with family members, but no public incidents.

LV: I assume that the opening scene in the film wasn't the first scene that you shot of Robert. How much planning went into the filming of *Southern Comfort*? Was the planning done with the "family" or mostly with Robert?

KD: The opening was part of the first shoot with Robert, where I landed at his little trailer home in the hills for an Easter weekend. After meeting Maxwell and Cass, I had a strong sense that the film should include them as parallel lives of TG men. This was underscored by Robert's talk about the group forming a "chosen family." And so I followed the others almost every time I came to Georgia. I tried to plan the shoots around pivotal events (such as Robert's parents visiting, or the convention); however, as with any vérité documentary, I had to keep my mind open during the shoots and give up on many preconceived ideas. In turn, some of my personally favorite scenes were the least planned.

LV: Much of *Southern Comfort* explores family relationships: Robert's "chosen family," Robert and his parents, Robert and his sons, and Robert and his grandson. In regard to his "chosen family"—Lola Cola, Maxwell, and Cass (I'm not sure if Tom and Debbie are part of the chosen family)—Robert is seen as "Big Daddy" because he takes care of everybody. Much of Robert's care seems to take the form of what some might call feminine, such as his "cooking up a feast" for his family. Could you explain some concerns that Robert demonstrated in regard to his chosen family that one might see as "traditionally" masculine?

KD: Robert was indeed a caretaker, taking on a mother role, to all of them. And I believe Robert was aware that he had taken on many classical traits from both genders. He once referred to transmen as GEMS, or Gender Enhanced Males. Before transitioning, Robert had been a nurse, again displaying his nurturing instincts. On the other hand, it seemed important to Robert that he show very clear signs of traditional masculinity, as when he always opened the door for a woman. His cowboy attire is another sign of this.

LV: Robert's parents apparently had difficulties with Robert's choice first to live as a gay woman and then with his decision to become male. Can you speak about the ways that Robert coped with his parents?

KD: I believe that Robert wanted to please his parents. It was in his nature to foster a strong sense of family. Being gay, as he says in the film, was a coverup, as it allowed him to live among women in a sexual context. But he finally decided to be truer to himself and in so doing jeopardized his relationship with his parents.

His parents could not conceive of his switching genders, and so Robert went along with their public statement that he was their nephew. Again, he just wanted things to work without conflict. Perhaps by doing so, his parents did come to accept him more, and, in the end, [they] call[ed] him Robert.

LV: Do you think that Robert's father might not be wrong when he says "I am proud because I know that in him [Robert] beats the heart of my daughter Barbara"?

KD: I think it is an interesting statement for what it reveals about Robert's father and his longing for the person he thought he raised and then lost. I can't really judge such a complex statement as wrong or right—that is not how I look at it. These things are not black and white, in any case.

Sure, Robert still has Barbara's heart in some way; they were one and the same person. Only the names were changed. Perhaps that means that Robert's father was "right," but that his daughter, from a young age, felt more like a Jim, Ted, or Robert. Robert's father simply did not know it until later.

LV: The relationship that Robert has with his son in the film demonstrates the division that exists for many transgender people between their present and former selves. His son, for example, always refers to Robert as "Mom," as when he says that if he were to marry he would "have chosen Mom to be my best man." Can you speak to what you observed about Robert's relationship with his son and the difference between that relationship and the one Robert had with his grandson?

KD: Robert cherished his relationship to his grandson, I think, in part because the child only knew Robert as one continuous character—his grandfather. So there was an unconditional love that likely never involved any questioning on the child's part. Robert's sons had to adjust, of course, and rethink the way in which they perceived their mother. However, at the core, love seems to know no gender bounds, from what I have observed, and the sons could reconcile their mother as a male. As Doug said, "My mother will always be my mother."

LV: Robert is the only female to male in *Southern Comfort* who has had children. How does that experience shape his perception of what it is to be a man?

KD: I really don't know. Maybe he just wanted kids more than the others. And once having them, maybe the experience helped him express his caretaking side. But then, that could happen with anyone, male or female, who opts for children.

LV: How much emphasis do stereotypical roles of masculinity and femininity play in transgender people's understanding of what they need to do to be what they want to be?

KD: Only a small minority of TG people I have met question the need to play out traditional gender roles. But indeed, some actively deny the basis for any gender-based behavior; Nancy Nangerone, for example, in *Transgender Revo-*

lution, insisted that there are no such things as girl toys or boy toys—they are just toys. And some feel like they are neither male nor female, but a mix, or simply themselves.

However, most people I encountered did exhibit classic gender traits, and though it baffled me at first (shouldn't they see how artificial some of this is?!) I now tend to feel that it makes sense for them. They do live in this world, after all, and the careful display of "appropriate" gender-based behavior, from how to hold your arms to how to apply lipstick, helps them fit in.

In other words, it is hard to generalize. For some, living out stereotypical gender roles affirms their sense of self; for others, such behavior is oppressive.

LV: Do you think that Robert dressed like a "good old boy" with his Richard Petty Stetson to fit into his rural culture or, perhaps, to critique the view that the "good old boy" represents the traditional view of a significant type of southern masculinity?

KD: I would tend to say that Robert felt his cowboy garb would help him fit into the rural scene and that he thought it gave him style. I doubt it was an ironic critique of anything. He was very sincere and tended to embrace others.

LV: How does the shot of Robert, Cass, and Maxwell, three females to males who have not had genital surgery, grabbing their "balls" reflect their attitudes about masculinity?

KD: They seemed to be comfortable about making fun of the classically male pose of grabbing one's crotch. They know all too well that genitals mean a LOT to men, and are tied to male identity. But for a host of reasons, they opted not to have "bottom surgery," as they call it. And yet they did not lose their sense of being men because of this. (Imagine the psychological work that it would take to get to that stage of self-acceptance.) I think this attitude gives them the intellectual and emotional strength to mock the macho male crotch-grabbing habit.

LV: All three of them also seem to find the presence of facial hair important to their sense of being a man. Can you comment on that?

KD: Like the cowboy hat, or holding open the door for a lady, growing beard hair is a clear and obvious way that transmen can assert their masculinity. Also, it is one of the most successful ways in which they may physically change with testosterone. After all, their feet can not grow five sizes, nor does their height shoot up a foot.

LV: How might the difference in age and experience account for the differences between Robert's and Maxwell's and Cass's attitudes towards their presentations of themselves?

KD: Robert seemed to enjoy his status as "grandpa," and he might have played up a little bit his status as the old wise man. He loved to council and had been through many stages in life, with many occupations, which helped him have a deep perspective on life and death. However, Cass, Max, and Robert all appeared to be very sure of their personal identity as male.

LV: Did Robert live most of his life in the South? The photograph of him when he was a young Barbara suggests that he lived then in a coal mining community somewhere in Kentucky or West Virginia. What do you think is "southern" about the way Robert chose to be a man? Lola speaks of Robert as "a real southern gentleman." Do you see a difference between Robert as "a good old boy" and as a "southern gentleman"?

KD: Yes, Robert did grow up in the South, spending his youth in West Virginia. He moved to Toccoa in part because it reminded him of his youth in the mountains. I have not had any direct experiences with what I imagine are good old boys. But certain things Robert did were clearly more typically southern than northern, or urban. For example, he loved his rifle and used to organize hunts with the boys every spring. And his cowboy attire was more indigenous to Toccoa than to, let's say, Cambridge, Massachusetts. His gentlemanliness came through when he brought Lola flowers, [he] never forgot to tell her how beautiful she looked, and he escorted her with an arm almost always. The men I have known in the Northeast sure did not show such displays of chivalry or classically male gestures of politeness toward women.

LV: Did Robert ever talk about the father of his children other than to say that his husband was "a man he could deal with"? What about masculinity do you think Robert learned from his father and from his husband?

KD: Robert was very critical of his former husband, though he did not love to speak about him. I gather things ended on a rather aggressive note. I sure cannot say what he may have learned from this man about male behavior. Robert's father, on the other hand, I have met several times, and my sense is that Robert may have learned to present himself with authority through his father. He worked for his father's car dealership and learned to deal with customers, etc. And when I was with them both, it was clear that Robert enjoyed his father's approval of his Southern Comfort speech, which I had given them on video.

LV: What did Robert learn about masculinity from his mother?

KD: I have no idea.

LV: One of the main problems for a transgender person would seem to be that of having to deal with a double self—in her youth longing to be a man and, once becoming a man, remembering his experiences in the other life. From your experiences in making *Southern Comfort* and *Transgender Revolution*, can you speak about your observations of that sense of one's divided self?

KD: Some of the TG people I met seemed very able to integrate their past with their present. I think Robert was a stellar example of this, as is Maxwell. Both would freely recall their roles as women and seemed pleased to have taken with them some more positive traits from female roles. Others, I think, had much suffering in their pretransition years, and for whatever reason, seemed less able to speak to their "other side."

Perhaps it comes down to how much one feels the need to reject one's past and memories in order to move on. This no doubt is played out on a very individual basis.

LV: Can you talk about Robert's and his chosen family's sense of the necessity they felt to choose a different life?

KD: My intuition is that people who feel from an early age as if they were physically born into the "wrong" gender don't want to pick a "different life," so much as that they want to grow into a truer life. In this sense it is not perceived as a choice. And so, if they do transition, their new lives might be seen as a natural and essential growth stage, like a butterfly emerging from a chrysalis, to use a common metaphor, among the postoperative. Their former lives, then, may be seen as an unnatural, almost dormant stage in which they were not truly alive. To call their transitions a choice is most often taken as a real insult.

LV: In what ways does the organization Southern Comfort help transgender people deal with their desire to be what they feel they are?

KD: There is almost no feeling, for me, like being among the TG community at a convention such as Southern Comfort. Here, some 700 people gather in a five-day period to revel in who they are, free from the social oppression they face most all of their lives. It is incredibly self-affirming, not to mention educational. They learn about a wide variety of topics regarding transitioning (from surgery to voice pitch to finding size-13 high heels) to relationship, employment, and political issues. Seminars crowd the days, and social fanfare goes well into the nights. In the end, it is about love and tolerance and the joy of being true to oneself. I always thought that if everyone outside the community could spend a few days at the conference, we'd have a different world, and a much more human one.

LV: How does Southern Comfort differ from other transgender organizations?

KD: Many of the TG conferences slant towards one arm of the community. It seems to me that the Southern Comfort Conference is very broad, and open to everyone, including cross-dressers, men, women, and everything in between, spouses, friends, and those who are sincerely interested in learning more.

LV: *Southern Comfort*'s opening scene raises the issue of the relationship between the medical profession and the transgendered when Robert says, "I wish I could understand why they did what they did and why they feel that way." Were the doctors who refused their services to Robert because he was a transsexual mostly urban? I ask this in part because Lola Cola mentions in an interview online that at the Sundance festival she met a doctor from Toccoa, Georgia, who approached her and said that he was appalled about the way the medical profession had refused to treat Robert for his cancer.

KD: I think that Robert was refused treatment because of a general ignorance on the part of the medical profession. That one Toccoa doctor feels bad says nothing about rural doctors versus urban doctors. There are humane, open-minded [professionals] and fearful and downright prejudiced professionals everywhere.

However, I think that, in big northern cities, like San Francisco [sic] or New York, where there are more LGBT groups, clinics, and so forth, the level of compassion for the plight of transgendered patients might be greater. This is not to say that southern physicians are evil or less humane, but they may have had less exposure to the issues and so may tend to want to pass a case off to someone else.

LV: The medical profession plays an important role in the lives of the transgendered, especially because of their desire to transform their bodies, yet the

medical profession, for the most part, has seemed not to enable those desir-
ing to change themselves. Throughout *Southern Comfort* there are discussions
about the poor quality of medical treatment transsexuals receive. Maxwell,
for example, comments about the poor quality of the phalloplasty when he
says, "You drop your drawers and people can tell right away that it ain't God
made." Could you talk about the medical profession's attitudes toward those
seeking drugs and, ultimately, surgery to change their physical appearances?

KD: There are a handful of wonderful surgeons across the United States and
Canada who devote themselves to helping the transgendered, but for many
doctors, phalloplasties and vaginoplasties are likely to be unknown territory.
The few centers that perform such surgeries are well known in the TG community, and the doctors apparently vary greatly in competence. I have heard
complaints that several charge too much (because they can), and some do
not do a good job. Botched operations are a real fear for preoperative transsexuals, who may lose sensation, or worse, may end up with lifelong painful complications (one female-to-male had a dozen subsequent urinary tract
operations).

In the film, Maxwell raises the idea that doctors may know less and/or
care less about male surgery—that phalloplasties are much more often badly
performed than are male-to-female operations. Max's own theory is that there
is a sexist component to this; that male doctors do not want genetic women
to compete in their area of masculinity.

LV: In your film, *Transgender Revolution,* you tell the story of Terry, who goes to
the Transitional Hospital in Tampa for genital surgery to become a male. I
thought the film suggested that that hospital specialized in transgender surgeries. Could you talk some about that hospital and about Terry's surgery, such
as its cost, the process, what sort of legalities he might have gone through,
and the fact that Terry had the surgery in order to legally become a male?

KD: There is a hospital in Florida that does specialize in sex reassignment surgery. (I forgot the name, actually.) And many transmen feel the need to have
"bottom surgery" before they feel fully male. The operations can cost from
$50,000 to $100,000, and are quite risky. Skin is taken from the forearm to
build up a penis, and rods may be inserted for a sort of permanent erection.
Other variations include an emphasis on the importance of urinating while
standing up, and so the urinary tract takes precedence over, let's say, the sex-

ual sensation. Again, many complications and infections may arise. And it is always painful, taking several weeks before one can comfortably walk.

For many transpeople, saving money for surgery is a full-time job. For others, the risks and expense are not worth it, and so one may become comfortable as a self-identified male or female regardless of the genital mismatch.

LV: Because Robert did not have genital surgery to become a male, was he "legally" a male?

KD: In some states Robert would have been considered a legal male, even while "in transition." It is widely recognized in the Harry Benjamin Standards, which are guidelines for the medical community, that female-to-males may be considered men if they have two out of three major surgeries (hysterectomy, mastectomy, and or phalloplasty). These rules differ for male-to-females, who must have all major surgeries in order to legally change genders.

LV: Robert says that "being a man or a woman has nothing to do with genitalia but with what's right here in your heart and mind," yet, doesn't the film suggest, when it shows the results of Cass's bungled mastectomy and Cori and Robert giving themselves hormone shots, that changing the body, if not the genitalia, is very important to Robert and his chosen family's understanding of themselves as male?

KD: Absolutely. There is a seeming contradiction in Robert's insistence that genitals do not matter, as gender is a mental state, while growing a beard apparently is quite important. I can only explain this by proposing that there is one main difference: one's genitals are a private matter. No one in public sees them, and whatever they are [is] invisible to the outside world; it is absurd that they should define a person. On the other hand, these folks do live in the public world, and so the pressure to conform visually to their gender is great. An Adam's apple, a high-pitched voice, breast shapes—any one of these things may be a dead giveaway, literally. They risk their lives just to claim their own identities. So I would imagine if Robert were asked, he would have suggested that the beard, cowboy hat, and all his "male" accoutrements also have nothing to do with his true identity (he had felt like a man since he was a little child in a dress, after all). And yet they helped him belong in his community, feel more the part, and live more free of ridicule.

LV: I hadn't realized the significance of the role that the psychiatric profession plays in the lives of those they identify as having Gender Identity Disorder

(GID). Am I correct in thinking that a person identified with GID can't have genital surgery unless a psychiatrist approves?

KD: The label *Gender Identity Disorder* has been attacked by TG political groups as being condescending. I am not sure if it is being used still by the APA [American Psychiatric Association]. But in any case, before having surgery, a transperson must undergo therapy for a year. This is, of course, a protection against rash decisions. The surgery is hardly reversible.

LV: I read in an interview with Lola Cola that Robert had gone to his doctor for a particular medication and the doctor suggested that he get the medication from the psychiatrist and that that doctor accused Robert of being sick, of not wanting to deal with the fact that he was a woman, and that he tried to have him committed. Can you talk about that situation and why it wasn't in the film?

KD: This verbal brawl between Robert and the doctor who told him his problem was psychiatric was one of Robert's most dramatic stories. I did not include it in the film purely for structural reasons. It played as too much of a backstory, and I wanted to root the film in the present tense. I felt the prejudice he encountered was clear enough in the fact that he was turned away by so many clinics and doctors. Still, I would love for others to have heard it, and so here is an excerpt from the transcripts, in Robert's own words:

ROBERT: I went down on a Friday to get the results of a routine MRI, found out there was a shadow on it that looked like it was on the bone. They wanted to do a bone scan. It was positive. I've got cancer of the bone at the base of my spine. That's not fun. That's very painful. If it gets into the spinal column it goes straight to the brain. That's not a real happy prospect. My doctor was concerned because I was already depressed. He brought it up to me, I admitted, yes, I'd been depressed. He asked me about suicide. I admitted honestly in the middle of the night at the height of the pain, yeah, I'd thought about it a couple of times, but I hadn't done it. He wanted me to see a psychiatrist. I told him I really didn't want to see a psychiatrist. I'd had some dealings with 'em before, and I wasn't real thrilled about it. I could use some antidepressants. I'd had a depression before with my back injury, and anti-d's helped me a lot. But it wasn't his field so he wanted me just to go see this guy. So against my better judgment, I agreed.

He calls him up, gets me worked in. I leave the office and go straight over to the psych clinic. I fill out the papers. I go back and talk to the first guy. He's kinda cool. We talk. I'm honest with him. I tell him about the depression. He mentions about going in the hospital so they could put me on some meds. I told him I am severely claustrophobic. I do not do hospitals well. I've just been told just thirty minutes prior that not only was my cancer spreading through the soft tissue, it was now in the bone. That I was facing something even worse than what I had to face before. The last thing I needed was to be stuck in a damn hospital. So he says let me talk to my head man, so he goes and gets this psych.

The guy walks into the room. I'm sitting there with my beard, my hat, my boots, and he calls me "Miss Eads." I say to him, "You've never seen me before; you're gonna call me Miss Eads. I don't think so." He proceeds to sit down, and he says, "You have cancer." And I said "Yeah." He says, "What kind of cancer?" I said, "I've just been told it went to the bone." He said, "No. What's your original cancer?" I said, "Original cancer was uterine and cervix, and it spread to the colon and the kidney." "Well, how does that make you feel?" I said, "How do you think it makes me feel? I've got cancer. It's spread; it's inoperable. Without treatment I'm gonna die." "No. How does it make you feel that your cancer's making you face the fact that you're not really a man, that you're living a fantasy? I think we need to put you in the hospital. I think we need to put you in the hospital for a couple of weeks and that's the issue we need to deal with to get you straightened out that you're not a man."

Needless to say this did not go over real well with me. I proceeded to tell him what an asinine homophobic jerk-off he was, and I didn't need to hear that right now, and I was leaving.

When I attempted to leave his office, he grabbed me and jerked me back and told the other guy to call security. That I was going to the hospital whether I liked it or not. I said a few choice words that I don't care to repeat. I pushed past him. I went out to the waiting room.

My friend Tom was waiting. I told him, "Come on, we're getting the hell out of here." The shrink comes out and grabs Tom. I said, "Don't talk to the homophobic son of a bitch. Let's get out of here."

I was out of the building, across the lot, and almost to my van when the cops caught me. The police catch me to tell me I have to go back. I explain to them, "Look, I'm not going to the hospital. I came down here to talk to—I'm dying of cancer, I'm depressed, yes. If I was gonna commit suicide, I just crossed three busy intersections, I could've been killed at any moment. I crossed 'em safely. I'm not going to the hospital." They said, "You gotta go back over there." So we walked back, and on the way over there I explained exactly what happened. We get over there—the doctor's totally irrational. It doesn't matter that I'm dying of cancer. The only thing that matters is the fact that I'm not dealing with the fact that, in his opinion, I'm not a real man.

He signs papers to commit me. I very nicely apologize to the officers and explain to them I understand the system. I know they've gotta do what they've gotta do, and I hope they understand I'm not going peaceful. And I've gotta do what I've gotta because if I agree to go over there of my own will, I'm not getting out. And I guarantee, you lock me up in that hospital, and I'll be dead within two days.

There's no way I could survive being put in that hospital. They apologize. They gotta do their job. I say, "I know, nothing personal." And a fight broke out. It took all three of 'em to get me down and handcuff me. In the course of the battle, my back is badly injured; my arm's fractured. I finally go with them willingly, but we go to the emergency room; we don't go to the other hospital. They take me to the emergency room. Back there for three or four hours, and an angel helped me out.

I can't go into exactly what happened because it would cost them their job, but an angel, one of God's real children, went for me to the mental hospital and talked to the doctor and explained the situation. The doctor told him, "Go back and tell him to come out here, let me talk to him. If what you're saying is true, I'm not going to admit him to this hospital." My angel came back to the hospital, snuck in, so that others who didn't need to know they were there, came back and told me what had occurred. I called the doctors and made them sign me out AMA [against medical advice]. They wanted me to stay and have more tests and X-rays. They were afraid I had a couple of ruptured vertebrae from the fight. I was in a hell of a lot of pain. I wasn't gonna risk the chance of this doctor getting off duty and having to deal with another one.

So the doctors finally signed me out AMA. We talked, had a nice chat. I explained what happened. She said, "I'm not admitting you; you're going home; you don't belong here." But if it hadn't of been for that one person, who understands about our community because they're a part of our community, a very closeted part, I wouldn't be sitting here talking right now, because if they'd locked me up in that hospital I'd have been dead.

LV: One of the distinctions that Robert stresses throughout the film in regard to Maxwell is that between intimacy and sex. Robert makes some comments, such as when he is looking at the piece of meat he is cooking and says to Lola "Isn't that the most beautiful piece of meat you ever saw next to you?" that suggests what might be a traditional view of a man's response to sex, but most of the talk of sex and suggestions of sex are seen in the actions of Maxwell and Cori. In making the film, did you want to emphasize what some might call Robert's more "feminine" view of the sexual relationship between man and woman as opposed to Maxwell's more "masculine" attitude?

KD: The argument over intimacy versus sex was intriguing to me. First of all, because it is such an age-old discussion, and one I thought a general audience could relate to. But also because it helped dramatize the dynamic between Robert and Maxwell. Robert enjoyed his stance as the wise one. And the quest for intimacy seems to occupy a higher ground than the hunt for physical satisfaction. I did not see Robert as more or less "feminine" than Maxwell, however. Rather, I feel we are all a bit of both and also full of contradictions.

LV: What about Lola Cola's and Robert's attitudes toward "John," Lola's other self? Lola speaks of "John" as a "construct," but couldn't some people argue that "Lola" is as much a construct as is "John"?

KD: To her, obviously John felt like a forced, unnatural role which she at times played. It is all a question of self-perception. Sure, from the outside we could argue that Lola is equally constructed, but then, so are all our identities. (When you buy a shirt, are you not consciously constructing a visual image of yourself?) What I believe is more important is to go beyond academic arguments to see that what we deem our "true" selves to be is a flexible, and relative, concept, and, of course, deeply personal.

LV: Would you say that one of the "themes" of Southern Comfort is to show Robert's striving to bring Lola into being herself? How successful do you think Robert was?

KD: I do think one of the main evolutions in the film is Lola's personal growth. The reason that this is important goes well beyond the "plot progression" level. I had hoped, during the editing, that as the audience identified with Lola (as someone who is funny, who is vulnerable, who is in love, who is facing loss, etc.), then they might go along with her ability to better accept herself as a female. In other words, Lola's own progress can mirror the audience's. And in the end, we become more enlightened and open-minded.

LV: What characteristics of Robert's attracted you to him?

KD: How do I begin? He was such an immediately accessible person. He had a mix of charm, wit, and wisdom that made him a magnet, in the best sense. He made people feel understood and loved. But I cannot overrate his inherent humor, which poured out of him up through his final days.

LV: I imagine that many people are curious about the film because of the irony of a man dying from ovarian cancer, but after seeing the film, does that interest remain the focal point of the audience?

KD: Each person sees a different film, and so I hesitate to say what "the audience" feels. But surely the initial ironies of Robert's situation, I hope, take a back-seat to the universal human plight of the characters. By the end, a man with ovarian cancer may be seen more as a person facing an untimely death.

LV: One of the qualities that I admire greatly about the film is that it shows how important gender is and, ultimately, how insignificant it is. To me that is the film's greatest irony. Do you feel similarly about that element of the film?

KD: I actually do. But in the end, I lean toward the sense that the importance we place on gender is sadly limiting, and painfully unnecessary. Somehow gender has become the great divide, the first line of identity, which, if crossed, is punishable by death. Aren't there more interesting ways to evaluate each other, which might have more to do with political views, personality, and such? Aren't these traits much more directly linked to who governs the country, who might be an ax murderer, etc? Yet for many, the most salient question is what initial (F or M) we were assigned at birth based on what is between our legs.

Doctor's Son

EDWIN T. ARNOLD

When I was very small, I sometimes confused my father with Mark Twain. This is not as improbable as it sounds. My father was born in 1910, the year Twain died, and I easily conflated these two events, imagining a transmigration of spirit, I suppose, engendered by Halley's Comet. I didn't know that Twain died in April, while my father was born in October, but it wouldn't have mattered. My father loved Twain, especially the stories of Tom Sawyer and Huck Finn (Pudd'nhead Wilson and the Connecticut Yankee came next), and he sometimes told us these tales mixed in with his own stories of boyhood in rural East Georgia, "God's Country," he called it. He had a book, *The Favorite Works of Mark Twain*, that he sometimes read, a big cloth volume that I would take down and admire, especially the illustration that graced the spine. It was Huck with a rifle in one hand and a lanky rabbit in the other, smiling at the reader from under his big hat. I have this book on my own shelf today, ripped and worn but still there, a presence and remembrance.

Also, my father, like Twain, wore white linen suits, to help ward off the stifling Georgia heat that took such a toll on him. He was a small-town doctor, a general practitioner, and this was his garb for most of the year. In his clinic he would sometimes work in a knee-length lab coat, stethoscope hanging from his neck, but it is the suit I best recall: baggy pants, wrinkled coat, topped off, before the first heart attack, by the habitual cigar. He looked nothing like Twain physically, no bushy white hair or electric eyebrows or luxuriant mustache. My father was always clean-shaven, neat, except during the short time he took up chewing tobacco after he had to quit smoking. My mother quickly put a stop to that, and I imagine he was uncomfortable with it, too, since it involved spitting, "expectorating," as he called it, which he considered a thoroughly nasty thing to do.

He was also something of a prankster, even a clown at times, who loved the outrageous. He told jokes to his patients, made them laugh, and, in turn, created funny stories out of his experiences with them which became a repertoire of amusing anecdotes he repeated time and again. When he wasn't dressed in white, he favored brightly colored plaid sports coats, the more extravagant the better. He liked to dress up and pose for the camera. He had a favorite pair of pince-nez glasses that he would sometimes wear, peering through them in an attitude of pretend seriousness, and his favorite photograph had him, dressed in white, with these pompously positioned on the end of his nose, a ribbon circling from them around his neck. He stares, unsmiling, his thinning hair standing up from his head in a plumage of static explosion. This picture accompanied a story in the local paper shortly after he was elected to the school board. He was mocking his own reputation in the photo and in the article, which I suspect he wrote himself. "Egad," the "reporter" observes at one point in the interview, "the old gentleman [he was in his forties at the time] goes on and on and on." Several years later, when he was sick, word got around town that he had died, and he gave another interview to the paper. This time he explained that he was recovering from his heart attack but that he was indeed back in practice. "The rumors of my death," he told the paper, channeling Mr. Twain again, "are only half-true."

Truth to tell, I don't remember this funny father very well. He suffered his first coronary in 1957, when I was ten; the second killed him fourteen years later; and the image I mostly recall is of the man in between. "I wish you could have known him before he got sick," my mother often said to me when we would talk about him, but from what I gathered he had always had a dark side, an emotional fragility and depressive nature that were exacerbated by the coronary and its aftermath. He had a temper that could eclipse his good humor in quick order. "Confound it!" was his common oath, for he rarely cursed in our presence beyond a muttered *damn* or *hell,* and he would never, under any circumstances, use the Lord's name in vain. But he could be thunderous, and former patients later told me of his rages, which were apparently more wind than lightning.

More insidious was the depression that overtook him. His mother, who died before I was born, was sometimes called "Black Mary" by other members of the family because of her "dark spells," and these he had inherited. I assume he had

had it all his life. My mother said that when World War II began, he "couldn't wait to get in and then immediately he couldn't wait to get out." As a medical doctor, he was given the rank of captain, and he made a handsome soldier, but he was a miserable one and was eventually discharged for emotional reasons. After the first heart attack, ravaged physically and psychically, he didn't stand a chance, and the black moods grew in occasion and duration. When I was a teenager, I would often come home from school to find him there, secluded in his room with the lights out, "exhausted," as he would say, or simply unable to keep from crying. My mother would meet me and my two brothers at the door on those days to warn us that he needed "quiet." That was the word: *quiet*. The word *quiet* is to this day one of the most ominous words I know.

Like preachers' kids, doctors' children find life difficult to negotiate in small towns. As it was when I was small, Hogansville, Georgia, is a place of some 3,000 inhabitants. "The City of Friendly People" is how we distinguished ourselves on the city limits signs, and, in general, that is probably an honest enough description. The town doctor in such places carried immediate status, and that status was transferred to the children as well, but only to a degree. While I was growing up, many of my friends were the children of textile mill workers. There were social distinctions there as well, of course, for some of my friends' parents were college graduates who were foremen or managers in the mill, while others worked manually at the looms. Many of them lived in "the Village" near the mills, made up of small company houses. Today, the mills are long gone, and many of those houses have been bought and renovated by investors or bedroomers who have discovered that Hogansville is just far enough away from Atlanta (about an hour) to serve as a quaint place to live.

In high school, however, the social world of Hogansville was divided between "uptown" and "downtown." It was actually more complex than this, because there was also "Colored town" across the highway, but some blacks also lived, largely in shacks, just off Main Street, near our house, for historical reasons. In the nineteenth century, this area had been part of the Hogan plantation that was the beginning of Hogansville, and slave quarters had been located in this area. Nevertheless, because we lived on Main Street, just two houses down from the old Hogan mansion, my family was definitely "uptown."

The unspoken irony was that, by the time I became aware of this distinction, my father made less money than the fathers of many of my Village friends, and while "hand-to-mouth" is too dramatic a description, there was always a financial dread hanging over our house. How many patients would make appointments? How many would he actually have the strength to see? How many would then be able to pay? The books my mother kept told an often-ominous story as my father borrowed from the bank, borrowed on his life insurance, borrowed, for all I know, from family and friends. He would sometimes send us, as children, to the bank with five or ten dollars to "put on the loan." At that time it seemed an adventure to walk up the stone steps, stand in line at the teller's window, and transact this grown-up business.

Although I recognized my father's social standing as doctor in the town, I never knew quite how to see him in relation to other men. I never thought of him as particularly "manly," certainly not like some of my friends' fathers, who hunted and worked with tools and drank, played poker, and cursed freely. They respected my father, but I never had the feeling they would necessarily have wanted him as part of their group. He and my mother belonged to a bridge club and sometimes played at the nearby Elk Club, but he didn't enjoy it particularly and would some-times arrange to receive phone calls from bogus patients to get him away. He was a deacon in the First Baptist Church, a godly man who kept the Bible by his bedside and, on Sunday nights, would listen to Billy Graham on the radio prophesying the end of the world. Billy Graham pointed out the signs, and my father took them to heart. He wanted to believe, and for the most part he did, but he was an intel-ligent man, and not everything added up. I have his Bible, and in the margins are occasional question marks or exclamation points that reflect his intellectual and spiritual struggle. He had earned his medical degree from the University of Chicago and was regarded as one of the smartest men in town, but he told us stories of his failures in school, classes he had to repeat because he had been a country boy unprepared by previous training either to live in the big city or to work at such a high level of academic expectation. Still, he said, he had the gift of diagnosis, an uncanny sympathy for illness that enabled him to intuit root causes. This skill impressed his professors, and he later contributed articles to medical journals advocating the importance of "listening" to patients, letting them talk as a contribution to their cure.

My father was, in other words, hard for me to figure out, a professional ad-mired but not embraced by the town in which he lived. As an adolescent, I tried to substitute Atticus Finch for Mark Twain as a model for understanding him. Once again, the white linen suit helped, especially after I saw Gregory Peck in the movie version. Scout and Jem had some of the same ambiguous feelings about their father's traditional manliness that I had for mine. The issue of race also arose here. I wanted to find in my father the racial sensitivity and understanding I saw in Atticus, but he was a man of his time. Although I never heard him refer to blacks in overtly degrading terms, he had many "funny" stories to tell about them. At his clinic in town he had segregated waiting rooms into the 1960s, with white patients entering by the front door and blacks by the side. I don't know on what basis they were seen. The same was generally true of people who would come to our house at night: whites might sometimes knock at the back door, but blacks always did. My father never refused to see a black patient or to visit one at his home. I sometimes went with him across the railroad tracks and highway that divided Hogansville into its primary racial regions and would either sit in the car or wait in the front room while he saw to his patient. I remember the smell, not unpleasant but close, earthy, real. You could taste it. I didn't consider the conditions that caused it. Blacks lived in poverty; it was the way of the world. I could see the respect they accorded my father, and it was a respect he expected and assumed, I think. One night in the early 1960s, as we drove up a dirt road to a house on this side of town, we passed a crowd of young black men drinking. They called out as we went by, and suddenly one of them ran after us and jumped on the back bumper of the car and bounced hard and yelled. My father was shaken by it. He talked about it when we reached the patient's house, and the family was outraged. "Those boys should have recognized the doctor's car." He agreed, but the world was changing on him, and he began to quote Billy Graham to us more often.

As for me, I was the eldest son. I had a sister, six years my senior, and two younger brothers, two years between each boy. Before I started school, I was typical of the neighborhood kids, at least as far as pictures from the time indicate. In them I have the standard 1950s GI haircut, the scabby knees, the missing teeth, the confident, even cocky smile, one eye squinted at the camera, head tilted to the side like a wiseacre. In the first grade I had my tonsils removed and began to gain weight. The two events became connected in my mind: I got fat because of the operation. Also, I began wearing glasses, and from that time on I dreaded the annual eye examinations that would inevitably mean a new prescription, thicker lenses. School pictures document the changes. In them, I take on a softness, a shyness. I still smile at the camera but hesitantly, quietly. I was not athletic, lacking in hand-eye coordination, and when all my friends went out for Little League, I held back. Both of my younger brothers would play when their time came, and they were good, but for me Little League season was a horrible time. I did go out once, had to wear a "hefty" uniform, went to practice sick to my stomach, even played in a game during which, at bat, I stood at the plate, heart racing, the ball a blur, never swinging until I was mercifully called out on strikes. I returned the uniform that night and put baseball behind me.

Adding to my discomfort was the fact that I began to mature sooner than most of my male friends. By the eighth grade I had dark hair on my legs and under my arms, and by the ninth I had the beginnings of a mustache. Once I surreptitiously shaved my legs, using my father's razor, but the hair came back blacker than ever. These were difficult issues to broach. Our family was unusually discreet, if not compulsively so, concerning matters of the body. We were clinical. When I had my sex talk with my father, he took me into his office and handed me a pamphlet he normally gave to newlyweds, complete with line drawings of a couple in various positions, and he asked if I had any questions. These drawings were actually pretty interesting, and I wouldn't have minded taking them with me for further inspection, but, no, I had no questions. My father retrieved the instructions, and we were done with sex. In our daily lives, we treated the body with similar clinical detachment. We had "bowel movements" or "BMs"; we "passed flatus"; we were obsessed with sanitation. A typical family story: as a child I run from the bathroom to the dinner table. "Did you wash your hands?" my father asks. "No, sir," I answer, "but it's OK. I didn't touch it." Big laugh, but not touching was important. My father let us know that this was a filthy world, filled with unsanitary people, and you needed to take care wherever you could. Even today I wash my hands as my father taught me, like a surgeon scrubbing before an operation. Public rest rooms are a challenge, especially those with hot air dryers rather than paper towel dispensers. Negotiations can be complicated in such circumstances. I instructed my own son to use his shirtsleeve or shirttail as protection while grabbing a bathroom door handle, and I still favor those restaurants that have the good sense to set their doors swinging outward so that you can just shoulder your exit with a push.

Because of my size and early physical maturity, I could not escape football as I had baseball, and in the eighth grade, although I still dreaded team sports, I found I had some small talent on the field. By the ninth and tenth grades, I had lost weight and gained confidence, a conventional enough story. However, I had also pretty much stopped growing at all, had stalled at five feet, nine inches, and 160 pounds, and I had to play without my glasses. Therefore, even though I was reasonably fast and better fit to be a back, I couldn't see well enough to do it and found a place as a guard instead. Our coach was Jim "Coon Dog" Davis, a former marine who had played college and semipro ball. He was big and thick and wore a flattop. When he was angry, his bottom jaw protruded, his face turned beet red, and he squeezed his hands into massive fists that he kept carefully at his side. I had never really known anyone like him, and he scared me plenty. Our house was only a block from the high school, and in August of each of my high school years, we had twice-a-day preseason practice, morning and afternoon. The walk there at sunrise was awful, the heat already beginning to build, the dread welling up in my soul.

Playing football, even at my small high school—I would never have made the team at any larger place—was my initiation into what I perceived to be manhood. It was physically demanding, and I took pride in being able to meet Coach Davis's expectations. He ran us hard and fed us salt tablets to ward off cramps, and occasionally he praised me for a block or tackle or, more often, a sweeping trap play, for I was quick and could stay low. But I was never the "man" I thought many of my teammates to be. I have yet another picture, me in the eleventh grade in my football uniform, taken at the beginning of the season. Number 60, right guard, but in the shot I'm smiling coyly at the camera, eye squinting and head tilted as when I was a child, instead of growling or grimacing meanly as my buddies did. I'm holding the helmet in the cool way we had all adopted—wrist threaded underneath the face mask and palm cupping the front curve of the helmet as it hangs by my side—but any pretense of toughness is debunked by that grin. I can't imagine a sweeter, less threatening football player.

But Coach Davis pushed me, us, and that junior year was a good one. We made the state playoffs for our division, and I was on the field a lot more than I probably should have been. When I sat on the bench, I would squint down the field toward the scoreboard and ask others how much time was left. I wasn't worried so much about the game and the score; I just wanted it to be over. This was the highlight of my athletic career. The next year, as a senior, I came down with mononucleosis and actually passed out after one of the first games while walking back to the gym to change. It was perfect in so many ways. I didn't have to play, but I had escaped without quitting. I had lettered and had a football jacket, but now I could sit on the bench with the others, wearing said jacket, and my glasses.

What I realize in recalling these events is that the construct of masculinity in this small southern town in the 1950s and 1960s was more inclusive than one might imagine, and it was possible to mix and blend with different degrees of acceptance. Certainly, I was not seen as the most masculine of boys—I was "pretty as a girl," as my sister's mother-in-law sometimes said. But I played football, dated and went to the prom, got in trouble at school, drank beer. I don't think anyone would have picked me as first choice to watch his back in a fight, but if I were there, I would have done it. And certainly there were boys less traditionally masculine than I. Here's where it gets complicated in my attempts to reconstruct the past. My memory is that the two or three boys pegged as probably or definitely gay—"queers" would have been the word we used—were not ostracized in any overt fashion. I'm probably wrong, and their memories would be important correctives to what I'm saying. One boy, whose parents worked in the mill, grew more and more flamboyantly feminine during high school. He employed comedy and outrageous behavior to make us laugh, but the guys he had grown up with in the village would allow only so much teasing or meanness toward him, for he was their childhood friend. He could also take up for himself; he was quick-witted and unafraid. After high school I lost contact with him, as with so many others who didn't go to college. I was told that he lived in Atlanta for a while and then had gotten a job at a box factory in a nearby town, a line job of some sort, and that he would sometimes come to work in drag. The person telling me this was laughing at his audacity, but he also said he admired the son of a bitch.

One of my closest high school friends finally understood, in college, that he was homosexual. It was no great surprise—teachers had always labeled him as "sensitive" and "artistic"—but, still, nobody had quite made the identification. He was a talented musician, a pianist and composer who moved to Los Angeles after school and once appeared on the *Tonight* show accompanying a well-known actress who was trying to become a singer as well. The whole town tuned in that night. Many years later I visited him in California. We went to his home and he introduced me to his companion, and we had dinner together. He told me that for a time, while he was discovering his sexual identity, he had wondered about my own. I remembered all the nights we would ride around together, go to movies and talk about them and about our own plans and dreams. Sometimes we double-dated—he had a girlfriend off and on for several years—but more often we would be alone. If anyone questioned the nature of our friendship during this time, I never heard of it. I would like to argue that it wouldn't have mattered. In 1995, our local high school was permanently closed as part of reorganization of the county school system. We had a huge reunion of all the classes, and each class selected a representative to address the audience. Our class chose my friend, now openly gay. I'm not sure what to do with this information, for I'm certain there are many ways to interpret it. Again, my point is that the response one might have expected in a small, conservative southern town did not always occur. Although the *idea* of homosexuality—and it was always male, never female—was often deplored and ridiculed, the behavior toward the individuals identified or imagined to be gay seemed much more accepting. I know it's more complex than I'm presenting it, and no one was asking for the right to marry, so maybe the perceived threat to the community wasn't as great. Maybe it is all in the memory.

My father had his first coronary when I was ten. It was late at night, and I heard the noise of people moving around in the house, but that wasn't unusual. Patients commonly came at all hours, and my siblings and I had learned to ignore nocturnal phone calls and rappings at the door that today would set my heart madly racing. But the sounds this night were different, and so I got up and came into the living room in time to see my father being wheeled out on a gurney to the waiting funeral hearse, used locally as an ambulance. He had begun to feel the chest pains early in the evening but had ignored them because he still had calls to make. He had medicated himself, and when he finally got home, he woke my mother to tell her that he might need help later on. Then he went to bed, in denial I suppose, and later they had to take him to the hospital, where he stayed for many weeks. I remember one visit to see him during that time. He was encased in an oxygen tent and could barely speak. I was sure he would die.

There followed a long, slow physical recovery as he adjusted to his reduced condition. He had bought a car on the day of his coronary—he always wanted new cars and dreamed of one that would make it to 100,000 miles, but none ever did—and the first matter of business was to see if it could be returned. One of the benefits of small-town life is that it could. He soon enough realized that he could no longer maintain his clinic downtown, and the decision was made to move his office into our house. My mother hated it, but there seemed to be little choice.

Therefore, the boys' room in the front of the house, where we slept on hospital beds, was taken over as his office, and the living room was made into the waiting room for his patients. During the day, this part of the house was off-limits to us. When he was just too exhausted or depressed to work, my mother simply shut the front door, and he retreated to his room.

One afternoon I came home from school, entering through the back door. As usual, I was wearing my football jacket. I stopped in the kitchen and cut a piece of dark angel food cake, then skirted through the dining room on my way to the bedroom. A man was sitting in a chair in the living room, waiting to see my father. We tried not to look at his patients, but as I passed through, I saw, peripherally, the man wrap his arms around his chest, squeeze, and then roll to the floor so slowly and gently that he could have been laying himself down as one would put a baby in a crib. I stopped and walked slowly back. He was alone, in the middle of the floor, and whether he was dying or dead, I didn't know. I had a mouth full of red cake turning to mud on my tongue; I stuffed the rest in the pocket of my jacket and turned to get my father. As I ran, I clipped the man's foot with my own and stumbled down the hall to the office. When he opened the door, my father looked first at me and then over my shoulder at the figure beyond, and I stepped aside as he rushed by. I watched him kneel and put his ear to the man's chest. When he raised his head, the look on my father's face was one of shame. Something awful had happened here in his own home, in the presence of his child, something ugly and unsanitary. Death had entered the house. That night my mother insisted that the office be moved, no matter the expense, and soon it was. But the damage was done, and the effects were lasting.

At some point—I'm not sure when—my father had begun electroshock treatments for his persistent melancholy. His physician was Dr. Corbett Thigpen, a prominent psychiatrist at the Medical College of Georgia in Augusta. My father had known him since childhood. In 1957, Thigpen and his associate Dr. Hervey Cleckley had published the famous case study *The Three Faces of Eve*—we had an autographed copy in the house—that brought to national attention the existence of multiple personality disorder. The Oscar-winning movie starring Joanne Woodward had made them even more famous. Much later the real "Eve" would write her own version of her story, and Drs. Thigpen and Cleckley would come under much criticism for their treatment and representation of her, but in the early 1960s they were stars, and my father felt that Thigpen could help him. Therefore, when this depression became too great, my mother would reluctantly drive him across the state for a "session." She thought they were barbaric, but my father was convinced they helped to "clear the cobwebs" from his head, as he put it.

When I got my driver's license, I was asked to make the trip, for my mother had always hated leaving us boys alone in the house for days at a time, as they had had to do whenever they went. One day after school Mother told me that my father wanted to talk with me in his room, where he had again retreated. We sat there in the dark while he tried to explain to me his helplessness, his confusion, and his sense of failure. At one point he began to cry, and I felt myself pulling back, shutting down: this was not something fathers should do in front of their sons. In some ways, I never completely opened up again after this day; never, I determined, would I appear so weak, so pathetic, so sad before someone I loved. This arrogant cruelty makes little sense to me now, but at the time it was my immediate reaction. Several mornings later we got up early and prepared to leave. My father lay down with a pillow in the back seat of the Oldsmobile and tried to sleep as I drove. We spent the night in Washington, Georgia, at the home of my aunt, the widow of my father's youngest brother, who had himself died of a heart attack several years earlier.

The next day, continuing from Washington to Augusta as the sun rose, my father began to speak to me. He was now anticipating what was to come, and he talked like a doctor, explaining the upcoming procedure to me. When we arrived, he said, they would take him away to prepare for the treatment. They would remove his glasses and his partial plate and his watch and wedding ring and give them to me to keep. I could go to the cafeteria, and they would find me there later. It was likely, he said, that I wouldn't quite recognize him when it was over, and he would himself be confused for some time. I shouldn't expect him to make much sense, but I needed to understand that soon he would be better, he would think clearer, and his mind would be free for a while of the dread and the clutter. This is what I remember he told me.

Driving home several days later, we went through the countryside in East Georgia where he had grown up, and he began to tell stories about his family. He talked about his uncle who had fought in World War I and had been gassed and came home an invalid and later died after inhaling a peanut and developing pneumonia in his ruined lungs. My grandfather had started out as a pharmacist, he said, but found the position too stressful and had then become a rural mail deliverer. As a boy, Daddy had ridden with his father along some of the same dirt roads we passed. The ruts were sometimes so deep that my grandfather could lock the tires in them and let his son pretend to steer the car as it followed its predetermined path. Years later, I drove with my wife, who was then pregnant with our son, back along this same stretch of road toward Washington to visit my grandfather in the nursing home. When we saw him, he thought I was my father, who had died more than a year earlier. He smiled, patted my hand, and called me "Ed," and I smiled back, debating whether to correct him or let it go. I let it go, partly because I didn't know how to explain I wasn't my father, wasn't my grandfather's son.

I know now that I am my father more than I ever admitted, and my attempts to be "stronger," less emotional, more "manly" than he was have had personal consequences that remain untold. He planted in me, and probably in my brothers as well, that we had to be ever alert for illness and weakness. He studied us as we grew up, looking for that nervous, depressive trait in us that he had seen in his mother and in himself, praying to God that we wouldn't have it. I know I've looked for it in my own children. I also know that the things that I've criticized most in my father and my son are exactly those characteristics I tried so hard to deny in myself, that fretful uncertainty, that emotional fragility that seemed wrong for a responsible man. At my father's funeral I gasped for breath and blubbered while my wife held my arm. After that I didn't cry again for many, many years.

It's no surprise that now I sympathize and acknowledge my father's courage. Once, while home from college, I sat at the dining table with him and my mother as he complained about his exhaustion. I erupted. "Well, why don't you exercise?" I demanded. "Why don't you just get out and walk? You're always so tired because you never do anything!" My mother called me from the table while he sat there in silence. "You have no idea," she told me. "Your father worries all the time about you and all of you. You don't know how he feels. He never knows when he can work or how many patients will come when he does work. Some days he sits there at his desk, waiting. Can you imagine what that is like?" She went on, pointing out these obvious facts, and I listened, determined to remain unmoved. But I know that my own life today has been directed in large part by a need for safety and security, a monthly paycheck and state-sponsored insurance. I know that my father took risks that I have never attempted, that he faced fears that I have never confronted.

I suspect there is very little that is original in the stories I've told here. They are fumbling attempts to explore the question of my own masculine construct while recognizing the artificial nature of that identity. There were certain standards of masculine behavior in the place where I grew up, to be sure, but many of us, probably most of us, failed to match those standards, and it's an oversimplification of southern life to assume that it made much difference. In *Outside the Southern Myth*, Noel Polk makes the essential point that, as a southern male, he rarely recognizes himself or his history in most popular representations of the white South. Coming at this issue from another direction, what strikes me is how similar all our stories are, no matter where we come from or the differences in individual details. As Polk says, middle-class life in the South was and is probably not all that different from life in "middle-class American towns everywhere" (xv). The same goes for young boys modeling their fathers in their attempts to become young men everywhere. We all are disappointed and disappoint, and we all question the image we finally develop.

A few years ago I spent a weekend with an old friend from high school. He had been a natural athlete, an outstanding baseball and football player. He had gone to college, gone into the army, served in Vietnam, gotten a job with the forestry service, had a brief marriage, and had known many women. He had no children himself but had remained close to his stepson. Now he was anticipating retirement, living alone off a dirt road, in a house he had partly built himself. He liked to hunt, and he owned enough land to do it pretty much when he pleased. If anyone fit the description of "traditional southern male," he was it. That weekend our old football coach, with whom my friend had faithfully kept in touch and who now lived nearby in that part of the state, drove over, and the three of us walked in the woods and drank beer and talked. Coach Davis was still powerful but had been sick and was slowing down. He and my friend clearly loved each other, and I was there as a guest as they recalled events I had long ago forgotten. I wondered why. At one point Coach Davis laughed about me as a player, shook his head at my general ineptitude but remembered my effort and determination. I didn't tell him how I longed for games to end, seasons to finish. He asked about my mother and spoke with respect for my father. "And you're a college professor," he smiled, his big red face beaming. He was proud of all of the boys who had stuck with him, no matter how they turned out.

That night after Coach Davis left, we opened the bottle of bourbon I had brought, and the talk became even more personal. "I'm so glad I'm getting old," my friend said. "I don't have to always be doing things, proving myself. I don't always have sex on the brain. I can just be who I am." "Who I am" is the central question of this essay. It's not a southern question, to be sure, but for me the South has framed the issue. Still, it's the South of my own experiences, one much more varied and complex than generally acknowledged in popular culture and yet, at the same time, I think, understandable and familiar to other men of my generation, no matter what their specific heritage. Since 9/11 and in the present political and cultural climate, we've witnessed a return to a simplified definition of manhood, encouraged by political and social needs. We want clear-cut examples. But there are very few clear-cut examples, and it's good that there are not. The inclusiveness of masculine values, southern or otherwise, offers us a much greater hope than the rigidity of narrower definitions. Our lives tell us so every day.

Drinking Poisoned Waters
Traumatized Masculinity and White Southern Identity in Contemporary Family Memoirs

JAMES WATKINS

Near the beginning of his 1997 memoir *Power in the Blood: An Odyssey of Discovery in the American South,* author John Bentley Mays describes his descent during his early adulthood into acute depression. Although the breakdown stemmed from his repressed grief over his parents' death when he was a child, Mays explicitly links it to his misguided, obsessional identification with a mythic South he associated with his father and the paternalistic social order he represented in the boy's mind. Mays's depiction of the episode's causes bears scrutiny because it points to a recently emerging trend in the representation of southern regional identity in which white autobiographers are moving away from emphasizing racial guilt as primary to their southern identity and adopting a more therapeutic model of self-narration in which southernness is figured in the language of pathology. More specifically, this shift suggests a turning away from what Fred Hobson calls the "white southern racial conversion narrative," a form of autobiographical narrative in which liberal writers, "all products of and willing participants in a harsh, segregated society, confess racial wrongdoings and are 'converted,' in varying degrees, from racism to something approaching racial enlightenment."[1] While examples of the racial conversion narrative continue to be produced, this moral, quasi-religious framework for representing white southern regional identity shows signs of being effaced by one in which writers like Mays articulate their ambivalent identification with the South in the discourse of the trauma recovery narrative. This type of autobiographical writing, which is informed by psychoanalysis, seeks to bring to light the author/narrator's repressed and painful memories—most often from childhood—of loss or physical and/or psychological violence and to foreground the therapeutic role that the writing of one's traumatic experiences plays in the process of recovery.[2]

For Mays, the deaths of both of his parents by the time he reached age ten served as the pivotal traumatic experiences of his childhood, but he makes it clear that these events alone were not responsible for his descent into acute depression in his early adulthood. Rather, he claims, it is the characteristically southern modes of attaching significance to those traumas, particularly to the sudden, mystery-shrouded death of his father—"what some called an automobile accident, and others thought was murder"—that results in his crisis.[3] An only child, Mays was born on his father's cotton plantation near Spring Ridge in northwestern Louisiana. He lived there until age seven when, upon the death of his father, he moved with his mother to his maternal grandmother's house in nearby Shreveport. While they were residing there, his mother was diagnosed with cancer and died within three years of her husband's passing. During that period in Shreveport, he writes, the farm at Spring Ridge loomed large in his imagination and "became less true place than a fantastical Eden simplified and internalized, made perfect and brittle by bleeding away all the colors that were ugly in the original fabric . . . In the aloneness of my dark room in the house where my mother lay dying, I would swim in bright fantasies of a southern boyhood in light" (18–19). A socially awkward child who already was temperamentally predisposed to shyness and introspection, Mays was encouraged to dwell in idyllic daydreams of his remembered childhood at Spring Ridge by his paternal grandparents and Aunt Vandalia, with whom he lived in Greenwood, Louisiana, after his mother's death. They immersed him in frequently retold stories about his father's childhood there in the house where he now dwelled: "The stories were not meant to deceive me: but they deceived us all. And gradually I began to believe that only here, where my father had been a radiant boy . . . could I be a Southern boy like him" (19).

Over the years, Mays's habitual escapes into fantasies of a return to his lost childhood innocence led to a corresponding identification with a version of the South he had come to associate with life on the plantation of his youth. "During my early twenties," he writes, "as part of my last attempt to protect the legion of nostalgia gnawing on my soul, I threw my whole heart into *being Southern*, in the sense I understood the phrase—living in an archaic, presumably noble past that was out of step with reality." The mental breakdown that soon ensued provided the "kindly crisis" that eventually allowed him, while "in the care of a wise and compassionate New York psychiatrist," to attribute his condition to what he characterizes as

> the peculiarly *Southern* cast of my childhood self-punishment—the poisoned vision of corrupted innocence that informed it, the obsessive posturing and withdrawal into fantasy that accompanied it. Our history since 1865 has made Southerners prone to this strategy . . . Hence the manufacture of such visionary ideals as the *Old South* and the *Lost Cause*—and hence the unreality that has long lain thick, like fog, in the hollows and bottomlands of the southern imagination. I had become ill by drinking the poisoned waters all around me; by *being Southern* in the dark sense of wounded, lamed by history, and by hankering after lost worlds. (20)

While this recognition occasions considerable relief from the acute depression he experienced as a young man, it fails to free him from the clutches of a chronic depression that dogs him throughout his adult life. *Power in the Blood* begins with the author's notification in 1990 of his Aunt Vandalia's death. Now an art critic in Toronto, where he has lived since shortly after his "kindly crisis," Mays undertakes a physical return to Louisiana to dispose of the house and his Aunts' belongings, which in turn initiates a parallel psychological journey into his southern past and the sources of his chronic depression. The resulting narrative combines genealogy, southern history, and autobiography to describe a process of psychological recovery in which the very act of writing his family history, a history of the region, and his personal history constitutes a significant part of the therapy.

Mays's conflation of the personal and the regional in the above-cited passage and throughout *Power in the Blood* aligns his text firmly in the tradition of modern autobiographical writing by southern white men, from William Alexander Percy's *Lanterns on the Levee* (1941) and Stark Young's *The Pavilion* (1949), to Willie Morris's *North Toward Home* (1968) and Harry Crews's *A Childhood* (1978), to Tim McLaurin's *Keeper of the Moon* (1991) and Reynolds Price's *Clear Pictures* (1994), to name just a handful of notable examples. Like his predecessors, Mays writes within the conventions of the family memoir, a distinctly intersubjective form of autobiography characterized by a strong focus on family genealogies, on the interpersonal and intergenerational dynamics within the narrator/protagonist's family, and/or on the autobiographical subject's relationships with individual family members. Southern writers from all backgrounds have found the family memoir to be a highly effective medium for representing selfhood as constructed primarily in relation to others and for showing the subtle processes by which it is shaped by specific geographic locales and the distinctive cultural practices associated with those locales.[4]

In many respects, the prominence of the family memoir in southern letters should come as no great surprise, given the degree to which family has functioned as an ideologically resonant image in what Jefferson Humphries calls the "discourse of southernness."[5] Arguing for the centrality of family to southern identity, Robert O. Stevens notes that "in southern history and culture, the family has served not as one among several supporting institutions but, in Andrew Lytle's now-classic recognition, as *the* institution of southern life."[6] Whether southerners have ever truly cared more about family than have nonsoutherners is highly questionable but ultimately irrelevant; few would contest the claim that family continues to operate as a central trope in the rhetoric of southern difference and as an icon of southernness from popular culture to highbrow literature. What may come as a surprise to some, though, is the extent to which white male autobiographers from the South have with such consistency and apparent ease adopted this female-centered discursive form as a medium for self-representation. Whereas the public memoir has typically been written by politicians, generals, and other figures who have acted in official, highly visible roles historically denied to women, and is thus seen as a more male-centered form of life writing, the family memoir is widely regarded as a more female-centered mode because of its emphasis on activity in the domestic sphere. Moreover, since memoir in general and family memoir in particular emphasize selfhood as constituted primarily in relation to others rather than as an autonomous entity, it is generally recognized in the field of autobiography studies as a form that is particularly well suited to representing women's experiences and concerns.[7] Yet, my own readings in southern autobiography have convinced me that white men have been as likely as white women to write their lives within the conventions of the family memoir and furthermore that they have skillfully used the form to articulate their ambivalence about and resistance to nationally dominant norms of masculinity. I should note here that the family memoir seems to be the preferred autobiographical mode for African

American women from the South, as well, but while some recent examples of these kinds of texts by their male counterparts can indeed be found, for instance, Clifton Taulbert's *Once upon a Time When We Were Colored* (1994) and Henry Louis Gates's *Colored People* (1995), compared to southern white men, southern African American men appear to find the form less useful.

It would be impossible to measure objectively the extent to which white southern masculinities differ from their nonsouthern counterparts, but a growing body of scholarly work has shed light on the historical conditions that helped to shape white male subjectivity in the South.[8] The most frequently cited of these, Bertram Wyatt-Brown's *Southern Honor: Ethics and Behavior in the Old South,* does not address regional differences in self-representational strategies but still offers some guidance in seeking an explanation of why southern white men have shown such a strong preference for writing their lives within the conventions of the family memoir. According to Wyatt-Brown, the cultural emphasis given in the Old South to the notion of honor meant that selfhood for most whites was "almost entirely external in nature" and was constructed within a system in which public shame, rather than private guilt, served as whites' primary mechanism of self-regulation.[9] To the extent that this formulation was especially true for southern white men, then, they would have found the introspective New England model of autobiographical practice, which had originated in the Puritan spiritual narrative, to be of little use in expressing their experiences of selfhood.

If the South lacked the strong religious emphasis on self-inspection that informed the New England autobiographical model, it also found itself increasingly at odds with the related ideology of autonomous individualism which emerged in the public discourse of the antebellum period as a defining difference between the North and South. Responding to abolitionists' attacks against the peculiar institution, southerners defended slavery by characterizing their society as a system of interdependent, albeit hierarchical, relationships in which personal freedom and autonomy were secondary to the fulfillment of personal responsibilities to one's subordinates, neighbors, and superiors. Although this paternalistic characterization of the slave society as one happy family bound together by filiations of mutual obligation glossed over the systematic mechanisms of oppression that lay at the heart of the institution, most white southerners—especially those of the slave-holding class—would, in their defensiveness against abolitionist criticism, have believed this description of their world and thus would have resisted overtly individualistic paradigms of selfhood. The Lost Cause mythology that emerged after the war ensured that this and other elements of perceived southern difference from national norms would persist into the present day.

Ironically, the strong preference white southern men have shown for the family memoir may well have resulted in their exclusion from the national canon of "classic" autobiography for many of the same reasons women writers have been excluded—at least in years past—from that body of works. That is, their failure to use the autobiographical occasion to celebrate autonomous individualism is notably distinct from the nationally dominant male autobiographical tradition canonized in such works as Jonathan Edward's *Personal Narrative*, Benjamin Franklin's *Autobiography*, Thoreau's *Walden*, and *A Narrative of the Life of Frederick Douglass*. An uncritical acceptance of this restrictive definition of autobiography can be seen in Lewis P. Simpson's assessment that "achievement in the formal mode of autobiography, in the artistically conceived and deliberately structured self-biography, while prominent in American literature . . . has not been notable in southern letters, not even in the 'glory' days of the twentieth-century 'Southern Renaissance.'"[10] Simpson's stipulative definition of "formal" autobiography as "artistically conceived and deliberately structured self-biography" implicitly excludes other-centered forms of life writing like the family memoir which fail to privilege autonomy over interdependence.

Rather than acknowledging and examining the large body of autobiographical works from the South which happen not to conform to the nationally dominant model, Simpson instead extends his discussion of the autobiographical impulse in the South by turning to the region's novelistic tradition and arguing that southern writers have shown a preference for couching autobiographical self-disclosure in the protective guise of fiction. But, as Philippe Lejeune has argued, autobiographical fiction does not make the kind of claims for referentiality that are made by texts in which the author, narrator, and protagonist are aligned in what he calls the "autobiographical pact."[11] In other words, autobiographical fiction, however closely modeled on real-life personages, lacks the "truth effect," or genre-specific referential authority, of autobiography. Yet it is precisely this truth effect that historically has allowed published autobiographies to successfully challenge standard histories and to subvert dominant ideologies of selfhood. Furthermore, in this so-called "age of memoir," where we are currently witnessing a virtual explosion of such works by self-declared southern writers, the authoritative truth claims of autobiography are playing an increasingly significant role in promoting continued perceptions of southern cultural distinctiveness. In critically acclaimed and popularly successful works like Edward Ball's *Slaves in the Family* and Rick Bragg's *All Over But the Shoutin'* and in lesser-known but equally powerful works like Mays's *Power in the Blood* and Clay Lewis's *Battlegrounds of Memory*, we encounter white men using the genre-specific authority of autobiography in ways that particularize and render visible whiteness and masculinity while simultaneously affirming the author/narrator's identification with the South.

The relatively recent appearance of trauma recovery narratives within the firmly established tradition of the southern family memoir reflects a broad-based trend in contemporary life writing in which Holocaust survivors and other victims of historical trauma as well as victims of childhood sexual abuse and/or domestic violence have told their stories as a form of therapy. According to Suzette A. Henke, author of *Shattered Subjects: Trauma and Testimony in Women's Life Writing*, trauma narratives are almost always concerned with taking repressed memories the author/narrator has experienced as highly disturbing recurring visual images and transforming those images into verbal form. Henke notes that "in pathological configuration, traumatic memories constitute a kind of prenarrative that does not progress or develop in time, but remains stereotyped, repetitious, and devoid of emotional conflict. Iconic and visual in form, these images relentlessly intrude on consciousness" until the subject asserts linguistic control over them by converting them into language and narrative."[12] (xvii–xviii). Crucial differences in severity of symptoms distinguish psychological trauma resulting from physical or emotional violence, on the one hand, and the sudden loss of loved ones, on the other. Nevertheless, bereavement can take the form of trauma, especially as it pertains to a pronounced identification with absence and loss.

For white southerners, identification with loss can take on broader cultural meaning in the form of Lost Cause mythology. As we see in the case of Mays, whose reaction to his parents' deaths centers around nostalgic fantasies of a prelapsarian wholeness symbolized by his father's plantation at Spring Ridge, personal responses to individual loss can be conflated with cultural responses to historical loss in ways that confuse the two and hamper recovery. In a recent essay in *Critical Inquiry*, Dominick LaCapra underscores the danger of "an overly generalized discourse of absence" in response to historical trauma in nations such as Germany and South Africa, warning that it "increases the likelihood of misplaced nostalgia or utopian politics in quest of a new totality or fully unified community. When loss is converted into (or encrypted in an indiscriminately generalized rhetoric of) absence, one faces the impasse of endless melancholy, impossible mourning, and interminable aporia in which any process of working through the past and its historical losses is foreclosed or prematurely aborted."[13] Although LaCapra never mentions the American South, the applicability of his remarks to white southerners' collective nostalgia about the Old South remains clear. Fortunately for Mays, he seems to have recognized as a young adult the impossibility of resolution inherent in his attempts to alleviate the pain of loss and mourning by identifying with a paternalistic myth of the plantation South. But despite his "kindly crisis" and subsequent renunciation of a self-consciously southern identity, he had failed to adequately step out of the grief structures that subliminally associated southernness with loss, and his return to the South and renewed investigations into the meaning of southern history are depicted as nothing less than a deferred process of self-therapy.

Because the trauma recovery narrative may focus on various forms of domestic abuse, its links to the family memoir are extensive. Elements of the southern family memoir as trauma recovery narrative can be found as early as 1949, in Lillian Smith's *Killers of the Dream*, where the author's long-repressed memory of her parents' complicity in a racial incident inside their home serves as the centerpiece of the book's first chapter, "When I Was a Child." In Maya Angelou's *I Know Why the Caged Bird Sings* (1970), the author recounts being raped at the age of eight by her mother's boyfriend and her subsequent loss of speech for several years. Nevertheless, these texts do not foreground the act of writing as a form of therapeutic self-recovery in response to trauma. The elements of the subgenre do not fully coalesce until the mid-1990s, in Dorothy Allison's autobiographical narratives in *Skin: Talking about Sex, Class, and Literature* (1994) and *Two or Three Things I Know for Sure* (1995).[14] To the extent that their gender constitutes one significant degree of removal from the southern patriarchy, white women's conflict with that tradition has been less internalized (though probably more bitter) than has been white men's. In these women's narratives, the authors seek either to disentangle themselves from the violence of their fathers, husbands, or other men in their lives or else they try to avoid the examples of their mothers, whose efforts to live within the self-denying roles of southern womanhood result in madness and suicide.

For male writers who have chosen to represent selfhood within the conventions of the southern family memoir as trauma recovery narrative, no such distancing by gender from the southern patriarchy is possible. The result in those male-authored texts is a more direct though also more deeply conflicted engagement with emotionally impoverishing or psychologically harmful attributes of southern masculinity (most notably alcoholism and violence), often associated directly with the author's father. While such father-son conflicts can be seen in earlier autobiographical works such as Crews's *A Childhood* and McLaurin's *Keeper of the Moon*, the discourse of self-therapy remains absent until the mid-1990s. In addition to *Power in the Blood* and Lewis's *Battlefields of Memory*, examples of the pattern can be found to varying degrees in Walter de Milly's *In My Father's Arms: A True Story of Incest* (1999), Lewis Nordan's *Boy With Loaded Gun* (2000), and McLaurin's *The River Less Run* (2001).

Nordan's *Boy with Loaded Gun* places at center stage the author's struggles against alcoholism and its effects upon his relationships with family members. At first glance its frequent humor would seem to make it an unlikely candidate for the designation of trauma recovery narrative, but like Mark Twain, Nordan uses humor to cover the black hole of loss and suffering that has plagued him and led him to chronic depression and alcoholism throughout his adult life: from the death of his father when the author was eighteen months old, to his wife's miscarriage of their second child in her ninth month of pregnancy, to his twenty-two-year-old son's death by suicide. In seeking to come to terms with that catastrophic event, he asks, "Who is at fault in my son's death? Isn't someone to blame for this horror besides the boy himself? I am. What is a responsible context for the writer to put that information into? Even random murder would be simpler to write about, somehow. Still—-no matter how much I have grown spiritually over the years since Robin died, no matter how much therapy I've had, no matter how much more I know about depression than I did then, still there are days when the only context that seems reasonable is that I was an inadequate father."[15] Nordan's dysfunctional behavior resulting from his alcoholism may well have played some part in his son's attraction to suicide, but so far as we can judge within the confines of the text, the father's sins were ones of omission, not commission.

Such cannot be said for the father of Walter de Milly III, whose *In My Father's Arms: A True Tale of Incest* relates in highly graphic terms a harrowing tale of sexual molestation at the hands of his father, a prominent Tallahassee businessman and church deacon. De Milly begins his narrative with a shocking recollection of a particular sexual encounter with his father in the family's fallout shelter. Beginning the account in first person, he describes how his father undresses, begins masturbating, then asks his son to touch him, at which point, de Milly writes, "I disappear."[16] From there the scene switches to third person and is rendered in fragmented, impressionistic images characteristic of repressed traumatic memories.

As an adult who is now living in an openly gay relationship, the author is presented with the opportunity to finally confront his father when the outraged father of a childhood friend calls to tell him he has learned that Mr. de Milly molested his son as well. In order to avoid arrest, the author's father agrees to undergo psychiatric treatment, where he is forced to acknowledge to his family the crimes he committed against his son and several of his son's friends. Incredibly, the doctor recommends castration as the most appropriate course of treatment, and the elder de Milly agrees in order to avoid public exposure as a pedophile. From this point on, the castrated father is shown more as an object of pity than of hatred, as the author delves into his father's southern childhood in an attempt to fathom how he could develop into the person he knew and knows. By the time of his father's death, a type of reconciliation has been reached, but the author must imagine for himself rather than actually hear his father's desire for atonement. "I believe that, in the final years of his life," he writes, "my father sought the place where this world ceases to exist. I imagine my father at this mystical boundary, where he stands alone, looking back upon himself. It is here, at the source of the river, that he accomplishes what is impossible on this earth: he repudiates his life" (118). As with the majority of autobiographers cited thus far, de Milly associates the father's inability to articulate his emotions with what he sees as specifically southern codes of masculine decorum (though reticence is likely a general masculine predisposition and not specific to southern men). Thus we are asked to see in the author's openness about the humiliations of childhood sexual abuse not only a break from the cycle of self-blame and guilt common to victims of child abuse but also a rejection of the southern tradition of masculine reticence.[17]

A rejection of certain forms of southern tradition figures in the recovery from childhood trauma in Lewis's *Battlegrounds of Memory* and Mays's *Power in the Blood*. For these authors, recovery is enabled by a complicated process in which the more obviously false mythologies of the South are rejected as self-destructive or illusory, then replaced by more judiciously chosen, supposedly objective versions of the South and its history. The process is essentially homeopathic, in that the cure for too much southern culture is more southern culture, though admittedly of a different variety. Lewis's *Battlegrounds of Memory*, like de Milly's *In My Father's Arms*, begins with an account of a traumatic encounter between the author and his father. While home in Ruxton, Maryland, from college on Christmas Eve, Lewis intervenes at his mother's bequest when his drunk father starts to abuse her. In a fit of rage he severely beats his father, then almost turns on his mother when she screams for him to stop. Bewildered and depressed by the sudden outpouring of rage, he remains confused about its sources. For years afterwards, he obsessively returns against his will to a mental reliving of that violent episode, while also set-tling into a pattern of alcoholism and depression. "This book," he writes, "which I have labored on for more than twenty years, attempts to understand the causes and consequences of that Christmas Eve forty years ago . . . Absolution for my sins . . . I have not found. Instead, I have found life-deep complicity in a heritage of loss, violence, and passion[18]."

Years after the incident, while reading Civil War history in the Ruxton public library, he realizes that upon the very spot where his family's house was built, the site of his battleground with his father, a furious artillery bombardment dur-ing the Civil War had taken place that leveled the homes that once stood there. More research spurred by this discovery reveals that, coincidentally, this particular battle at Ruxton was among those in which his Mississippi ancestors had fought. The extensive and meticulous genealogical and historical research Lewis initiates after making this discovery seems nearly as obsessive and unhealthy as his earlier fixation on the encounter with his father. But at least his new obsession allows him the therapeutic benefits of anchoring his personal identity and experiences of selfhood in a continuum of time and place which, in turn, displaces the frag-mented, recurring image of father and son locked in combat. "Finding the impress of inheritance," Lewis writes, "the exact figure of despair and hard yearning that comes down to you through the workings of time, history, and family, is to find one's self. To begin to find true freedom" (219).

For Bentley and Mays, then, freedom from depression and from recurring im-ages of violence and loss, respectively, is found in a reimagined relationship to time and place through history and genealogy. With respect to autobiography's therapeutic potential to emancipate its writer from the death grip of a traumatic past, the usefulness of genealogy would appear to be limited, as it emphasizes an identification with a patrimonial line of descent which would seem to circumscribe identity and channel it into the rather narrow form of family name, even as it authorizes the self and anchors it to the tangible reality of bloodlines. As theoretician Julia Watson has noted, "genealogy detects the recorded past while autobiography pursues the desire for creation of free, agentified subjectivity."[19] Perhaps in tacit acknowledgment of the essentially conservative thrust of genealogy, Mays, an art critic, musters the opinions of postmodernists like Susan Sontag, Berthold Brecht, and Michel Foucault to help explain the efficacy of this "saving of our intimate histories, the stories of our ground and blood" (*Power in the Blood* 24).

At the heart of Mays's autobiographical journey lies a rejection of the monolithic notion of history invested in Lost Cause mythologies. "In my distraught early years I had tried to resolve the tension between myself as *free* and myself as *southern* by extinguishing the second term of the opposition" (*Power in the Blood* 54). But that false dichotomy is now replaced by a conception of truth that is commensurate with—rather than in reaction to—postmodernity. He writes:

> The essential truth about myself, or any text, *anything*, is not a simple kernel locked away inside a worthless, obfuscating husk . . . Rather, ultimate realities of both life and art are all on the surface: plural and various, conflicting, coinciding. *Truth* is, or should be, a plural noun, denoting shifting ground plans and patterns of reality, iridescent, revealing and disclosing continually. From this it follows that the only worthwhile way of knowledge is *knowing*, as one knows another person, not prying and studying, but joining in the endless mirror play of options and opposites and changes that constitute the truth of any friend, lover, or enemy. And that surely constitutes whatever reality we'll know. (51–52)

While Mays's pronouncements could hardly be said to reflect widespread conceptions of truth and knowledge in the recent South, his rejection of traditional epistemology does point the way into a new millennium in which tortured identification with the region will likely become much less common as perceptions of regional differences fade and as the history of the South remains subject to competing interpretations in an increasingly multicultural America. Whether or not the trauma recovery narrative will soon pose a serious challenge to the preeminence of the racial conversion narrative in the autobiographical writing of southern whites remains to be seen, but as memories of the Jim Crow South recede into the past and regional racial practices become less out of step with those of the rest of the nation, we will almost certainly see a continuing effacement of the white/black racial binary that historically has dominated the discourse of southernness. Furthermore, it seems a commonplace of contemporary America that traditional masculine reticence—arguably more pronounced in the South still, where honor-based conceptions of selfhood hold some sway even today—is giving way as men show more willingness to "open up" and articulate "soft" feelings (instead of only "hard" ones like anger, frustration, and jealousy). To the extent, then, that the trauma recovery narrative provides a socially sanctioned means of expressing masculine interiority, there is little reason to doubt that white men from the South will continue to use this particular autobiographical form for representing their selfhood and that they will do so in ways that bear the marks of southern regional identity.

NOTES

1. Fred Hobson, *But Now I See: The White Southern Racial Conversion Narrative* (Baton Rouge: Louisiana State University Press, 1999), 1–2.

2. For discussions of the trauma recovery narrative, see Roberta Culbertson, "Embodied Memory, Transcendence, and Telling: Recounting Trauma, Re-establishing the Self," *New Literary History* 26 (1995): 169–95; Suzette Henke, *Shattered Subjects: Trauma and Testimony in Women's Life Writing* (New York: St. Martin's, 1998); and Dominick LaCapra, "Trauma, Absence, Loss," *Critical Inquiry* 23 (Summer 1999): 696–727.

3. John Bentley Mays, *Power in the Blood: An Odyssey of Discovery in the American South* (New York: HarperCollins, 1997), 17. This work is cited parenthetically by page number throughout the chapter.

4. Other autobiographical forms besides the family memoir that constitute recognizable, albeit often overlapping, generic patterns within the broader category of southern autobiography include, most notably, the slave narrative (probably the richest and easily the most carefully studied of the subgenres of southern autobiography) and its modern descendents, the apology, the diary and journal, the travel narrative, the aforementioned white racial conversion narrative, and the oral history.

5. Jefferson Humphries, "The Discourse of Southernness: Or How We Can Know There Will Be Such a Thing as the South and Southern Literary Culture in the Twenty-First Century," in *The Future of Southern Letters,* ed. Jefferson Humphries and John Lowe (New York: Oxford University Press, 1996).

6. Robert O. Stephens, "Family," in *The Companion to Southern Literature: Themes, Genres, Places, People, Movements, and Motifs,* ed. Joseph M. Flora and Lucinda Mackethan (Baton Rouge: Louisiana State University Press, 2001), 248.

7. See Susan Stanford Friedman, "Women's Autobiographical Selves: Theory and Practice," in *The*

Private Self: Theory and Practice of Women's Autobiographical Writing, ed. Shari Benstock (Chapel Hill: University of North Carolina Press, 1988), 35–61. Friedman notes that the fundamental inapplicability of individualistic paradigms of the self to women and minorities is twofold. First, the emphasis on individualism does not take into account the importance of a culturally imposed group identity for women and minorities. Second, the emphasis on separateness ignores the differences in socialization in the construction of male and female gender identity.

8. See Bertram Wyatt-Brown, *Southern Honor: Ethics and Behavior in the Old South* (Oxford: Oxford University Press, 1982); Ted Ownby, *Subduing Satan: Religion, Recreation, and Manhood in the Rural South, 1865–1920* (Chapel Hill: University of North Carolina Press, 1990); and Kenneth Greenberg, "The Nose, the Lie, and the Duel in the Antebellum South," *American Historical Review* 95, no. 1 (1990): 57–74.

9. Wyatt-Brown, *Southern Honor*, 33.

10. Lewis D. Simpson, "The Autobiographical Impulse in the South," in *Home Ground: Southern Autobiography*, ed. J. Bill Berry (Columbia: University of Missouri Press, 1991), 63–64.

11. Philippe Lejeune, "The Autobiographical Pact," in *On Autobiography*, ed. Paul John Eakin, trans. Katherine Leary (Minneapolis: University of Minnesota Press, 1989), 4.

12. Henke, *Shattered Subjects*, xvii–xviii.

13. See La Capra, "Trauma, Absence, Loss," 699–701.

14. Other examples include Mary Carr's *The Liar's Club* (1996) and *Cherry* (2000), Judith Patterson's *Sweet Mystery: A Book of Remembering* (1996), Connie May Fowler's most recent publication, *When Katie Wakes* (2002), and Karen Salyer McElmurray's *Mother of the Disappeared: An Appalachian Birth Mother's Journey* (2002).

15. Lewis Nordan, *Boy with Loaded Gun* (Chapel Hill, NC: Algonquin, 2000), 214.

16. Walter de Milly, *In My Father's Arms: A True Story of Incest* (Madison: University of Wisconsin Press, 1999), 4. This work is cited parenthetically by page number throughout the chapter.

17. For discussions of masculine reticence, see Peter Middleton, *The Inward Gaze: Masculinity and Subjectivity in Modern Culture* (London: Routledge, 1992), especially 166–232.

18. Clay Lewis, *Battlegrounds of Memory* (Athens: University of Georgia Press, 1998), 5. (This work is cited parenthetically by page number throughout the chapter.)

19. Julia Watson, "Ordering the Family: Genealogy as Autobiographical Pedigree," in *Getting a Life: Everyday Uses of Autobiography*, ed. Sidonie Smith and Julia Watson (Minneapolis: University of Minnesota Press, 1996), 300. Near the end of her essay, Watson concedes the liberatory value of genealogy to autobiography, noting that it may indeed become, "for the reflective subject, a means of getting a new life" (316).

Ratliff and the Demise of Male Mastery

Faulkner's Snopes Trilogy and Cold War Masculinity

SUSAN V. DONALDSON

When William Faulkner talked in the 1950s about the Snopeses, characters who had haunted his imagination throughout his long career, he resorted to words and images that resonated with the language of cold war fears and anxieties.[1] At the University of Virginia interview sessions, he noted that the Snopeses represented "the idea of a tribe of people which would come into an otherwise peaceful little Southern town like ants or like mold on cheese."[2] One of the Snopeses' two great opponents, attorney Gavin Stevens, uses much the same language in *The Town* to describe the seemingly endless stream of poor whites who emerge out of the village of Frenchman's Bend. "They none of them seemed to bear any specific kinship to one another," Stevens observes; "they were just Snopeses, like colonies of rats or termites are just rats and termites."[3] Stevens's primary ally, the sewing machine agent V. K. Ratliff similarly cultivates, in the words of Stevens's nephew Charles Mallison, "the idea of Snopeses covering Jefferson like an influx or snakes or varmints from the woods" (*The Town*, 98). To a striking degree, Faulknerian descriptions of the Snopeses as infestations of vermin and/or faceless, soulless creatures bring to mind vivid allegories of internal and external threats to American security represented in 1950s films like *Them!*—focusing on an invasion by giant ants—or the more infamous *Invasion of the Body Snatchers*, which gave voice to American fears about insidious communist takeovers.[4]

On the face of things, analogies of this sort—Snopeses as faceless, relentless, interchangeable ants—would seem to link the Snopeses with the fabled conformity of the 1950s—whether that of communist hordes or of the new corporate flunkies lamented in William H. Whyte's *The Organization Man*, C. Wright Mills's *White Collar*, or Sloan Wilson's *The Man in the Gray Flannel Suit*.[5] One of *The Town's* narrators, Chick Mallison, even appears to confirm this suspicion when he observes, "that was our trouble with Mr Snopes: there wasn't anything to see even when you thought he might be looking at you" (*The Town*, 147). Flem Snopes, invariably linked with blandness and grayness, suggests nothing so much as the kind of invisibility and facelessness popularly associated with that supposedly archetypal man of the 1950s, the Man in the Gray Flannel Suit.[6] Yet Faulkner also tended to associate Flem Snopes with a kind of flinty individualism and with a roguishness appropriate for tracing a portrait of the artist as nonconformist and outlaw. "But a first-rate scoundrel, like a first-rate artist," Faulkner observed at the University of Virginia, "he's an individualist, and the pressure's all against being an individualist—you've got to belong to a group. It don't matter what group, but you've got to belong to it; or there's no place for you in the culture or the economy." Faulkner himself rather admired Flem, he told the students at Virginia, "until he was bitten by the bug to be respectable, and then he let me down." If anything, Faulkner tended in interviews to voice preference for "an out-and-out blackguard or rascal" rather than someone who had succumbed to respectability, which he associates throughout the Snopes trilogy with consumerism, domesticity, and, by implication, women.[7]

Contradictions of this sort suggest that we can read the Snopes trilogy as a meditation and commentary on competing versions of white masculinity—ranging from frontier horse-trading and eye-gouging competitiveness to post–World War II domesticated, consumer-oriented masculinity—in a midcentury America increasingly preoccupied with what was perceived as a crisis in white masculinity.[8] For, like the country at large, Faulkner was deeply concerned with the emergence of a new postwar masculinity that at once stressed conformity, domesticity, and consumerism and lamented older forms of entrepreneurial individualism. Faulkner was, though, equally troubled by the personal costs of traditional masculine competitiveness—by what appeared to be the sheer vulnerability of a competitive form of manhood requiring an unending ordeal of display, performance, and achievement dating back to elite duels choreographed by antebellum codes of honor as well as to those biting, eye-gouging contests between southern backcountry white men that Elliott Gorn so vividly chronicled in his famous 1985 *American*

Historical Review essay.[9] The result in the three Snopes novels—*The Hamlet* (1940), *The Town* (1957), and *The Mansion* (1959)—is a somewhat unsettling picture of Faulkner's own complicity in the discourse of cold war masculinity. For what wins out in Faulkner's saga of the Snopeses and their adversaries is not the competitive individualism of Flem Snopes but a reduced, domesticated, commodified form of masculinity represented by Gavin Stevens and his ally V. K. Ratliff—a masculinity signaling in some respects an acknowledged loss of mastery—for men in the Snopes novels and for Faulkner himself.[10]

A good many Faulkner scholars have already pointed out the peculiarly male motifs and perspectives emphasized throughout the Snopes trilogy, among them Panthea Reid Broughton, Noel Polk, Gary Lee Stonum, and Joseph Urgo. They have done so in part by giving heed to Gavin Stevens's comment in *The Town* that "apparently all Snopes are male . . . as if *Snopes* were some profound and incontrovertible hermaphroditic principle for the furtherance of a race, a species, the principle vested always physically in the male, any anonymous conceptive or gestative organ drawn into that radius to conceive and spawn, repeating that male principle and then vanishing" (*The Town*, 120–21).[11] Urgo points out rightly enough that even in *The Hamlet* women characters like Mrs. Tull and Mrs. Littlejohn shrewdly (and resignedly) "recognize the Snopeses as prototypically male."[12]

In particular, *The Hamlet*, which opened the Snopes trilogy in 1940, seems to be a peculiarly male world, dominated by the lusty, practical-minded backwoods squire Will Varner, "the largest landholder and beat supervisor in one county and Justice of the Peace in the next and election commissioner in both, and hence the fountainhead if not of law at least of advice and suggestion to a countryside which would have repudiated the term constituency if they had ever heard it."[13] Secure in his economic preeminence as owner of the country store, cotton gin, and combined grist mill and blacksmith shop, Will Varner leaves his small empire's everyday operation—and the competition it requires—to his son Jody, a perennial bachelor who takes on the responsibility of matching wits with and emptying the pockets of tenant farmers, mortgage seekers, and general store shoppers. Indeed, Jody's early encounters with the Snopes family, headed up by the reputed barnburner Abe Snopes and his eldest son Flem, fairly crackle with male rivalry, but those early sharp-trading endeavors soon give way to the central competition between the aspiring Flem, who sets his sights on Varner property, and the traveling salesman Ratliff, who prides himself on his ability to turn a neat profit and to collect community gossip, especially about the Snopeses.

From the beginning of that novel, in fact, Ratliff makes shrewd note of Flem's systematic usurpation of his nominal employer Jody Varner as Will's heir apparent, and Ratliff himself comes to see Flem as his archrival in the art of making a deal.[14] Fairly early on, though, the sewing machine agent senses that Flem is far more ruthless than Ratliff is in pursuit of a profit. After nearly being bested in an early scheme to buy fifty goats, Ratliff thinks, "I quit too soon. I went as far as one Snopes will set fire to another Snopes's barn and both Snopeses know it, and that was all right. But I stopped there. I never went on to where that first Snopes will turn around and stomp the fire out so he can sue that second Snopes for the reward and both Snopeses know that too" (97–98). By the end of the novel, Flem has soundly trounced Ratliff by tricking him into buying an abandoned plantation carefully salted with gold and has gained a foothold in the nearby town of Jefferson by buying out Ratliff's interest in a small restaurant. Only Flem, the inhabitants of Frenchman's Bend declare, could have beaten Ratliff at a deal, and by doing so the up-and-coming Snopes effectively removes the sewing machine agent from the field of competition. Ratliff himself admits as much, in a roundabout fashion, when he indignantly declares, "I never made them Snopeses and I never made the folks that cant wait to bare their backsides to them" (355).

Not incidentally, Flem also manages to capture the prize that eludes all the men in Frenchman's Bend, save one, who measure their own masculinity by her worth: the luscious and pregnant Eula Varner, whose father effectively trades her off to Flem to ensure that her unborn child has a name. So powerful is Eula's sexuality that she defines to a great extent the masculinity of the men and boys who swarm around her and test their manhood against one another in competition for her favors.[15] Indeed, she seems to possess the very power to bring their masculinity into being by exciting "the simple male hunger which she blazed into anguish just by being, existing, breathing" (The Town, 117). In many respects, her presence defines the far reaches of masculine dreams of femininity as it emerges in local gossip: "the word, the dream and wish of all male under sun capable of harm—the young who only dreamed yet of the ruins they were still incapable of . . .—the word, with its implications of lost triumphs and defeats of unimaginable splendor—and which best: to have that word, that dream and hope for future, or to have had need to flee that word and dream, for past" (The Hamlet, 164–65).

It is, in fact, something of that elusiveness that defines her worth for the hapless schoolteacher Labove, who is drawn to the little school in Frenchman's Bend by the eleven-year-old Eula, representing for him his own "pagan triumphal prostration before the supreme primal uterus," a prostration that is transformed into humiliation and defeat when the teenage Eula dismisses his violent advances as the inept fumblings of an Ichabod Crane (*The Hamlet*, 126). But the sexual dreams and desires that Eula inspires are fulfilled neither for Labove nor the country swains who later flock around her for a few summers. She does briefly choose Hoake McCarron, who fathers her child, but it is the "cold and froglike" Flem, conniving as always to make a deal, who wins her hand in marriage. Ratliff finds this specific form of success particularly galling in part because of Flem's behind-the-scenes maneuvering to clear the field of competition and in part because Flem himself appears to be nowhere near the equal of Eula herself: "What [Ratliff] . . . felt was outrage at the waste, the useless squandering: at a situation intrinsically and inherently wrong by any economy . . . as though the gods themselves had funneled all the concentrated bright wet-slanted unparadised June onto a dung-heap, breeding pismires" (*The Hamlet*, 176).

Flem's success, coupled with Eula's larger-than-life allure, nonetheless imposes a certain sense of vulnerability upon Ratliff, who feels that Eula is far beyond him: "it would have been like giving me a pipe organ, that never had and never would know any more than how to wind up the second-hand music-box I had just swapped a mail-box for, he thought" (*The Hamlet*, 176). Accordingly, Ratliff's subsequent retreat to what the narrator of *The Hamlet* calls "ungendered peace" is particularly significant for the way that Ratliff sees his own sense of masculinity because sexuality by the end of the nineteenth century and the beginning decades of the twentieth century had become such a crucial part of defining American manhood (216).[16] Historian George Chauncey declares, "Middle class men increasingly conceived of their sexuality—their heterosexuality, or exclusive desire for women—as one of the hallmarks of a real man. It was as if they had decided that no matter how much their gender comportment might be challenged as unmanly, they were normal men because they were heterosexual."[17] E. Anthony Rotundo in *American Manhood* says much the same thing, as does Richard Dyer, who observes quite simply that "sex was seen as perhaps the most important thing in life in fifties America."[18]

Masculine vulnerability, particularly in the area of sexuality, seems to suggest the netherside of the highly competitive world of the Snopes trilogy, which in many respects reminds us that Faulkner himself was heir to a regional tradition of white male honor charged with manhood-threatening competitiveness. Historians of white southern masculinity like Ted Ownby, Edward Ayers, and Elliott Gorn, as well as Bertram Wyatt-Brown, who has written the definitive study of white southern honor, have emphasized that honor depended in part upon the esteem of one's fellows. Hence, self-regard depended upon one's performance in a never-ending cycle of competition.[19] "The glue that held men together," Gorn asserts, "was an intensely competitive status system in which the most prodigious drinker or the strongest arm wrestler, the best tale teller, fiddle player, or log roller, the most daring gambler, original liar, skilled hunter, outrageous swearer, or accurate marksman was accorded respect by the others."[20]

Winning, though, could also mean the possibility of losing, and it was in losing, whether to other men or even to women, that white southern men revealed their vulnerability in a world in which status could shift abruptly and one's very masculinity could be held up to ridicule.[21] If winning marks the rise of Flem Snopes in the Snopes trilogy, losing—as well as the revelation of vulnerability—defines two parallel narratives in The Hamlet—those of Jack Houston, Mink Snopes, and their respective love stories, thereby reminding us, in Chauncey's words, that if "manhood could be achieved, it could also be lost."[22] Jack Houston, the arrogant and well-to-do landowner eventually shot by Flem's besieged and desperately poor cousin Mink, finds himself in a war of sorts with his future wife to maintain his "unbitted" masculine freedom. Marriage means, in Houston's terms, becoming "bitted," relinquishing "that polygamous and bitless masculinity" that he prizes (The Hamlet, 237, 238). It is hardly surprising, then, that Houston's prized stallion, which represents nothing so much as that "bitless masculinity," abruptly kills the wife he loves but has dodged for so long, and Houston himself remains inconsolable after her death. Similarly, Mink, who feels compelled to kill Houston over a dispute of livestock and male honor, finds sexual happiness with his wife but can never reconcile himself to her own past sexual experience. He was, the narrator tells us, raised to believe irrevocably in the value of female virginity, and hence he feels not just cuckolded by the ghosts of his wife's sexual past but feminized by their presence, "as if he and not she had been their prone recipient" (245). That feeling in turn extends to his sense of being under siege at every turn, for Mink lives and breathes by a conviction that there exists both in the land itself and in the surrounding community "a conspiracy to frustrate and outrage his rights as a man and his feeling as a sentient creature" (242).

Most vulnerable of all, though, is the idiot Ike Snopes, enamored of a cow, who becomes the object of a peep show run by his unscrupulous cousin Lump. Reduced to a sideshow for the benefit of the men of Frenchman's Bend, Ike serves as a dirty joke, the negative by which the men who look at him define their own sense of manhood and sexuality. It is significant, I think, that it is Ratliff, already on the losing end of his competition with Flem Snopes, who is outraged by the spectacle and who puts an end to it. For what Ratliff sees when he looks at Ike and his cow is an image, in a sense, of himself, of defeated manhood, of the loser in unceasing male competitions: "it was as though it were himself inside the stall with the cow, himself looking out of the blasted tongueless face at the row of faces watching him who had been given the wordless passions but not the specious words" (*The Hamlet*, 217). So shocking is this revelation that it has a good deal to do, I would argue, with Ratliff's eventual retreat from economic competition with Flem and his resorting, with Gavin Stevens and Chick Mallison in *The Town* and *The Mansion*, to the telling of stories about Flem's economic rise. At the end of *The Hamlet*, we see Ratliff eventually succumbing to Flem's manipulative ruses and to his own greed and buying, against all commonsense, the Old Frenchman place from Flem, who has salted the grounds of the ruined mansion with gold. In his last direct contest with Flem, Ratliff is unmistakably the loser and by implication the lesser man—as duped and bested by Flem Snopes as is Ratliff's temporary partner-in-greed Henry Armistead, who is last seen "spading himself into the waxing twilight with the regularity of a mechanical toy" (*The Hamlet*, 405). So Ratliff himself is perceived, reduced to an object of derision and humor by the community that once valued his gossip and his deal making: "Couldn't no other man have done it. Anybody might have fooled Henry Armistid. But couldn't nobody but Flem Snopes have fooled Ratliff" (*The Hamlet*, 405).

In the second and third volumes of the Snopes trilogy, Ratliff exchanges direct economic competition with Flem for storytelling competition with Gavin Stevens. Urgo has argued that *The Town* focuses on epistemological issues—how people come to know what they know and how they exchange information—but I think it might be more accurate to say that *The Town* and *The Mansion* to a certain degree are about reading Flem Snopes in particular and masculinity in general. Indeed, masculinity seems to be changing before the eyes of Faulkner's storytellers and Snopes-watchers, from early versions of backwoods finagling, bartering, and horse-trading to more subtle and urbane maneuvers in a small-town economy.[23] What preoccupies Ratliff and his fellow narrators of Snopes's rise are Flem's motives—why Flem undertakes the schemes that he does, how he manages to better his situation with each scheme, what he hopes to gain in the end, and ultimately what matter of man he is in his climb out of Frenchman's Bend into twentieth-century Jefferson, Mississippi.

A good deal of their attention, of course, is taken up by the two femmes fatales linked with Flem—Eula Varner Snopes and her daughter Linda Snopes Kohl—who both provide scales of sorts for weighing the masculinity of men around them. As Chick Mallison observes of the townsmen who watch Eula dance with her paramour Manfred De Spain, the men of Jefferson in contrast were "all the other little doomed mean cowardly married and unmarried husbands looking aghast and outraged in order to keep one another from seeing that what they really wanted to do was cry, weep because they were not that brave, each one knowing that even if there was no other man on earth, let alone in that ball room, they still could not have survived, let alone matched or coped with, that splendor, that splendid un-shame" (*The Town*, 66). To Gavin, Eula represents all he yearns for and can never have—a peerless abundance of female sexuality and a wistful notion of himself as a knight errant fighting for her honor—and even Ratliff, who has long sought shelter in "ungendered peace," arranges his parlor in his tiny house as a shrine of sorts to Eula.

In this respect, *The Town* and *The Mansion* make liberal use of certain film noir conventions, not the least of which is the detached and cynical stance of the hard-boiled detective. His is a perspective skeptical of domesticity and both wary of and lured by the indispensable figure of the femme fatale, whose "transgressive sexuality," Robert J. Corber observes in *Homosexuality in Cold War America*, "eventually displaces the crime as the object of the hard-boiled detective's investigation."[24] For, as immersed as Ratliff and Gavin are in the task of charting Flem's rise in Jefferson and speculating on his next move, they are equally drawn to the mesmerizing spectacle of first Eula and then her daughter Linda, who, Ratliff says, "had inherited her maw's fatality to draw four men anyhow to that web, that one strangling hair."[25] To ponder both women—and to test their own masculinity against their lure—preoccupies both men throughout the last two novels of the Snopes trilogy, but it is significant that neither man feels fortified enough to rise to the challenge. Made wary by his own early contests with Flem, Ratliff, for one, is content to remain on the sidelines and observe, and Gavin Stevens, though he feels compelled to indulge in adolescent contests with Eula's lover Manfred De Spain, is far too intimidated by Eula to accept her casual offer of sexual favors. Faced with Eula's direct gaze, "with that blue envelopment like the sea, not questioning nor wait-ing, as the sea itself doesn't need to question or wait but simply be the sea," Gavin feels far too diminished to accept what Eula offers—"too small to hold, compass without one bursting seam all that unslumber, all that chewed anguish of the poet's bitter thumbs which were not just my thumbs but all male Jefferson's or actually all male earth's by proxy, that thumb being all men's fate who had earned or deserved the right to call themselves men" (*The Town*, 81, 80). Gavin's sister and Chick's mother, on the other hand, is far more direct about the nature of Gavin's plight. "You don't marry Semiramis: you just commit some form of suicide for her. Only gentlemen with as little to lose as Mr Flem Snopes can risk Semiramis" (*The Town*, 44–45). If, as David Savran suggests in his book, *Taking It like a Man*, gen-der identities are indeed "based . . . on fantasy, desire, and disavowal," it appears all too apparent that for Gavin and Ratliff, Eula does indeed suggest that curious mixture of "fantasy, desire, and disavowal," the object of yearning and fear, desire and repudiation.[26] So too does Gavin resist any real sexual engagement with Linda Snopes Kohl once she returns a widow, deafened from her time in the Spanish Civil War. His nephew Chick speculates that Gavin's reluctance might be due to the silence in which she is now enshrouded, or perhaps her strange new duck's voice, or perhaps even more to the point her usurpation, as a war veteran in her own right, of the role of the "hero," the role that Gavin himself has always longed to play for her and for her mother.

For the most part, though, Ratliff and Gavin are preoccupied with Snopes-watching, what Gavin calls their "constant Snopes-fear and dread, or you might say, Snopes-dodging" (*The Mansion*, 595). It is, as Chick Mallison says, "like a game, a contest or even a battle, a war, that Snopeses had to be watched constantly like an invasion of snakes or wildcats and that uncle Gavin and Ratliff were doing it or trying to because nobody else in Jefferson seemed to recognise the danger" (*The Town*, 94). Their conversations and exchanges are certainly comic at times, but there is something distinctly unsettling in the strong resemblance that Snopes-watching bears to the 1950s preoccupation with surveillance over communists, sexuality, and the nuclear family. This was the period, after all, when "the national agenda," as David Savran points out, was dominated by "the baiting and brutaliza-tion of 'Communists and queers.'" For "when the architects and administrators of the Cold War turned their attention to policing the American body politic,"

Savran notes, "they aimed precisely at Communists and homosexuals in the conviction that both groups were plotting to undermine and destroy the American
way of life."[27] Curiously enough, Faulkner makes oblique reference to this national
preoccupation in *The Mansion* in a brief episode about a "gray" FBI agent making
inquiries into Linda Snopes Kohl's reputed Communist background (549). Loyal
to Linda, Gavin refuses to respond to the agent, but he does ponder telling the FBI
that Flem Snopes has a Communist Party card.

Ratliff and Gavin's surveillance of Flem in particular results in markedly different assessments of his motives, and Ratliff for one notes with a certain satisfaction
that Gavin's preoccupation with Flem's "Rapacity . . . Greed. Money" makes Gavin
overlook other motives—like the quest for "respectability" that Ratliff sees driving
Snopes toward the end (*The Town*, 134). But what emerges from their collective
portrait of Flem Snopes is a picture of a humorless, ruthless, faceless driven man
whose sole criterion and interest is the making of money for its own sake rather
than for the luxury goods it can possibly buy. Flem himself remains remarkably
simple in his needs, retaining his "snap-on-behind bow tie" to the end and exchanging only his "little cloth cap" for a "broad black felt kind which country
preachers and politicians wore" (*The Town*, 121–22, 122). He is the quintessential
self-made man, defining himself by the criterion of financial success and allied
with the sort of entrepreneurial masculinity that had become a commonplace by
the late nineteenth century. It is only later, Ratliff maintains—and Faulkner confirmed in interviews—that Flem becomes ensnared by the need for respectability
and hence the imperative of removing embarrassing relatives like the enterpris-
ing pornographer Montgomery Ward Snopes from the environs of Jefferson. As
Faulkner himself noted at the University of Virginia, "to gain what he wanted,
he had to assume all sorts of things that had never occurred to him in his wildest
dreams that he would have to. Like respectability, for instance. That he still clung
to his undeviating aim, but he had to take on all sorts of what he considered fool-
ishness and extra baggage in order to stick to it."[28] Hence Flem eventually acquires
the De Spain family home and transforms it into a southern mansion, complete
with oversized pillars, but to the end acquiring consumer goods seems something
of a distraction to him, as does the existence of a family. "But it was jest the house
that was altered and transmogrified and symbolised," V. K. Ratliff tells us: not
him" (*The Mansion*, 470). Flem was content, he adds, with cosmetic changes to the
house's exterior, but the interior—and Flem himself, for that matter—remained

the same as it was the day Flem bought the house from De Spain, save for "a little wood ledge, not even painted, nailed to the front of that hand-carved hand-painted Mount Vernon mantelpiece at the exact height for Flem to prop his feet on it" (*The Mansion*, 471).

By the time Flem has become the leading banker of the town, he has also become something of an anachronism, a dinosaur from the age of individualism and entrepreneurship, a self-made and relatively ascetic money man in a period of emerging consumerism and domesticity "who had begun life as a nihilist," Chick Mallison observes, "and then softened into a mere anarchist and now was not only a conservative but a tory too: a pillar, rock-fixed, of things as they are" (*The Mansion*, 530). As the narratives of *The Town* and *The Mansion* progress, in fact, Flem emerges as something like a negative form of masculinity against which to define the postwar model of masculinity with which Gavin Stevens and V. K. Ratliff come to be implicitly allied. Faulkner himself, as biographers like Judith Wittenberg have acutely observed, had distinctly Flemlike qualities—including a never-ending preoccupation with making money, especially during the writing of *The Hamlet*.[29] Moreover, he had a certain admiration for Flem's ruthlessness and drive for mastery, as Urgo has argued and as Faulkner himself acknowledged.[30] But Faulkner was also quite critical of the cult of success and argued in his 1955 National Book Award speech that maybe "one of the things wrong with our country is success." He added: "Perhaps what we need is a dedicated handful of pioneer-martyrs who, between success and humility, are capable of choosing the second one."[31]

Perhaps more to the point, it is striking that characters in *The Town* and *The Mansion* repeatedly draw attention to Flem's impotence—first Eula, then obliquely Flem's cousin Montgomery Ward Snopes, and finally Gavin Stevens—with no small satisfaction, I might add. To dwell on Flem's impotence in the 1950s, when impotence was a topic of considerable cultural concern, as Steven Cohan has argued in his study of masculinity and the decade's movies, is to situate Flem as masculinity's other, the negative that helps determine the shape and boundaries of the norm.[32] Since the late nineteenth century, defenders of bourgeois society had traditionally tended to define males on the margins—vagrants and homosexuals among them—as deficient in manliness. In the 1950s, when mass-circulation magazines frequently gave voice to popular anxieties about "The Decline of the American Male," no surer way existed to question an individual's manliness than through the accusation of impotence.[33] It was, after all, a decade replete with the "trappings of gender failure," in Michael Kimmel's words—when men were pronounced failures by virtue of being homosexuals, juvenile delinquents, or Communists.[34] To stress the sexual failure of the highly successful Flem Snopes, then, was to bring attention to the "disavowals," as Judith Butler pronounces them, through which Ratliff and Gavin stressed Flem's utter otherness and defined their own notions of manhood.[35]

Indeed, through their objectification and othering of Flem, oddly prescient of the sort of "spectacularized" objectification of men Paul Smith sees as so typical of late twentieth-century American films, Ratliff and Gavin assert their own sense of masculinity as the norm.[36] That masculinity, strangely enough, seems associated with the very "respectability" for which Faulkner expresses so much contempt in his interviews and that Gavin Stevens himself denounces as "that damned female instinct for uxorious and rigid respectability which is the backbone of any culture not yet decadent, which remains strong and undecadent only so long as it still produces an incorrigible unreconstructable with the temerity to assail and affront and deny it" (The Town, 161). It was a respectability that Faulkner himself also darkly associated with consumer products and advertising, and that respectability in turn evokes a form of masculinity—cooperative, domesticated, woman-allied, consumer-oriented—emerging as the dominant form in the 1950s, when definitions of white masculinity appeared to reorganize themselves to become better suited to a corporate age valuing subordination, consumerism, and cooperation, values of Whyte's Organization Man, over the competitiveness and individualism of an earlier entrepreneurial masculinity.[37] This was a model of masculinity, Paul Corber argues, that focused on the virtues of domesticity and even discouraged the sort of aggressiveness earlier associated with male competitiveness.[38] Indeed, one of the most striking features of the Man in the Gray Flannel Suit seen as so representative of the 1950s was how advertising directed at this figure assumed his implicit feminization—linked as he was with the feminine sphere of shopping and consumption and with submission to the hierarchies of corporate structure.[39]

From the perspective of a domesticated masculinity that is attuned to the needs of the organization, then, a competitive, money-driven individualist like Flem Snopes, despite his tentative overtures toward respectability, does appear to be something of a dinosaur. The narrator of The Mansion tells us that at life's end, Flem "had no auspices either: fraternal, civic, nor military: only finance; not an economy—cotton or cattle or anything else which Yoknapatawpha County and Mississippi were established on and kept running by, but belonging simply to Money" (706). In contrast, by the end of the Snopes trilogy, Gavin and Ratliff have both exchanged economic competition for storytelling rivalry, more content with their surveillance of Flem than with direct competitive engagement. Perhaps even more striking is their happy association with the world of postwar consumerism. By the end of *The Mansion*, Ratliff has become a radio company agent, and his truck with its little imitation house now sports a radio and a demonstrator sewing machine, and "two years more and the miniature house would have a miniature TV stalk on top of it" (618). Ratliff himself has also become the proud owner of a designer tie from New York City that he displays in a glass case in the parlor of his immaculately kept little house. As for Gavin Stevens, he has married into money and now resides on an old cotton plantation renovated to look like a Long Island horse farm. The goddess of female sexuality for which they both have yearned has been reduced to a subdivision that bears her name—Eula Acres, where ex-GIs with their arms full of children wait impatiently for the next bungalow to open up for sale.

In this new world of consumerism—of installment plans and refrigerators full of canned beers—Faulkner himself had become something of a commodity, his reputation revived as a powerful symbol of American individualism to serve quite effectively as a weapon in the cultural skirmishes of the cold war. "Like Jackson Pollock and the abstract expressionists," Lawrence Schwartz tells us, "Faulkner became universalized as an emblem of the freedom of the individual under capitalism, as a chronicler of the plight of man in the modern world. Faulkner was seen to exemplify the same values that Western intellectuals saw in capitalism which made it morally superior to communism."[40] In the aftermath of World War II, as Urgo reminds us, Faulkner's body of work was "revived and reorganized by literary critics to serve the interests of the cultural Cold War abroad and cultural hegemony at home."[41] This was a time, after all, when Faulkner did extensive traveling for the State Department as a representative of U.S. capitalism and culture, who seemingly exemplified the virtues of individualism arrayed against communism. It was also a time, significantly enough, when he increasingly feared that he had lost his artistic mastery, written himself out, just as he had come increasingly to question, as Noel Polk and Karl Zender have suggested, so many of his assumptions about the privileges of white male authority.[42] Zender even goes so far as to say, "A tragedy at the heart of Faulkner's fiction—at the heart, one is tempted to say, of his anger—is the suspicion that all (male) development is a form of psychic imperialism, a co-optation of some 'other' (generational, sexual, racial) in the service of the self."[43] In this respect, the refrain "the pore sons of bitches" that Ratliff and Gavin repeat toward the end of *The Mansion* carries a certain personal and powerful resonance—as much Faulkner's lamentation for himself toward the end of his life as for the diminished expectations his fictional men faced in a newly emerging corporate age valuing group cooperation over individual mastery.[44] As if to underscore those waning powers, Urgo shrewdly observes, Faulkner found himself struggling in the copyediting stages of the publication of *The Mansion* for control of the narrative. Two powerful editors at Random House, Albert Erskine, and a young academician named James B. Meriwether, were brought in to ensure that at least a measure of consistency in facts and names would help forge the links between the last volume of the Snopes trilogy and its predecessors. That struggle ironically replicates the economic competition lying at the heart of *The Hamlet* and the storytelling competition driving the narratives of *The Town* and *The Mansion*.[45]

Still, a footnote of sorts is left by the character of Mink Snopes, who represents in many ways an even older form of masculinity than Flem's entrepreneurial and money-hungry individualism. By *The Mansion*, Mink is something of a frontiersman cast adrift in postwar America, defined by a powerful sense of white male southern honor and an unrelenting feeling of being under constant siege by unknowable and impersonal forces determined to test his manhood at every step. That his particular version of white southern manhood is outmoded is underscored by his sad and comical quest, upon his release from prison after decades of confinement, for a weapon with which to shoot Flem Snopes for failing to come to his rescue thirty-eight years before. In a new postwar landscape defined by money, which he decidedly lacks, and by overabundant consumer goods, like soda pop, tempting him, Mink manages to buy a gun—and a poor one at that—with the greatest of difficulty and after considerable travail. The time for avenging insults to male honor, those difficulties implicitly suggest, is definitely past, but Mink nevertheless manages to fulfill his mission and shoot Flem. That he is able to do so with the behind-the-scenes help of Flem's daughter Linda, who signs the petition for Mink's release from prison and eventually shows him the way out of the Snopes house after the shooting, says a good deal about Mink's flinty integrity and single-mindedness but also suggests that the help, even direction, of a woman is essential to his success. And if we have any doubt that Mink's shooting of Flem is something like a last hurrah of frontier masculinity long since outmoded by a world brimming over with consumer products designed to make the domestic sphere all the more alluring, we have only to remember that Linda purchases a British Jaguar in anticipation of Flem's death—and leaves Jefferson with a flourish in the most conspicuous of consumer goods, as though to underscore for good measure her own sense of agency made possible by the world of money and her freedom from the romanticized scenarios of male sexual desire and competitiveness.

NOTES

1. Joseph Urgo rightly notes that the Snopes saga represented "the one fictional project that occupied Faulkner's attention and sustained his creative interests throughout his career" (*Faulkner's Apocrypha: A Fable, Snopes, and the Spirit of Human Rebellion* [Jackson: University of Mississippi Press, 1989], 168).

2. Quoted in *Faulkner in the University: Class Conferences at the University of Virginia, 1957–1958*, ed. Frederick L. Gwynn and Joseph Blotner (Charlottesville: University of Virginia Press, 1959), 33.

3. William Faulkner, *The Town*, in *Novels, 1957–1962* (New York: Library of America, 1999), 36. This work is cited parenthetically by page number throughout the chapter.

4. See Steven Cohan's discussion of *Them!* in *Masked Men: Masculinity and the Movies in the Fifties* (Bloomington: Indiana University Press, 1997), 130–31. See also Michael Kimmel, *Manhood in America: A Cultural History* (New York: Free Press, 1996), 242.

5. See William H. Whyte, *The Organization Man* (New York: Simon and Schuster, 1956); C. Wright Mills, *White Collar: The American Middle Classes* (New York: Oxford University Press, 1951); and Sloan Wilson, *The Man in the Gray Flannel Suit* (New York: Simon and Schuster, 1955). For the context of these works of and in the 1950s, see Barbara Ehrenreich, *The Hearts of Men: American Dreams and the Flight from Commitment* (New York: Anchor-Doubleday, 1983); and Elaine Tyler May, *Homeward Bound: American Families in the Cold War Era* (New York: Basic Books, 1988). See as well Cohan's discussion of masculinity in 1950s films and Robert J. Corber, *Homosexuality in Cold War America: Resistance and the Crisis of Masculinity* (Durham, NC: Duke University Press, 1997).

6. See Cohan, *Masked Men*, xvi.

7. Quoted in Gwynn and Blotner, *Faulkner in the University*, 33 and 32.

8. Historians like Clyde Griffen have explicitly criticized the tendency to see crises in masculinity in one historical period after another. See, e.g., Griffen's "Reconstructing Masculinity from the Evangelical Revival to the Waning of Progressivism: A Speculative Synthesis," in *Meanings for Manhood: Constructions of Masculinity in Victorian America*, ed. Mark C. Carnes and Clyde Griffen (Chicago: University of Chicago Press, 1990), 183–84. Still, a strong case for widespread anxiety about white masculinity after World War II with the rise of corporate and consumer culture is made by Kimmel, *Manhood*, 237; Cohan, *Masked Men*, x–xi; and Corber, *Homosexuality*.

9. See, in general, Elliott Gorn's "'Gouge and Bite, Pull Hair and Scratch': The Social Significance of Fighting in the Southern Backcountry," *American Historical Review* 90 (1985): 18–43. See also Bertram Wyatt-Brown's *Southern Honor: Ethics and Behavior in the Old South* (New York: Oxford University Press, 1983); and Kenneth Greenberg, *Honor and Slavery: Lies, Duels, Noses, Masks, Dressing as a Woman, Gifts, Strangers, Humanitarianism, Death, Rebellions, the Proslavery Argument, Baseball, Hunting, and Gambling in the Old South* (Princeton, NJ: Princeton University Press, 1966). Noel Polk talks about the sexual and masculine vulnerability defining the men of Frenchman's Bend and of Jefferson in their encounters with Eula Varner's larger-than-life sexuality in his essay "Testing Masculinity in the Snopes Trilogy," *Faulkner Journal* 16 (2000/2001): 11–13.

10. Susan Faludi makes an interesting case for a loss of mastery suffered by contemporary American men in *Stiffed: The Betrayal of the American Man* (New York: William Morrow, 1999).

11. See, in general, Panthea Reid Broughton, "Masculinity and Menfolk in *The Hamlet*," special issue on William Faulkner, ed. James B. Meriwether, *Mississippi Quarterly* 22 (1969): 181–89; Polk, "Testing Masculinity in the Snopes Trilogy," 3–22; Noel Polk, "Around, Behind, Above, Below Men: Ratliff's Buggies and the Homosocial in Yoknapatawpha," in *Haunted Bodies: Gender and Southern Texts,* ed. Anne Goodwyn Jones and Susan V. Donaldson (Charlottesville: University of Virginia Press, 1997), 343–66; Noel Polk, *Children of the Dark House: Text and Context in Faulkner* (Jackson: University Press of Mississippi, 1996); Gary Lee Stonum, *Faulkner's Career: An Internal Literary History* (Ithaca, NY: Cornell University Press; and Urgo, *Faulkner's Apocrypha,* 171–81.

12. Urgo, *Faulkner's Apocrypha,* 172.

13. William Faulkner, *The Hamlet: The Corrected Text* (New York: Random-Vintage International, 1990), 5–6. This work is cited parenthetically by page number throughout the chapter.

14. Noel Polk has a provocative and fascinating reading of this rivalry in "Around, Behind," 343–66.

15. George Chauncey notes that "collective sexualization and objectification of women" served as one of the "rituals" establishing manhood for nineteenth-century working men in particular. See his *Gay New York: Gender, Urban Culture, and the Making of the Gay Male World, 1890–1940* (New York: Basic, 1994), 81.

16. See Kimmel, *Manhood,* 100.

17. Chauncey, *Gay New York,* 117.

18. E. Anthony Rotundo, *Manhood in America: Transformations in Masculinity from the Revolution to the Modern Era* (New York: Basic, 1993), 276. Richard Dyer is quoted in Cohan, *Masked Men,* xiv.

19. See, in general, Edward L. Ayers, *Vengeance and Justice: Crime and Punishment in the Nineteenth-Century American South* (New York: Oxford University Press, 1984); Greenberg, *Honor and Slavery;* Ted Ownby, *Subduing Satan: Religion, Recreation, and Manhood in the Rural South, 1865–1920* (Chapel Hill: University of North Carolina Press, 1990); and, in particular, Gorn, "Gouge and Bite," 18–43. See also Wyatt-Brown, *Southern Honor;* and Rhys Isaac, *The Transformation of Virginia, 1740–1790* (Chapel Hill: Pub. for the Institute of Early American History and Culture by the University of North Carolina Press, 1982).

20. Gorn, "Gouge and Bite," 42.

21. Ownby, *Subduing Satan,* 13.

22. Chauncey, *Gay New York,* 80.

23. Urgo, *Faulkner's Apocrypha*, 184.

24. Corber, *Homosexuality*, 16.

25. William Faulkner, *The Mansion*, in *Novels, 1957–1962* (New York: Library of America, 1999), 484. This work is cited parenthetically by page number throughout the chapter.

26. David Savran, *Taking It like a Man: White Masculinity, Masochism, and Contemporary American Culture* (Princeton, NJ: Princeton University Press, 1998), 10.

27. David Savran, *Communists, Cowboys, and Queers: The Politics of Masculinity in the Work of Arthur Miller and Tennessee Williams* (Minneapolis: University of Minnesota Press, 1992), 5, 4.

28. Quoted in Gwynn and Blotner, *Faulkner in the University*, 119.

29. Judith Wittenberg, *Faulkner: The Transfiguration of Biography* (Lincoln: University of Nebraska Press, 1979), 181.

30. Urgo, *Faulkner's Apocrypha*, 162.

31. Quoted in Joseph Blotner, *Faulkner: A Biography*, 2 vols. (New York: Random House, 1974), 2:1525.

32. Cohan, *Masked Men*, 29. Judith Butler makes a similar argument, albeit a much more complicated one, in "Melancholy Gender/Refused Identification," in *Constructing Masculinity*, ed. Maurice Berger, Brian Wallis, and Simon Watson (New York: Routledge, 1995): "If a man becomes heterosexual through the repudiation of the feminine, then where does that repudiation live except in an identification that his heterosexual career seeks to deny? Indeed, the desire for the feminine is marked by that repudiation: he wants the woman he could never be; indeed, he would not be caught dead being her" (26).

33. Angus McLaren, *The Trials of Masculinity: Policing Sexual Boundaries, 1870–1930* (Chicago: University of Chicago Press, 1997), 35; Cohan, *Masked Men*, 6.

34. Kimmel, *Manhood*, 237.

35. Butler, "Melancholy," 33.

36. See in general Paul Smith, "Eastwood Bound," in Berger, Willis, and Watson, *Constructing Masculinity*, 77–97.

37. Gwynn and Blotner, *Faulkner in the University*, 32; Corber, *Homosexuality*, 6.

38. Corber, *Homosexuality*, 5–6.

39. Cohan, *Masked Men*, 19.

40. Lawrence H. Schwartz, *Creating Faulkner's Reputation: The Politics of Modern Literary Criticism* (Knoxville: University of Tennessee Press, 1988), 4.

41. Urgo, *Faulkner's Apocrypha*, 9.

42. Polk, *Children of the Dark House*, 162.

43. Karl F. Zender, *Faulkner and the Politics of Reading* (Baton Rouge: Louisiana State University Press, 2002), 30.

44. Joseph Urgo observes, "'The poor sons of bitches' is a signal throughout *The Mansion* for a sense of shared oppression or a common foe" (*Faulkner's Apocrypha*, 202).

45. Ibid., 195–96. See also Blotner, *Faulkner*, 2:1729–30, 1734–35.

Where Has the Free Bird Flown?

Lynyrd Skynyrd and White Southern Manhood

BARBARA CHING

When Neil Young sang "Southern Man" (1970) and "Alabama" (1971), the songs that provoked Lynyrd Skynyrd's "Sweet Home Alabama" (1974), he provided the most obvious in what was (and would be) a host of insults and boasts from the Los Angeles–based country rockers who dominated California country rock music in the late 1960s and early 1970s.[1] According to Young, *After the Gold Rush*, the album featuring "Southern Man," expressed "the spirit of Topanga Canyon," the L.A. exurb where he and many others in the country rock scene settled. While "Southern Man" evoked an antebellum world of white male privilege, Young's first-person perspective and penchant for social commentary gave the song a contemporary twist. The singer testified to hearing bullwhips and screams.[2] "Alabama" clearly expressed Young's view of the South as a cradle of regression held back by the simpleminded corruption of the white man. In this folksy lament, Young takes the role of an enlightened guide, speaking of his desire to befriend the backward, Wallace-governed state. Indeed, he believes he speaks for the majority; the last verse criticizes the state's resistance to change and asserts that "the rest of the union" is ready and willing to help.

With similar assurance about their roles as benevolent leaders, Crosby, Stills, Nash, and Young (Neil again) sang, "We are stardust, We are golden," in Joni Mitchell's "Woodstock" (1970), summing up not only this musical enclave's vision of itself but also the self-suspended halo that supposedly enlightened the (white) men of the counterculture. Jackson Browne, a David Crosby discovery, released "Red Neck Friend" (1973), purportedly a song about his unruly penis. Famed for his sensitive southern California crooning, he cast the organ of his manhood as a white male southerner, the enemy of all the trendy mellowness he otherwise embodied. (Eagles cofounder Glenn Frey sang harmony.) Barney Hoskyns, the best chronicler of the L.A. scene, defined *mellow* as a "combination of bland tunefulness and harrowing introspection" (213); he also notes that "mellow" conveyed "post-hippie" masculinity—whether in Neil Young's "wavering falsetto" (204) or Jackson Browne's WASPy photo on the cover of *The Pretender* (280).[3] No wonder Skynyrd's "When You Got Good Friends" concluded that Los Angeles "never cared for me."[4]

If California was cool, these southerners were steaming. The difference in emotional temperature reveals much about what the counterculture and its aftermath did to shape contemporary perceptions of the white southern man. By the time "Sweet Home Alabama" filled the airwaves, the ethos of California country rock had prepared the rock establishment and hipster wannabes to hear Skynyrd as the epitome of white southern manhood, an unreconstructedly macho and fascinating barrier to progress. Whereas Ted Ownby has convincingly defined and described the masculinity of southern rock by contrasting its themes to those of country music,[5] I focus on its contrast with California's mellow country-inflected rock of the 1970s, particularly the Eagles' music. This contrast allows the defeat and anger of the marginalized southern male to be heard far more clearly than Ownby's approach, which emphasizes southern rock's rebellion against the southern ideology of evangelical domesticity. By comparing the careers, reception, and music of Lynyrd Skynyrd to those of the Eagles, I show how California-based "free birds" triumph in their projection of masculinity, while Lynyrd Skynyrd still represents the struggle over the role and meaning of white southern manhood.[6] The Eagles, although they often thematically allied themselves to life in California's fast lanes, also successfully named themselves after an American national symbol.[7] Every song an anthem could have been their motto. Grace Lichtenstein praises the Eagles for just this reason: *Hotel California*, she says, "is about modern America. *Desperado* . . . is about America both past and present."[8] In effect, the Eagles became an enormously popular band without regional connotation to limit or qualify that popularity. Lynyrd Skynyrd, in contrast, remained marked: they were southerners first and foremost (although New Jersey–born Ed King, who played guitar in the band between 1973 and 1975, came from the L.A. psychedelic band Strawberry Alarm Clark). The Eagles were country rock, and their country was America; Skynyrd was southern rock in a country ruled by the Eagles.[9]

Skynyrd's detractors unflinchingly resorted to ad southern hominem attacks to frame their opinions. In a review of Skynyrd's 1976 *Gimme Back My Bullets*, Lester Bangs called the group "crude thunderstomper hillbillies whose market value rested primarily on the fact that they could play their instruments about like they could plant their fists in your teeth."[10] That same year, Mitch Glazer's *Crawdaddy* article on the group emphasized not the music but "One Mo' Brawl from the Road," a play on Skynyrd's 1976 *One More from the Road*.[11] A *Creem* profile by Jaan Uhelszki also called attention to redneck stereotypes of drunken violence and hedonism with the title "Lynyrd Skynyrd: Fifths and Fists for the Common Man" (1976). Self-consciously female and Yankee, she claims she expects guitarist Gary Rossington to tell her "some juicy tales of nigger skinnings."[12] Even after the 1977 plane crash that killed Skynyrd leader Ronnie Van Zant and two other band members, Warren Zevon implicitly answered the question of "Free Bird"—"If I leave here tomorrow, would you still remember me?"—with a trite satire on southern incestuousness and squalor. The chorus of his "Play It All Night Long" (1980) had Lynyrd Skynyrd providing the soundtrack to this bathos: "Sweet Home Alabama / Play that dead band's song" it began. Jackson Browne sang harmony.

Even praise for the band cast Skynyrd as savage and regressive. Al Kooper, the band's first producer and a rock star in his own right, reported that a friend who loved the band thought Kooper mishandled them by letting them dress in twentieth-century garb: "they should come out with just loincloths on and their guitars should be shaped like clubs."[13] In a quandary over the band's relation to George Wallace, Robert Christgau (who calls himself "the dean of American rock critics") confessed in the *Village Voice* that he "love[d] Lynyrd Skynyrd, a band that makes music so unpretentious it tempts me to give up subordinate clauses." As a New Yorker, he somehow felt "obliged to come to terms with [Skynyrd's] Southernness," but he certainly didn't expect the southern man to approach political issues with "values that are analytic, modern, Northern."[14] In *Stranded*, in which Greil Marcus asks a host of rock critics to name the album that they would take with them to a desert island, everyone can live without Skynyrd, while several members of the L.A. country rock coterie get cast away with Marcus's select group of rock crit intellectuals such as Lichtenstein. Nevertheless, in his appendix, Marcus praises the 1977 album *Street Survivors* in language that again emphasizes savagery: "the guitars [are] striking fire and drawing blood" (278). Everywhere, one sees the trademark triple guitar virtuosity christened the "guitar army."

Of course, the band lent credence to such descriptions. Witnesses and police reports attest to their brawling, although any rock fan can name other bands that engaged in similar displays of machismo.[15] On their first two album covers, the letters in the group's name were drawn to look like bones. Al Kooper takes credit for the image, saying it seemed appropriate "because they got into fights all the time" (181). Their publicity photos and album covers displayed sullen and grungy band members in kudzu-choked landscapes.[16] On the back cover of *Nuthin' Fancy* (1975), pianist Billy Powell makes an obscene gesture (at the camera? at fans devoted enough to buy the record?). The huge Confederate flag they used as backdrop to their live performances reinforced their redneck image.[17] The mock-didactic title of their first album, *Lynyrd Skynyrd (Pronounced Leh-nerd Skin-nerd)* suggested that the band came from a South so deep that even the language was incomprehensible (1973); *Second Helping*, the next year's album (which contained "Sweet Home Alabama") seemed to offer southern hospitality, while the third release, *Nuthin' Fancy* used dialect to signal deference and diffidence to rock's standards of glamour. "Gimme Back My Bullets" (1976) played on their rowdy image but also on the violent lingo of success; the title refers to the *Billboard* top 40 chart symbolism, where songs marked with a "bullet" indicated a quick rise to the top. A record painted as a practice target shot full of holes adorns the cover of *The Eagles Greatest Hits, Volume 2* (1982). In other words, bullets lead to hits—whether they are called "Peaceful Easy Feeling" or "Saturday Night Special" (a 1975 single about handguns).[18]

In fact, California country rock and Skynyrd's southern rock shared several significant traits. Both were male-dominated, and both were hybrids of country and rock.[19] As Kooper put it, all of contemporary country music "is founded on" either Skynyrd's *Second Helping* or the Eagles' *Hotel California* (187–88).[20] The Byrds became the first rock band to play on the Grand Ole Opry stage thanks to *Sweetheart of the Rodeo*, their 1968 album stuffed with classic country covers and Gram Parsons originals. Throughout his nearly forty-year career, Neil Young has played both country and rock. He outwailed Don Gibson when he included the country star's "Oh Lonesome Me" on *After the Gold Rush*. "Are You Ready for the Country?" he asked in 1972; in 1976 country superstar Waylon Jennings put his version of the song in the country chart's top ten. The early Eagles anthologized southern California's country rocking techniques with their lovely vocal harmonies, acoustic bravado (including the banjo and steel guitar), and frequent use of a relaxed mid tempo. But unlike the hardest country singers, the Eagles communicated no redneck shame or defensive pride. They never headed south thematically, preferring a romanticized alienation best expressed in the concept album *Desperado*, which conflated the band with long gone Wild West outlaws (1973). As Christgau put it in his critique of their first album, "the Eagles' hip country music excises precisely what it is deepest and most gripping about country music—it's adult working class pain" (268). They embodied "the ultimate in California dreaming," he concluded (269). Thus "Take It Easy," a Jackson Browne / Glenn Frey collaboration, was their first single and perpetual signature tune.

Paradoxically, Skynyrd *sounded* more rock in spite of growing up with the kind of working-class pain Christgau misses in the Eagles.[21] With three guitars alternating lead *and* a Jerry Lee Lewis–style pumping piano, Eagles-esque lavish harmony would have been an effete affectation (although backup singers, three women called the "Honkettes," were later added to the band). In typical rock production style, Van Zant's vocals were seldom foregrounded in the studio mix; in contrast, country songs and California country rock were usually engineered to allow the vocal track to predominate. You never heard a steel guitar or a banjo on a Skynyrd record, either.[22] Still, their "Gimme Three Steps" tells the story of an ignoble honky-tonk contretemps over one Linda Lou, and throughout their career, they alluded to their ties to country music. In "Railroad Song," on *Nuthin' Fancy*, the singer praises rock and roll while promising "to ride this train . . . until I find out what Jimmie Rodgers and the Hag was all about" (King–Van Zant). " I'm a Country Boy" makes a predictable contrast between Dixie and New York City (Collins–Van Zant). *One More from the Road* had a cover of Jimmie Rodgers's "T for Texas"; *Street Survivors* featured "Honky Tonk Night Time Man," by Ronnie's hero Merle Haggard (Ballinger 93). "Jacksonville Kid," a *Street Survivors* outtake, uses Haggard's melody to support Ronnie's autobiographical musings. But unlike the Eagles and the rest of country rock California, Skynyrd sang the blues, too, an important distinction that I return to in the end.

Most importantly, Skynyrd and the country rockers shared a fascination with flight imagery. Flight is the defining trope of country rock, with its cosmic cowboys, grievous angels, flying burrito brothers, flying machines, and eagles. Los Angeles, the home of this sound, is the City of Angels, and, as Joni Mitchell put it in "Free Man in Paris" (1974), the home of the "star-making machinery behind the popular song" (250). The Byrds introduced the orthographic eccentricity of the *y* as well as the flight theme, used not only in nomenclature but also in song.

Skynyrd is ostensibly more down to earth, but the name reaches for the *sky* with similar orthographic games. The band tells a story that, as long-haired students at Robert E. Lee High in Jacksonville, Ronnie Van Zant, Gary Rossington, and original drummer Bob Burns were frequently reported to school authorities by gym teacher Leonard Skinner. After numerous suspensions, they simply dropped out of school to pursue their music. Although the band called themselves many names, their hometown audience gave them such a good response when they introduced themselves as "Leonard Skinner" that they decided to stick with it, changing the spelling slightly to avoid further trouble with the coach.[23] The choice of the *y* nevertheless resonates with country rock, since the band could just as easily have deformed the coach's name with many other letters. The boys in the band were casting their lot with the counterculture, not with the rules of Robert E. Lee. When Crosby, Stills, Nash, and Young sang David Crosby's "Almost Cut My Hair," they congratulated themselves on their fortitude in the face of persecution; by resisting the pressure to visit the barber, long-haired white men let their "freak flag fly" (1970). Strangely, outside of Robert E. Lee High, the band's hair was tantamount to flying the Confederate flag. In the words of Diane Roberts, "Skynyrd had the kind of long hair that should have been against the law"; long hair looked sexy on Dylan, Jagger, and Jim Morrison, she claims, but "trashy" on the boys from Jacksonville. "Their hair was an outer manifestation of their Rebel cap–cherishing, gun-fascinated inner selves."[24]

Flight represented not only motion through the sky or solar system but also the counterculture's supposed transcendence of the drab demands of middle America. Country music always has had its responsibility-free, roving boozers; in rock and roll, drugs offered the most thrilling experience of this escape. Rather than the down-and-out ramblers portrayed by traditional country stars, California country rockers got high. "See how high she flies," sang the Eagles of "Witchy Woman," the enticing heroin-empowered heroine on their 1972 debut album (Henley-Leadon). In the drug-induced vision of "After the Gold Rush," Young sings about "flying mother nature's silver seed" to the sun. After such trips, the workaday world looked even worse—at least that's what the Byrds sang in "Eight Miles High" (Clark-McGuinn 1966). The singer in Jackson Browne's "The Road and the Sky" prefers gliding in the spot where the "road and the sky collide" to working for a living. His personal pleasure acquires universal significance when apocalyptic rain engulfs the planet. It might be heaven or hell, he speculates, but his jaunty tone suggests that he considers *himself* saved (1974; Don Henley of the Eagles sings harmony). Most blatantly, the Eagles' "Earlybird" contrasts the poor fools scrabbling around for worms with the Eagles' ascendance to country rock power. "High up on his own, the eagle flies alone and he is free" (Leadon-Meisner 1972). We're even better than stardust and golden, they seemed to be saying. And then there's "Free Bird"; in concert, when Ronnie Van Zant asked the crowd what song they wanted to hear, that was always the answer. My favorite, "Call Me the Breeze" (J. J. Cale 1971, covered on Lynyrd Skynyrd's 1974 *Second Helping*), also evokes flight.

The Eagles finally recognized the laws of gravity but sang as if they were somehow exempt. In "On the Border," the singer refuses to hear about "law and order," concluding the chorus by claiming to work Christlike miracles—changing "water to wine" (Henley-Leadon-Frey). Their 1976 masterpieces in this genre, "Life in the Fast Lane" and especially "Hotel California," bespeak a jaded experience with druggy excess but also a mastery over it, as if they were giving flying lessons. The first verse and chorus of "Life in the Fast Lane" introduce a pair of doomed hedonists cruising down the freeway (Walsh-Henley-Frey). Then instructor Henley checks in with his pupils: "Are you with me so far?" The much more ambiguous "Hotel California" preaches in apocalyptic tones, wondering, like Jackson Browne, whether Golden State hedonism is heaven or hell. The "feast" at the end of the "desert highway" turns out to be a "beast" that no knife can kill. Far from "Sweet Home Alabama," the luxurious hotel turns into a prison where you can always check out "but you can never leave" (Felder-Henley-Frey).[25] The Eagles themselves, though, seemed to simply leave the runway behind.[26] In fact, they left country rock for rock pure and simple. The title track and opening cut of their next album, *The Long Run*, coincidentally released the day of the Skynyrd plane crash (October 20, 1979), positioned the Eagles as survivors. It's a love song, but it also speaks of quitting the "high time" in favor of going the distance (Henley-Frey). The last song, "The Sad Café," mourns the early days of the country rock fraternity. The Eagles then disbanded, but fourteen years later, when they reunited for a lucrative tour, they had clearly broken with the mellow. In "Get Over It," one of the new songs written for the occasion, Henley snarls to a nation of complainers, "I'd like to find your inner child and kick its little ass" (Henley-Frey). Still, they continued to crow about their supernatural powers by labeling the tour "Hell Freezes Over."

The free bird's flights conferred no such distinction. Instead, Lynyrd Skynyrd cast their fates on the airwaves by complicating their roles as rednecks. They didn't get the haircuts and high school diplomas that would have ensconced them in working-class Jacksonville, but their flight never put them among the people who, Skynyrd implies, have the power to address the world's problems (poverty in the ghetto, environmental degradation) but instead "just get high" (Rossington–Van Zant, "Things Goin' On," 1973). "Whiskey Rock A Roller" (1975) expresses the fear that even if women can't restrain the high-flying rockers, divine retribution will. In fact, the freedom Lynyrd Skynyrd portrayed seemed to require the redemptive process of crashing and burning. "The Needle and the Spoon" compares drug addiction to "a trip to the moon" *and* a tearful reunion with Mama, which brings the user to the recognition that this kind of flying leads to death (Collins–Van Zant, 1974). "Simple Man," on Skynyrd's first album along with "Free Bird," sonically tells the first chapter of this story. Mama, country music's perennial transmitter of social norms, begs the singer to be a simple man—God-fearing, monogamous, and uninterested in worldly wealth. Anyone familiar with country music narratives knows that country men, no matter how much they revere their mamas, don't want to be mama's boys. When country met rock, that story just got louder. As Ted Ownby notes, Van Zant's persona dramatizes his reluctance to accept Mama's "low expectations" by struggling with the high notes that convey the title (372–73). Likewise, the rock sound effects, particularly the ponderous bass line, pelt the front-porchy picking that mimics Mama's point of view. Ultimately, Skynyrd fights Mama's teaching by flight. "Was I Right or Wrong" sketches a similar conflict. The singer imagines his homecoming as a rich rock star only to find his father, who had warned him against leaving home, dead and unable to witness his son's rise in the world. In a graveside monologue, the singer asks the title question. "First I got lost then I got found," he tells the tombstone, but it's not clear whether he's talking about his success or his homecoming (Rossington–Van Zant).[27]

The lyrics to "Free Bird" further unbalance the country rock equation of flight with freedom. In his liner notes to the Skynyrd box set, John Swenson notes that in this song the man's departure *appears* to be from his lover but ultimately must be from life itself. The singer "ironically profess[es] his freedom while at the same time admitting that his nature is predestined."[28] "Lord knows I can't change," the singer tells his beloved. Those are the choices: live simply or die. Well before the plane crash, the band publicly dedicated the song to Duane Allman of the Allman Brothers band, dead in a motorcycle accident in 1971 at only twenty-four years old. Even without tragedy as a reference point, the song unfurls like a southern rock dirge. The first lines wonder about resonance, if not immortality: when I'm gone, the singer wonders, "would you still remember me?" Kooper's organ introduction reinforces the funereal theme. While the lyrics proceed with a down-home dignity similar to that of "Simple Man," the last half of the nine-minute song enacts an exhilarating electric guitar flight. The song, then, is structured as a memory of a fatal flight, four minutes of exuberant freedom that can only be experienced as defeat and commemoration.

Ironically, like the Eagles, Lynyrd Skynyrd eventually presented themselves as a band who had lived to tell tales of their descent from the stratosphere. The cover of their 1977 album *Street Survivors* portrays the group emerging from an urban blaze.[29] Three of them wear conciliatory messages on their T-shirts: drummer Artimus Pyle's announces that he is a vegetarian; bass player Leon Wilkeson's proclaims "my grass is blue"; Ronnie's bears the cover of Neil Young's keep-off-heroin, keep-on-rocking opus *Tonight's the Night*. This time Ronnie also had a similar message. "That Smell" begins by alluding to one of the band member's drunken car wrecks, then runs through a menu of dangerous drugs that evoke "the smell of death" (Collins–Van Zant). (It's worth noting that "Hotel California" opens with a reference to the "warm smell" of "burning" drugs.)[30] At the same time, "You Got That Right" raucously pledges allegiance to the rock and roll road show, complete with the promise of an early death. The notion of survival, though, took on a cruel irony when the band's plane crashed fewer than two weeks after the album's release. "Free Bird" became Ronnie Van Zant's eulogy and "That Smell" his prophecy.[31]

The free bird needn't worry about being forgotten. Some days, the classic rock station in Memphis seems to play all Skynyrd all the time; commentators elsewhere have made similar observations. Roberts suspects "karmic torture plotted by FM station managers all over the world" (156).[32] Sheer repetition renders Skynyrd innocuously contemporary and anesthetizes us to the words and music as soon as we recognize the groove; we take the flight and then it's over. Remarkably, the Drive-By Truckers, an Athens, Georgia, alt. country band, aestheticized *and* historicized Skynyrd in their *Southern Rock Opera* (2001), making it possible to listen with new ears. Two themes intertwine: the insistence that Lynyrd Skynyrd be heard simultaneously as a product of the 1970s and as an ongoing expression of "the duality of the Southern thing"—pride and shame, the experience of the white southern male and the representation of it. Drive-By Truckers leader Patterson Hood's father played in the rhythm section in the famed Muscle Shoals Sound Studio, and three of the other five group members grew up in the area, so they have personal experience with both themes. Like Skynyrd, the redneck is their central image, although their use of it is more overtly parodic.[33] Still, with the ostensibly burlesque title *Southern Rock Opera*, they offer a tribute to Skynyrd's unflinching wit.[34]

Act I presents the unnamed hero, an aspiring rock star. The centerpiece, a lengthy recitative, "The Three Great Alabama Icons," explores the role models available for white men in the 1970s South: George Wallace, Bear Bryant, and Ronnie Van Zant. The singer hates football, so he dismisses Bryant quickly. The opening cut, "Graduation Day," puts the emphasis on Van Zant. The hero loses his best friend in a car wreck (significantly, the car "went airborne") the night before the class of 1979's graduation; at the ceremony, the rumor circulates that when the ambulance arrived, "Free Bird" was pouring from the car stereo. "You know it's a very very long song," the last line grimly states. What follows demonstrates just how enduring it is. The hero leaves home and takes up punk rock as a way of "rebelling against the music of my high school parking lot." Like Skynyrd themselves, though, he eventually embraces southern rock as a way to address "the duality of the southern thing." "Ronnie and Neil" provides one example of it as it contrasts Birmingham's history of racial violence with nearby Muscle Shoals' literal creation of racial harmony. As "Sweet Home Alabama" says, "in Birmingham *they* love the governor" (emphasis mine). (They finish this line by booing.) The next line asserts that they did what they could—although they don't say what that is.

The last verse praises the blues-curing sounds of the Muscle Shoals "swampers." The "sky runs blue" in "Sweet Home Alabama" because of the *blues.* The Drive-By Truckers offer details: with Wilson Pickett and Aretha Franklin, the mostly white musicians in this north Alabama town created scores of great records. While critics make much of British Invasion influence on Skynyrd (O'Brien, unpaginated; Ballinger, x), the band doesn't sing about John Mayall or Mick Jagger. In "The Ballad of Curtis Loew," the singer praises an old black man at the corner store as "the finest picker to ever play the blues" (Collins–Van Zant, 1974). "Swamp Music" likens Skynyrd's sound to "Son House singin' the blues." Canadian/Californian Neil Young, they claim, heard only about Birmingham. When he heard "Sweet Home Alabama," he loved it, and supposedly wrote his "Powderfinger" for Skynyrd.[35] Ultimately, the song is named after both Neil and Ronnie because, to the

Truckers, the exchange between them illustrates the blending of voices that makes rock what it is (or should be): "Speaking their minds on how they feel / Let them guitars blast for Ronnie and Neil."

Skynyrd's 1976 version of Robert Johnson's "Crossroads" brought them to the mythic origin of the blues, the Delta road where Johnson sold his soul to the devil in exchange for the music.[36] According to the Truckers, George Wallace cut a similar deal in the late 1960s and early 1970s, trading his progressive ideals for racist votes. In "Wallace," the devil eagerly awaits his arrival. "Thanks to George Wallace," says the singer in "The Three Great Alabama Icons," the global problem of racism gets portrayed "with a southern accent." In "Birmingham" and "The Southern Thing," the Truckers' would-be rock star blames poverty and the class system for much of the South's racial tension. Ironically, much of the Truckers' inspiration for these songs comes from the Los Angeles singer-songwriter Randy Newman's 1974 concept album *Good Old Boys*. In typical L.A. fashion, the album features three of the Eagles as backup singers, but according to Hoskyns, "Newman was an entirely atypical example of the L.A. singer-songwriter" (207).[37] Newman's "Birmingham" is the home of a steel factory worker who expresses a rather hollow pride in his city; in later songs we learn of his self-hatred and alcoholism. The first song, "Rednecks," conveys Newman's judgment on this situation. The first verse describes Lester Maddox's treatment by "some smart-ass New York Jew" talk-show host who laughed at his guest. The chorus articulates the stereotype of "rednecks," who "don't know [their] ass from a hole in the ground," but they're "keeping the niggers down." In the last verses, the singer angrily plays with the notion that African Americans can escape racism after leaving the South by listing horrific ghettos from California to Boston. *Good Old Boys* also includes a Huey P. Long campaign song, "Every Man a King," and "Kingfish," Newman's own song about populism, to illustrate the appeal of such politics to white southern working men. The temptation to sell one's soul to the devil seems constant.

While Wallace burns in hell, Act II of *Southern Rock Opera* depicts the hero and his band's Skynyrd-like rise to fame. (The synopsis says that "our hero might have sold off a little of his [soul] too.") While the Drive-By Truckers create many Skynyrdesque sounds with their three guitars, in this act, Hood literally combines Ronnie and Neil by singing the first song, "Let There Be Rock," in a Neil Young–like waver. The last five songs are literally about Skynyrd; then Hood sings like

Ronnie Van Zant. In the last song, "Angels and Fuselage," angels wait for the dead band members. Apparently, Wallace was not the only white southern soul the devil wanted, so the Skynyrd angels crashed, burned, and are airborne again. "Free Bird," after all, is a very, very long song. In the artwork that accompanies *Southern Rock Opera*, the free bird is an owl, a night-flying symbol of wisdom, drawn so perhaps because it takes a long time to really *hear* the song. What better proof, though, that understanding comes with time than a February 2002 article in *Spin* on the "50 Greatest Bands of All Time"? Skynyrd was among them, praised as "complex" *and* "drunk-ass."[38]

NOTES

1. The connections are so numerous that books have been written about them: see John Einarson, *Desperados: The Roots of Country Rock* (New York: Cooper Square Press, 2001), and Barney Hoskyns, *Waiting for the Sun: Strange Days, Weird Scenes, and the Sound of Los Angeles* (New York: St. Martin's, 1996). Pete Frame draws family trees showing the connections between the Byrds; Crosby, Stills, Nash, and Young; the Eagles; et al. in his lovely and obsessive *Rock Family Trees* (London: Omnibus, 1993), 8, 17–18, 36.

2. Jimmy McDonough, *Shakey: Neil Young's Biography* (New York: Random House, 2002), 338. McDonough is quoting a 1975 interview by Cameron Crowe.

3. Specifically, Hoskyns notes that Browne, enacting a line in the title tune about the pretender's evening stroll, is the sole WASP among "shabbier looking black and Mexican pedestrians" (*Waiting*, 280). Bruce J. Schulman reproduces the album cover in *The Seventies: The Great Shift in American Culture, Society, and Politics* (New York: Free Press, 2001) with the comment that Browne exemplified a "new, more sensitive male" archetype (unpaginated photo signature between pp. 110–11). Surely, there's more to be said about the connotations of the word *pretender* as both an heir to the throne and sham.

4. The good friends in the title were fellow southerners such as Charlie Daniels. This song was not released in Van Zant's lifetime; it appeared on *Legend* (1987), a collection of B-sides and unused recordings.

5. Ted Ownby, "Freedom, Manhood, and White Male Tradition in 1970s Southern Rock Music" in *Haunted Bodies: Gender and Southern Texts*, ed. Anne Goodwyn Jones and Susan V. Donaldson (Charlottesville: University Press of Virginia, 1997), 369–88. See also Mike Butler, "'Luther King was a Good Ole Boy': The Southern Rock Movement and White Male Identity in the Post–Civil Rights South," *Popular Music and Society* 23, no. 2 (1999): 41–61.

6. While the band reformed in 1987 with Johnny Van Zant replacing his brother as lead singer, I consider here only the original Lynyrd Skynyrd. Marly Brant's *Freebird: The Lynyrd Skynyrd Story* (New York: Billboard, 2002) provides an exhaustive account of the original and the reformed band.

Paul Wells discusses later Skynyrd (and other southern rockers) as a "contemporisation of a Civil War ethos as a mode of identity" in "The Last Rebel: Southern Rock and Nostalgic Continuities," in *Dixie Debates: Perspectives on Southern Cultures*, ed. Richard H. King and Helen Taylor (New York: New York University Press, 1996), 115–29. Mark Kemp's excellent *Dixie Lullaby: A Story of Music, Race, and New Beginnings in a New South* (New York: Free Press, 2004) offers both a professional and personal reflection on southern rock and white masculinity. Kemp tells how listening to the Allman Brothers and Lynyrd Skynyrd helped him and his high school friends in Asheboro, North Carolina, cope with both the joys and difficulties of becoming southern men. As a high-profile music journalist, Kemp was able to interview key players in the southern rock scene, including the Drive-By Truckers, to confirm that the music was informed by the complicated history that brought white ears and black music together in the South.

7. Robert Christgau notes that "the eagle roams the sky . . . in search of fresh prey, which is why he is such an apt symbol of American imperial power" (267). "Trying to Understand the Eagles," his alarmed analysis of the Eagles' debut, originally printed in *Newsday,* October 1972, is reprinted in his *Any Old Way You Chose It: Rock and Other Pop Music,* expanded ed. (New York: Cooper Square Press, 2000), 265–69.

8. Grace Lichtenstein, "Desperado," in *Stranded: Rock and Roll for a Desert Island,* ed. Greil Marcus (New York: Knopf, 1979), 87. Marcus introduced the notion of rock stars as "symbolic Americans" in *Mystery Train: Images of America in Rock 'n' Roll Music,* rev. ed. (New York: Dutton, 1982), 5.

9. Although he fails to give southern rockers any credit for critical distance, Robert Duncan otherwise puts it well in *The Noise: Notes from a Rock 'n' Roll Era* (New York: Ticknor and Fields, 1984): "A corollary to the rise of country-rock was the rise of what became known as southern rock, in which southerners unironically plumbed their roots themselves. Southern rock was also young people restaking claims to America—but as southerners, not as young people. These young people were primarily responding not to their alienation from their elders—that was simply a given at the time in rock 'n' roll—but to their alienation from the rest of the counterculture" (219).

10. Lester Bangs, "Heavy Metal Brontosaurus M.O.R.," *Creem,* May 1976, 57.

11. Mitch Glazer, "One Mo' Brawl from the Road," *Crawdaddy,* November 1976, 18–19.

12. Jaan Uhelszki, "Lynyrd Skynyrd: Fifths and Fists for the Common Man," *Creem,* March 1976, 48–50, 69–70.

13. Al Kooper, *Backstage Passes and Backstabbing Bastards* (New York: Billboard Books, 1998), 103.

14. Robert Christgau's 1975 column is reprinted as "A Boogie Band that Loves the Governor (Boo Boo Boo): Lynyrd Skynyrd," in *Grown Up All Wrong: 75 Great Rock and Pop Artists from Vaudeville to Techno* (Cambridge: Harvard University Press, 1998), 144–49.

15. See Marc Eliot, *To the Limit: The Untold Story of the Eagles* (Boston: Little Brown, 1998) for several accounts of the Eagles fistfights among themselves, and McDonough for a brief account of guns and fights on a Crosby, Still, Nash, and Young tour (*Shakey,* 453–54).

16. All the album covers and a good selection of publicity photos are available at www.skynyrd.com.

17. According to Ron O'Brien and Andy McKaie, MCA, Skynyrd's record company, added the flag

to their act in 1974, after the success of "Sweet Home Alabama"; the group dropped it sometime in 1976. "American by Birth . . . (Southern by the Grace of God)," liner notes to *Lynyrd Skynyrd Box Set* (MCA Records MCAD3–10390, 1991).

18. "What kind of redneck writes an anti-gun song?" Ed King wonders in Lee Ballinger, *Lynyrd Skynyrd: An Oral History* (New York: Avon, 1999), 98.

19. See Peter Doggett, *Are You Ready for the Country: Elvis, Dylan, Parsons and the Roots of Country Rock* (London: Viking, 2000) for a discussion of the country elements in both genres. Most definitions of southern rock describe it as an innovative fusion of country and blues with post-British invasion rock. See Michael Bane, *White Boy Singin' the Blues: The Black Roots of White Rock* (New York: Penguin, 1982), 213–27; Frye Gaillard, *Watermelon Wine: The Spirit of Country Music* (New York: St. Martin's Press, 1978), 147–62; Martin Popoff, *Southern Rock Review* (Burlington, Ontario: Collectors Guide, 2001), 5–7. Marley Brant focuses on the relationship to the blues in *Southern Rockers: The Roots and Legacy of Southern Rock* (New York: Billboard, 1999), 22–25. She also includes a collection of statements from the musicians involved; most deny the existence of "southern rock" (11–13).

20. There's no better proof of this statement than two tribute albums compiled by Nashville's brightest stars: *Common Threads: The Songs of the Eagles* (1993) and *Skynyrd Friends* (1994).

21. To Charlie Daniels, this experience defines southern rock: "The genre was a *genre of people* that were all basically raised the same way . . . Everybody was raised in a blue collar situation, came up listening to the same music, eating the same food, going to the same type of churches. We were all street people" (cited in Ballinger, *Lynyrd Skynyrd,* 2; emphasis in original).

22. They did occasionally use dobros and mandolins. Moreover, outtakes such as "No One Can Take Your Place" (ca. 1970, on *Lynyrd Skynyrd Collectybles*) and "When You Got Good Friends" reveal that they could play full-ahead country but chose not to release such material.

23. The story is recounted in nearly any discussion of Skynyrd. I am relying on Ballinger, *Lynyrd Skynyrd,* 12–16.

24. Diane Roberts, "Song of the South," *Oxford American 5th Annual Music Issue* (2001), 156–58.

25. You can find lively debates and line-by-line parsings (ranging from wacky to wonderful) of this song on the Internet. For starters, see http://forums.gardenweb.com/forums/load/prairie/msg0823111116210.html (accessed June 5, 2002). In contrast, on the Eagles official website, Glenn Frey all but states that the lyrics are meaningless; see www.eaglesmusic.com/HotelCal/hotelcal.html (accessed June 5, 2002).

26. Robert Christgau's attack puts it most personally and succinctly in his capsule review of the album *Hotel California:* "Don Henley is incapable of conveying a mental state as complex as self-criticism—he'll probably sound smug croaking out his famous last words ("Where's the Coke?")." See www.robertchristgau.com/get_artist.php?id=1423&name=The+Eagles (accessed June 5, 2002).

27. The song was originally recorded in 1974 but not released until 1978. "Don't Ask Me No Questions" (1974) and "Am I Losin'" (1975) express similar concerns about the impact of fame.

28. John Swenson, "Lynyrd Skynyrd: Swamp Music," liner notes to *Lynyrd Skynyrd Box Set* (MCA Records MCAD3–10390, 1991).

29. The cover was redesigned to remove the flames shortly after the plane crash (Brant, *Freebirds,* 167) although the original design is used on the compact disc.

30. Sound engineer Barry Rudolph claims to have consciously developed the parallel between the songs: "I heard 'That Smell' as 'Hotel California' for that band . . . I was going for that sort of production" (Ballinger, *Lynyrd Skynyrd*, 187).

31. For an elaboration of the notion of Ronnie Van Zant as prophet, see Jaan Ulhelszki and Ben Edmonds, "The Southern Death Cult," in *Mojo,* November 1997, 48–63.

32. Philosopher Crispin Sartwell makes this observation at http://www.crispinsartwell.com/truckers.htm (accessed June 5, 2002).

33. See S. Renee Dechert and George H. Lewis, "The Drive-By Truckers and the Redneck Underground: A Subcultural Analysis" in *Country Music Annual 2002,* ed. Charles K. Wolfe and James E. Akenson (Lexington: University Press of Kentucky, 2002), 130–50.

34. "Even the seemingly irreverent title is in keeping with the spirit of the band that performed 'That Smell' and the man who wrote the line 'oak tree you're in my way' to tell of his band mate's near fatal collision. We hope that it is taken as the absolute highest possible form of flattery and honor." Patterson Hood, epilogue to liner notes to *Southern Rock Opera* (Soul Dump Music 005, 2001).

35. In fact, at some point, Young renounced the sentiments expressed in "Southern Man": "I don't sing it anymore. I don't feel it's particularly relevant. It's not 'Southern Man'—It's White Man" (McDonough, *Shakey,* 338).

36. The lyrics of the song don't mention this deal, but Van Zant knew the legend (Ballinger, *Lynyrd Skynyrd,* 64).

37. Hood told S. Renee Dechert that "Newman 'got it right.' He adds 'it was like taking lessons from the master.'" See S. Renee Dechert, "Setting a Trailer House in the Rich Part of Town," available at www.popmatters.com/pm/music/reviews/16495/drivebytruckers-southern/ (accessed June 5, 2002). Surely Newman's *Faust* also taught them much (1993). In this concept, Don Henley plays Faust as a rock star.

38. See http://www.spin.com/new/features/videofeatures/february2002top502.html (accessed June 5, 2002).

Contributors

EDWIN T. ARNOLD is Professor of English at Appalachian State University in Boone, North Carolina. He has published widely on southern authors including William Faulkner, Cormac McCarthy, Erskine Caldwell, and Donald Harington. He is presently coeditor with Michael Zeitlin of the *Faulkner Journal* and is working on a study of a series of lynchings that occurred in Georgia in 1899, tentatively titled *"What Virtue There is in Fire": Southern Justice, Sam Hose, and the Making of a Black Martyr.*

COURT CARNEY is Visiting Assistant Professor of History at Texas A&M University. His research has also appeared in the *Journal of Southern History* and *Popular Music and Society.* He is currently writing books on the image of Nathan Bedford Forrest and on jazz and American culture in the 1920s.

BARBARA CHING is Associate Professor of English and Director of the Marcus W. Orr Center for the Humanities at the University of Memphis. She is the author of *Wrong's What I Do Best: Hard Country Music and Contemporary Culture.* She coedited, with Gerald Creed, *Knowing Your Place: Rural Identity and Cultural Hierarchy.*

SUSAN V. DONALDSON is National Endowment for the Humanities Professor of English at the College of William and Mary. She wrote *Competing Voices: The American Novel, 1865–1914*, and coedited, with Anne Goodwyn Jones, *Haunted Bodies: Gender and Southern Texts.* Her current book projects focus on the politics of storytelling in the U.S. South and on William Faulkner, Eudora Welty, Richard Wright, and the demise of Jim Crow.

STEVE ESTES is Associate Professor of History at Sonoma State University. He is the author of *I Am a Man!: Race, Manhood, and the Civil Rights Movement* and editor of *Ask and Tell: Gay and Lesbian Veterans Speak Out.*

ANTHONY JAMES teaches at Coastal Carolina Community College. He holds a Ph.D. from the University of Mississippi. His dissertation was entitled "The De-

fenders of Tradition: College Social Fraternities, Race, and Gender, 1945–1980."
His research has also appeared in *The Historian* and the *Journal of Mississippi History*.

TED OWNBY is Professor of History and Southern Studies at the University of
Mississippi. He is author of *American Dreams in Mississippi: Consumers, Poverty, and
Culture, 1830–1998*, and *Subduing Satan: Religion, Recreation, and Manhood in the
Rural South, 1865–1920*, and editor of *Manners and Southern History*.

K. MICHAEL PRINCE is a freelance writer and translator, currently living
in Munich, Germany. A native of South Carolina, he is the author of *Rally 'Round
the Flag, Boys! South Carolina and the Confederate Flag*, the first book-length history
of that state's long struggle over the display of the rebel flag. Current scholarly
interests include the experience of war and its impact on political and historical
identity. He is now completing a book on World War II and German memory.

BROCK THOMPSON, a native of Conway, Arkansas, holds degrees from Hen-
drix College and the University of Arkansas. He is a doctoral candidate in American Studies at King's College, University of London. His research focuses on gay
and lesbian southern history, identity politics, and queer theory.

LARRY VONALT was chair of the Department of English and Technical Com-
munication at the University of Missouri-Rolla until his death in December 2006.
Vonalt had wide-ranging interests in the history, literature, and other arts of the
American South. His published work includes essays on the novelist Donald Harington and the photographer Shelby Lee Adams.

JAMES H. WATKINS is Associate Professor of English, Rhetoric, and Writing at Berry College in Rome, Georgia. His work on autobiography and literature
of the American South has been published in the *Southern Quarterly*, the *North
Carolina Literary Review*, the *Marjorie Kinnan Rawlings Journal of Florida Literature*,
the *American Indian Culture and Research Journal*, *The Companion to Southern Literature*, *The History of Southern Women's Literature*, and *The New Encyclopedia of
Southern Culture*. He is the editor of *Southern Selves: A Collection of Autobiographical
Writing*.

ADAM WATTS is a scientist at the Florida Cooperative Fish and Wildlife Research Unit in Gainesville, Florida, where he coordinates a research program using unmanned aerial vehicles (UAVs) for ecological surveys. Previously he studied restoration ecology at the University of Florida, worked as an alligator biologist, and spent two years in Guinea as a Peace Corps volunteer. His work has been published in *In the Land of Fire and Water: Proceedings of the Florida Dry Prairie Conference* and *Ecology and Society.*

TRENT WATTS is Assistant Professor of American Studies at the University of Missouri–Rolla. His research has also appeared in *Southern Cultures.* He is an Associate Editor of the *Mississippi Encyclopedia* and a member of the editorial board of the *Journal of Mississippi History.*